Legal Argumentation Theory: Cross-Disciplinary Perspectives

# Law and Philosophy Library

VOLUME 102



For further volumes:
http://www.springer.com/series/6210

Christian Dahlman • Eveline Feteris
Editors

# Legal Argumentation Theory: Cross-Disciplinary Perspectives

Springer

*Editors*
Christian Dahlman
Faculty of Law
Lund University, Lund
Sweden

Eveline Feteris
University of Amsterdam
Amsterdam
The Netherlands

ISSN 1572-4395
ISBN 978-94-017-8235-7 ISBN 978-94-007-4670-1 (eBook)
DOI 10.1007/978-94-007-4670-1
Springer Dordrecht Heidelberg New York London



Printed on acid-free paper

Springer is part of Springer Science+Business Media (www.springer.com)

# Introduction

Legal argumentation theory is a cross-disciplinary research field where theoretical tools for analyzing and evaluating legal argumentation are developed and applied. Due to its cross-disciplinary nature, legal argumentation theory has become a meeting point for scholars with a background in argumentation theory, logic, artificial intelligence, rhetoric, legal theory, cognitive psychology, communication studies and many other disciplines.

This volume brings together two theoretical approaches to legal argumentation theory: the first approach is based in general argumentation theory and contributes to the study of legal argumentation by developing general argumentation theory in application to law, the second approach is based in legal theory and contributes to the study of legal argumentation by developing legal theory with regard to argumentation. The chapters in this volume illustrate how research from one approach complements research from the other approach, and show how they can be fruitful for each other.

The papers that belong to the first approach take their point of departure in the analysis of a certain kind of argument, a specific argumentation fallacy, a rhetorical strategy or in certain rules for a rational discussion, and apply this theoretical analysis to legal argumentation. Each of the first four contributions concentrates on a specific form of argument: the argument from consequences, the argument *ad absurdum*, the argument from precedent and the argument *ad hominem*. The authors propose an integration of ideas from argumentation theory and legal theory to develop tools for analyzing and evaluating arguments of this kind in legal argumentation.

In her contribution, Flavia Carbonell investigates 'consequentialist arguments' in legal reasoning. She analyzes the diverse approaches to consequentialist arguments given by MacCormick's theory, Wróblewski's theory and Feteris's pragma-dialectical theory, with the purpose of, firstly, comparing, at a theoretical level, the strengths and weaknesses when arguing by consequences is at stake. For testing the scope of the proposals, the paper, secondly, uses the selected theories in a study of the consequentialist arguments used in a ruling of the Chilean Constitutional Court. The theoretical comparison, together with the outcomes to which the analysis of judicial argumentation leads, sheds light on the capacity and efficacy of these tools in guiding the rational construction and evaluation of judicial reasoning.

In his contribution, Thomas Bustamante concentrates on a specific form of argumentation in which judges refer to the consequences of application of a legal rule, in this case the unacceptable or 'absurd' consequences of application of the rule in the specific case. He explains that the *ad absurdum* argument can be understood either as a strictly logical tool, which is equivalent to a proof by contradiction, or as a pragmatic argument about the desirability or undesirability of a given proposition. Yet, in legal reasoning lawyers tend to use it, at least in the vast majority of cases, only in the latter sense. The *argumentum ad absurdum*, he argues, can be classified as a special kind of pragmatic argument whose specific feature is its special argumentative strength in comparison with generic consequentialist argumentation. Once we are able to grant that premise, the chapter intends to explain the most important rules of interpretation that may be used to determine the conditions under which the *ad absurdum* argument can be correctly deployed in legal reasoning.

In his contribution, Fred Schauer investigates the argument from precedent. Schauer argues that it is a mistake to see the argument from precedent as a special case of the argument from analogy, and demonstrates that there are fundamental differences between the two argument types. An argument from precedent claims that the present case must be decided in the same way as a previous case, since there are no relevant differences between the cases. An argument from analogy claims that there is an important similarity between the present case and the previous case, but does not claim that the cases are identical in all relevant aspects. Furthermore, Schauer points out that a decision maker may disagree with the decision in the previous case and still make an argument from precedent, since an argument from precedent is made for the sake of consistency. This is not possible with an argument from analogy.

In their contribution, Christian Dahlman, David Reidhav and Lena Wahlberg develop a theoretical framework for evaluating an argument *ad hominem*. This is highly relevant for legal argumentation, as lawyers often use arguments *ad hominem* to cast doubt on the reliability of a witness. The authors propose a general definition of ad hominem arguments, and a general framework that identifies the different ways in which ad hominem arguments can go wrong. According to the authors, an argument ad hominem is an argument that makes a claim about the reliability of a person in the performance of a certain function, based on some attribute relating to the person in question. On the basis of this definition, the authors identify seven different ways that ad hominem arguments can go wrong, and classify them as seven different ad hominem fallacies: false attribution, irrelevant attribute, overrated effect, reliability irrelevance, irrelevant person, insufficient degree and irrelevant function.

The following two contributions start from a specific argumentation-theoretical approach, the pragma-dialectical approach, and explain how legal argumentation can be analyzed and evaluated from this perspective as a constructive contribution to a rational legal discussion. Harm Kloosterhuis starts by giving a description of the pragma-dialectical approach to legal argumentation in which the justification of a judicial decision is considered as part of a critical discussion. In this approach it is assumed that legal argumentation theory should integrate descriptive and normative perspectives on argumentation. Legal discourse should be studied as a sample of normal verbal communication and interaction and it should, at the same time, be measured against certain standards of reasonableness. This implies first a philosophical ideal of reasonableness, second a theoretical model for acceptable argumentation and third tools to analyze actual legal argumentation from the perspective of the model. Analyzing argumentation in judicial decisions from the ideal-perspective of a critical discussion is sometimes criticized. One of the main objections is that a judge does not have a standpoint in a critical discussion, but simply decides a case. As a result, the critical norms for evaluating argumentation are not applicable to a legal decision. In his contribution, the author tries to refute these two objections by showing how the ideals of a critical discussion relate to the ideals of the Rule of Law, and how these ideals function as starting points in analyzing and evaluating legal decisions, focusing on the reconstruction of standpoints in legal decisions.

Eveline Feteris gives a further explanation of the pragma-dialectical approach and presents an analysis of the discussion strategy of the Dutch Supreme Court in the famous case of the 'Unworthy Spouse'. The author explains how the theoretical starting points of the pragma-dialectical theory can be used in the analysis of the strategic maneuvering of the Dutch Supreme Court in a case in which there is a difference of opinion about the argumentative role of certain legal principles. In its discussion strategy, the Supreme Court aims at maintaining the decision of the court of appeal while at the same time making a correction so that the decision is in line with the way in which the Supreme Court wants to make an exception to a statutory rule about the division of the matrimonial community of property. The discussion strategy consists of a specific, systematic and coordinated choice of the dialectical possibilities in the different stages of a critical legal discussion, consisting of particular choices of common starting points and particular choices in the evaluation of the argumentation. These choices are aimed at steering the discussion in a particular direction so that a particular result is reached that would be desirable from the perspective of certainty, from the perspective of justice in the specific case, and the perspective of the development of law with respect to the role of general legal principles and reasonableness and fairness.

The chapters that are based in legal theory investigate legal argumentation in the context of various key issues in legal theory: the normativity of legal argumentation, the nature of legal justification, the nature of legal balancing, the formation and revision of normative systems and the relation between law and truth.

The contribution by Carlos Bernal discusses the different relations between legal argumentation and the concept of normativity. On the one hand, legal norms are elements of the arguments which go together to make up legal discourse. On the other hand, legal argumentation plays an important role in grounding the normativity of legal norms. Bernal considers four aspects of the relation: the normativity of the different kinds of legal norms, the rules of legal argumentation, the role played by the rules of legal argumentation in grounding the normativity of legal norms and the role played by legal norms in legal argumentation.

The contribution by Bruce Anderson begins by arguing that the key elements in any analysis of weighing and balancing are questions, insights and judgments of value. This position is used to critique the role Marko Novak assigns to rationality in balancing and Robert Alexy's idealized weight formula. Finally, by examining the relation between deliberation and expression, he argues that a written legal decision represents the possibility of someone understanding and evaluating that decision. Expressions, in whatever form, do not justify legal decisions.

The contribution by Jaap Hage discusses the theories known as 'legal constructivism' and 'ontological constructivism'. According to legal constructivism, the legal consequences of a case are what the best legal arguments say that they are, and this means that legal judgments can be 'true' even in hard cases. Critics of legal constructivism say that there is no such thing as a 'best legal argument' in a hard case, and that judgments in such cases therefore cannot be 'true'. Hage concludes that legal constructivism is a view that can neither be verified nor falsified, and moves on to discuss ontological constructivism. According to ontological constructivism, the legal consequences of a case depend on the best possible legal argument. Hage points out that this view incorrectly presupposes that the law is a closed domain.

Marko Novak discusses the problem of the separation between the context of discovery and the context of justification of legal decisions, one of the basic themes in legal argumentation theory. Whereas the context of discovery focuses on the process of reaching a legal decision, which concludes a decision-making process, the context of justification is concerned with justification of the legal decision through the application of relevant legal arguments. The majority of legal theorists interested in legal argumentation theory support the position that the mentioned two contexts are rigidly separated, in the framework of which the process of discovery is mainly studied by psychologists while the process of justification is the only area that should be relevant for legal argumentation theory. The author opposes such a rigid separation between the two contexts and views it as a position that is too idealist. Instead, he supports a more realistic position of their moderate separation, whereby he recognizes the importance of the discovery context while still insisting on the major relevance of the justification context.

The contribution by Antonino Rotolo and Corrado Roversi proposes a framework for reconstructing legal arguments that support an extensive or restrictive interpretation of a legal provision. According to Rotolo and Roversi, these interpretative techniques correspond to revision operations in systems of constitutive rules. Extensive and restrictive interpretations of legal concepts require expansions and contractions in the constitutive rules that define them. The advantage of the proposed framework is that it makes these arguments more transparent and provides criteria for evaluating them.

Jan Sieckmann's contribution discusses legal justifications where normative arguments are balanced against each other. Sieckmann claims that a legal justification of this kind cannot be reconstructed as a deductive argument where a conclusion is drawn from certain premises. Balancing is a different method for justification. According to Sieckmann, balancing is a rational method for justification in its own right, since the balancing of normative arguments includes an element of autonomous choice, subject to constraints of rationality.

In his contribution, Giovanni Tuzet discusses the role of facts in legal argumentation, and the function of trials with regard to the truth. Tuzet criticizes the view that trials do not aim at the truth, and cannot aim at the truth. According to Tuzet, truth is a necessary condition for justice.

Most chapters in this volume were presented at a workshop on legal argumentation theory at the Goethe Universität in Frankfurt am Main (Germany) on 18–19 August 2011. The workshop was organized by Christian Dahlman (Lund University) and Eveline Feteris (University of Amsterdam) as a special workshop at the IVR World Congress for Philosophy of Law and Social Philosophy. The participants to the workshop included scholars from Germany, Canada, Brazil, The Netherlands, Italy, USA, Sweden, Chile, Poland and many other countries.

Christian Dahlman
Eveline Feteris

# Contents

# Chapter 1
# Reasoning by Consequences: Applying Different Argumentation Structures to the Analysis of Consequentialist Reasoning in Judicial Decisions

**Flavia Carbonell**

## 1.1 Introduction

Theories of legal argumentation, as many scholars point out, arise in legal theory as an echo of the argumentative turn in philosophy of language and as a middle way between the idea of a mechanistic judge and an arbitrary judge with absolute discretion. These theories propose a diverse range of criteria both for guaranteeing rationality and reasonableness of legal decisions – especially judicial ones – and for enabling intersubjective scrutiny or public control on the process of adjudication (García Amado 1986:152–154).

Among these criteria, one that has received special attention is the argument from consequences, also called pragmatic argument or consequentialist reasoning. This argument is generally used in the context of judicial hard cases – that is, when problems of interpretation, relevance, classification or proof arise, according to MacCormick's classification[1] – where judges have to justify their decisions using different types of argument and where the efforts are directed at reinforcing the chain of arguments. The theoretical proposals concerned with the argument from consequences consider diverse elements and variables that are necessary for assuring the correct, strong and sound construction of this argument and its proper use.

Even if consequentialist reasoning is not a new technique in legal argumentation, its use in justifying legal decisions, particularly judicial decisions, is not exempt from criticisms, nor has it had a homogenous reception within legal theory and judicial practice. The criticisms refer to different problematic aspects of consequentialist

[1]The first two of these problems have to do with the major premise (law), and the others with the minor premise (facts). See MacCormick (1997:65–72, 87–97).

F. Carbonell (✉)
Faculty of Law, University Alberto Hurtado, Santiago, Chile
e-mail: fcarbone@uahurtado.cl

C. Dahlman and E. Feteris (eds.), *Legal Argumentation Theory: Cross-Disciplinary Perspectives*, Law and Philosophy Library 102, DOI 10.1007/978-94-007-4670-1_1,

arguments, such as insufficiently backing the prediction of future consequences, the extension of the consequences to be considered, proof of the causal relation between an act and its foreseen consequences, the parameters to evaluate or assess consequences against other values, interest or goods, and the question for what or for whom are the consequences favourable or unfavourable, among others. In the legal sphere we can add questioning about the legitimacy of judges incorporating extra-legal consequences as reasons for deciding in one way or another and problems of excessive judicial discretion and weak accountability mechanisms when these sorts of arguments are at stake.[2] This paper will not discuss all of these issues.[3] Thus, i.e., I will not develop at large the issue of whether judges do, can, must or should not use consequentialist extra-legal argumentation. Instead, the starting-point is that since judges use the argument from consequences to justify their rulings, it would be relevant to identify which are the theoretical tools that help them to make a better use of this argument. With this as the premise, I will focus specially on the different parameters proposed by legal theorists to evaluate the use of the argument from consequences, pointing out the problems derived from these proposals and offering a possible solution to them or at least a way of mitigating them.

The aim of this paper is to perform a preliminary comparison among the theoretical approaches to consequentialist reasoning developed by three scholars – MacCormick, Wróblewski and Feteris – bearing in mind the common purpose of legal argumentation theories in order to provide tools for constructing good or correct arguments, or indicators for improving, modelling or guiding the practice. The comparison will be done considering a ruling of the Chilean Constitutional Court. This case-study will be useful to identify strengths and weaknesses of the three theoretical proposals.

The structure of this contribution will be the following. I will first consider very briefly two aspects of consequentialist arguments (a concept and a distinction), and I will highlight the central points of each of the theoretical proposals. Secondly, I will apply these proposals to the evaluation of some consequentialist arguments of a recent decision of the Chilean Constitutional Court. The final section will offer some conclusive remarks.

## 1.2 Theories on Consequentialist Reasoning

In this section, I will explain the concept of the argument from consequences and I will outline a distinction that is relevant when applying this argument to legal reasoning. Second, I will briefly describe the way in which three scholars that

[2]Dworkin tackles this problem by saying that consequences-based reasoning denies past judicial and political decisions and displaces the conception of welfare of the community by the judge's own conception (1986:101; 152ff).

[3]For a panorama of the debates in legal scholarship on the argument from consequences see Bengoetxea (1993b); for an introduction to the philosophical consequentialism – non-consequentialism debate, see Scheffler (1988); Sinnot-Armstrong (2006); Slote (1992).

have delved into the analysis of the argument from consequences have tackled the problems and elements involved in the argument's use.

By "consequentialist argument" I refer to an argument that takes into account the positive or negative consequences that a particular legal decision may produce as a reason to support or reject that decision.[4] From this definition, it is relevant to emphasise that, on the one hand, consequences are brought forward as reasons to support decisions or, most of the time, to reject decisions with unacceptable, harmful or unfavourable effects, either for the legal system or for the society, i.e., consequences are a factor or a reason for making a decision[5]; however, on the other hand, those consequences that act as reasons for the decision are future and hypothetical ones, that is, they are only foreseen or foreseeable. In what follows, I will be using as interchangeable the expressions "consequentialist reasoning," "argument from consequences" and "argument referring to consequences." I will also circumscribe the analysis to judicial decisions as a paradigmatic case of legal decisions.

Concerning the argument from consequences in the legal sphere, it is interesting to distinguish – following the suggestions of several scholars[6] – between two types of consequences: legal and extra-legal ones.[7] *Legal consequences* are the effects of a decision inside the legal system or the possible legal implications of a decision internally (Bengoetxea 1993a:256). In this sense, the use of the argument from legal consequences looks for consistency and coherence of a ruling with the Constitution and the rest of the norms of the legal system and, at the same time, tries to avoid legal gaps and deregulation. Thus, consequentialist argumentation appears frequently together with arguments based on coherence, and it is used mainly to dismiss solutions that produce effects that are incoherent with the legal system as a

---

[4]The argument from consequences has been generally conceptualized as "the argument for accepting the truth (or falsity) of a proposition citing the consequences of accepting that proposition (or of not accepting it)" (Walton 1999:252). This same argument, under the name of "pragmatic argument", is defined by Perelman as the one that enables to evaluate an act or event in accordance with its favourable or unfavourable consequences (Perelman and Olbrechts-Tyteca 1969:266ff).

[5]MacCormick differentiates between the result of a decision – understood as the legal effects that must be applied to a case when the factual and normative requirements prescribed by the rule are met – and its consequences as a factor for deciding (MacCormick 1983:246).

[6]Bengoetxea, following MacCormick, distinguishes, in my view, between these two types of consequentialist arguments, even when not with this terminology: (a) those consequences that refer to the possible internal juridical implications of a legal decision, that is, within Law as a legal system; and (b) those consequences that might follow a judicial decision in Law that refer to the results or repercussions (in behavioural terms), for example, consequences in the economy or in Law as a social system or in other systems (Bengoetxea 1993a:256ff). See also the distinction between juridical and behavioural consequences in MacCormick (1983:251). An analogy could also be made with the categories "normative" and "factual" consequences within the trilogy proposed by Wróblewski (1984:151ff).

[7]Scholars have also elaborated other classifications that, although interesting, will not be developed here: causal and remote, favourable and unfavourable, foreseeable and certain, particular and systemic. See, for example, Perelman Olbrechts-Tyteca (1969:266ff), Gottlieb (1968:76), and MacCormick (1997:150).

whole or with the specific principles of a branch of law (Bengoetxea 1993b:48). Some examples of the use of the argument of legal consequences are: to avoid legal uncertainty, to avoid normative gaps, to avoid empting the content of a legal competence, to avoid injuries to the rights of third parties in good faith, and to reject generic appeals to future damages.[8]

On the other hand, *extra-legal consequences* are all those repercussions that a judicial decision may have in the extra-legal social reality or outside the legal system. Like the argument from legal consequences, an argument referring to extra-legal consequences is commonly a negative one. That is, the argument is incorporated in judicial reasoning to justify the rejection of a competing decision because of that decision's unfavourable or undesirable consequences. Some examples of extra-legal consequences are: the economic consequences, for the local government, of reviewing or annulling a town-planning administrative permission; the impact in the public funds derived from the duty of the state to return taxes paid on behalf of a statute declared void; the variations produced by a decision on the economic and financial state policy; the negative political effect of the failure to comply with an international duty; the changes in the logic of the democratic system; the social consequences produced by changes introduced in the labour policy.[9]

The relevance of distinguishing among these types of consequences is twofold. Firstly, the argument referring to legal consequences is less controversial than the argument referring to extra-legal consequences. This is so since legal consequences are usually articulated, in the law-adjudication justificatory discourse, by other elements coming from the corresponding legal system that are easily identifiable or the belonging of which to the system and its importance are not controversial. It would be difficult for someone to deny that legal certainty is an aim protected by legal systems, leaving aside the issue that the expression "legal certainty" is a vague one which may have multiple meanings. In contrast, it is generally contentious whether the positive or negative effects of an unwritten social, economic or political principle or value can be used as a reason for adopting or rejecting a certain decision. Thus, e.g., it is not clear if "economic stability" can be brought forward in a decision as a reason for deciding one way or the other – and it is even less clear if judges are the ones entitled to do this balancing of values, principles and interests of a given society – despite the fact that it seems, at first glance, a positive and desirable status for a society to reach. Moreover, the analysis would be incomplete if one argues that economic stability is desirable, without mapping out whether there is some legal principle or legally-protected interest that is being defeated, unapplied or overruled

[8]These type arguments come from an analysis of a set of rulings of the Spanish Constitutional Court that I did a couple of years ago. Following the order of the text, these rulings are: STC 45/1989, de 20th February; STC 195/1998, 1st October; STC 75/1984, 27th June; STC 37/1981, 16th November; STC 178/2004, 21st October; STC 184/2004, 2nd November.

[9]These examples are taken from the study of a set of rulings of the Spanish Constitutional Court mentioned in the previous footnote. Following the order of the text, these rulings are: STC 54/2002, 27th February; STC 13/1992, 6th February; STC 155/2005, 9th June; ATC 135/2004, 20th April.; STC 22/1981, 2nd July.

by the desirable extra-legal effect that the decision may carry. In short, the problem of extra-legal consequences in judicial argumentation is that the justification of the desirability or positive character of them is not a straightforward issue. Further, in many cases this argument is dressed as one of common sense or authority which, at the end, hides both the existence of a fundamental disagreement on the matter and the reasons that really justify the decision (Bell 1983:36).

Secondly, the distinction is also useful to identify criteria for assessing the argument from consequences that are problematic, especially when applied to extra-legal consequences, and to consider the need of having both common and differentiated criteria for each type of consequences.[10] However, in some cases there is no clear dividing line between legal and extra-legal consequences, or the latter are redirected to legal principles or norms.

Keeping in mind the concept of the argument referring to consequences and the two types of consequences that play a role in legal argumentation, the following sections will expose the main points of consequence-based reasoning in the three authors under study: MacCormick, Wróblewski and Feteris.[11]

### *1.2.1 MacCormick's Theory*

In MacCormick's theory, the argument from consequences acts as a second-order justification, which consists of the material justification of the normative and factual premises. This second-order justification follows the deductive syllogism (first-order justification) when the latter is insufficient for solving a hard case or when there is a problem of interpretation, relevance, proof or classification. At this second level, three elements have an important role to play, which are consistency, coherence, and consequences of the alternative decisions. The first two are requirements of the decision making sense within the given system, while the latter looks for the decision to make sense with the perceptible world (MacCormick 1997:132).

[10]In my view, this is the proposal of Bengoetxea. Some of the common criteria for assessing consequences that he points out are the *unity* among the parts of the argument, the *consistency* or absence of contradictions among the elements of the argument, the *coherence* of the argument with the legal system, and the *completeness*, that is, that the argument gives account of all its premises. Concerning the different criteria, the parameters of evaluation of legal consequences are: substantive equality, the goals and purposes of the norm or branch of law, institutional values, constitutional principles or general principles of law. Extra-legal consequences, in turn, are assessed through axiological criteria such as economic stability, good international relations, and protection of the social welfare of the society or of a certain group. The problem is, precisely, that with the consequences being hypothetical, there is no possibility of an empirical evaluation when they are used as an argument; instead, their assessment is always made *a priori* and abstractly, which prevents the rational control of those hypotheses (Bengoetxea 1993b:46ff).

[11]I borrow this expression from Péter Cserne (2012).

MacCormick is especially interested in the justification of the second level because if the premises are well-justified, a formally correct deduction from the premises will lead to a justified or rational conclusion, interpretation, or decision. Consequences are brought into the theory as a reminder that legal decisions, and particularly judicial decisions, do not impact only on the shape of the legal system, but also – and maybe mainly – directly on people and other dimensions or subsystems within society.

Following a suggestion of Rudden (1979), the Scottish scholar distinguishes between juridical and behavioural consequences. Juridical consequences, or consequences with logical implications relevant for legal justification, are those that have effects within the legal system. Behavioural consequences, on the other hand, are those effects that the decision produces in the world, in the behaviour of individuals and of economy and society (MacCormick 1983:251).

There are other important aspects in MacCormick's writings about consequences. According to his view, some types and ranges of consequences are *necessary* and *relevant* in the justification of decisions, and, thus, should be included. This is the result of placing his proposal as a middle-way between two extreme views: justification only based on consequences – with the main criterion here being the cost-benefit ratio – and justification that guarantees the nature and quality of the decision (1997:101–102).

However, incorporation of consequences in judicial reasoning cannot ignore a crucial rule applicable to legal argumentation in general: that the legal answer "always has to be capable of being framed in terms of the law, through interpretation of statues or of precedents, or of legal principles developed through reflection on law as practically coherent normative order". In this vein, a primary requirement of legal reasoning is to show that the ruling "does not contradict validly established rules of law". A second requirement is to show that the decision is supported by established legal principles. When both requirements are not sufficient or conclusive in favour of a single ruling, then consistency and coherence need to be complemented by the argument about consequences (MacCormick 2005:101, 104).

Together with the requirements just mentioned, the justification process should lead to the universalisation of the reasons involved in the decision, which is a way of realizing formal justice or the egalitarian character of the rule of law (MacCormick 2005:230–231).[12] The universalisation requisite applies also to consequentialist reasoning, which means that one criterion in the evaluation of the reasoning should be its capacity of being universalised, i.e. of becoming a general norm of the

[12]By universalisation or universalisability in adjudication legal theorists refer to the fact that the judge that adopts a decision in a particular case has to be ready to give the same solution to all future cases with analogous relevant features. Uniformity in judicial decisions is a requirement also of consistency and coherence of the legal system, at the same time as being an expression of the rule of justice that "requires that those who are essentially similar should be treated alike". Perelman calls it the rule of *formal justice*, "because it does not tell us *when* beings are essentially similar nor *how* they must be treated" (Perelman 1977:81–82; 1974:28).

system.[13] In the same sense, one should understand MacCormick's claim as saying that relevant consequences are those that are based on a general rule and not only on the specific effects produced by the decision over the parties (1997:150).

Finally, MacCormick identifies the determination of the criteria for assessing consequences as a "trap" of consequentialism. Without distinguishing among juridical and behavioural consequences, he says that this exam should be done in the light of criteria such as "justice", "common sense", "public policy", and "convenience" (1997:150; 1983:255). Evaluation, then, considers a plurality of values that law aims to uphold, and not only utility or a cost-benefit relation. This is why consequentialist argument cannot be strictly assimilated into utilitarian reasoning. Assessing consequences is not only done according to a plurality of values, but, in the words of this scholar, it is at least in part subjective, because different judges can attribute different weights or importance to the diverse evaluation criteria. He even raises the following question: can these criteria be redirected to a single metric or should one accept that they are incommensurable? This question, however, is left relatively unanswered. There are values, he argues, that are "imperfectly commensurable even situationally"; on the other hand, there are irresolvable contentious cases where the disagreement is a reasonable one (2005:117). The suggestion seems to be that in these last cases, judges can justify their rulings in several directions, and logical form, universability and completeness act as basic argumentative requirements that only guarantee a *minimum* of "correctness".

### *1.2.2 Wróblewski's Theory*

Firstly, it is advisable to note that Wróblewski uses the term "consequences" to describe two different operations: the "choice of consequences" and the "justification through consequences". The first use of the term refers to the competence that certain norms confer on judges for particularizing the consequences of their decisions, with this determination being inside their discretionary powers by explicit recognition of the legal order (Wróblewski 1992:189ff). The typical example is criminal rules that enable judges to decide the years of imprisonment within an established range. However, the exercise of this competence does not necessarily involve consequence-based reasoning but rather is just the use of a judicial power.

Wróblewski's second use of the term "consequences" is the one of interest here. Justification through consequences, as Wróblewski explains, is justification that includes consequences among the reasons for justifying a decision or, in other words, reasoning that justifies a decision or an action "by the evaluation of its consequences" (1984:141). The author differentiates this type of justification from

[13]Some authors have pointed out that universability is a feature of rationality of argumentation according to the great majority of theories of practical reasoning. Wróblewski says that even if the former idea could be debated, universability can be nevertheless understood as a requirement of its legality (1984:160–161).

"justification through principles", which is a justification where the principle stands as the *ultima ratio* of the decision. Nonetheless, both types of justification are interrelated in three senses: first, because the classification of consequences is based on the category of principles; second, since "a justification through consequences is needed when the principles used in justification refer to consequences, or when the choice of these principles depends on the evaluation of their consequences"; and third, since they are likely to operate jointly, particularly in hard cases (1984:156).

Wróblewski classifies consequences in the categories of logico-semiotical, normative and factual (1984:151ff). As has been said, the classification is related to three types of principles: (a) principles as a rule of justificatory reasoning (PRR), for example principles of logic, rhetoric, argumentation, *topoi*; (b) an enacted norm and/or its formal consequences or interpretative consequences treated as valid rules having some special relevance (PN); and (c) a rule which is related with enacted norms but is neither their formal neither their interpretative consequence (PR). In this last case, the expression "principle" stands for the reasons of the norms, their rationalisation or their axiological grounds.

As to the first classification, *logico-semiotical consequences* are those inferred from the rules or decisions according to the rules of justificatory reasoning, that is, inferred from the first type of principle just mentioned (PRR). Formal consequences (i.e. those inferred from norms through formal logical calculi) and interpretative consequences (i.e. those that are the results of interpretation of enacted legal norms) are examples of this category. *Normative consequences* are of two types: (a) logico-semiotical consequences considered to be valid rules according to an accepted concept of validity or rule of recognition; and (b) consequences of rules or decisions in terms of rights or duties ascribed to subjects or that qualify their behaviour. Lastly, there are *factual consequences* of rules and decisions, which are identified and analysed on a socio-psychological empirical level of the phenomena and have a space-time dimension. This last type would be part of what I have called extra-legal consequences.

In his analysis, Wróblewski assumes "that the justification should include *inter alia* a reference to valid legal rules, to facts, and evaluations, and that the rules of reasoning and premises of the decision that are used could be controlled" (1984:140). This assumption is a rather relevant one, since it presupposes several choices, e.g., the determination of the criteria of validity of legal rules and the decision of incorporating evaluations in processes of legal justification. It also reinforces the idea of making explicit in the decision several elements with the purpose of enabling its control. Choices, in turn, reveal theoretical options (e.g. how to understand the legal system) or even an ideology, in Wróblewski's words. His own theoretical framework for analysing justification contains choices and stands on two basic values: legality and rationality. Legality implies a decision according to law, i.e. that "(a) the decision does not create the law, but applies it; (b) the scope of law is determined, and (c) the decision implements the axiology of applied law" (1984:158–159). Rationality refers to the formal conditions for the internal and external level of justification, which are consistency between the premises and the decision, consistency of the premises themselves and consistency between the premises and their justification (1974).[14]

Wróblewski's proposal to evaluate consequences identifies internal, external and mixed criteria. The internal criterion evaluates consequences in relation to the elements of the system, and has as sub-criteria consistency, normative coherence and formal justice. Coherence requires that the argument, the chain of arguments and the decision resulting from it are axiologically coherent with the respective legal order (Wróblewski 1984:153), the verification of which demands the identification of the values underlying rules, principles and legal institutions. The external criterion uses values that enable the assessment of a legal decision from outside the system, substantive justice being the most important one. The mixed criterion is acceptability (Aarnio 1987:185ff) and consists of the approval or rejection of the consequences by a concrete audience, i.e., the one that has particular social features and shares a certain axiological consensus. The better – justified decision will be the one that achieves the adherence of the universal audience. Thus, the judge should ask himself if the consequences of his decision would be accepted or rejected by the parties and/or the public opinion. The acceptance of the decision depends on several factors, such as the amount of harmful consequences, any damages to goods, rights or interests that could be affected, and any unacceptable consequences (Wróblewski 1984:153).

### *1.2.3 Feteris' Pragma-Dialectical Proposal*

The main purpose of the pragma-dialectical theory applied to legal proceedings is to reconstruct the argumentation of the parties and of the judge as part of a critical discussion subjected to rational control (Feteris 2005:462)[15] In several articles, Feteris applies and specifies the pragma-dialectical model to the analysis and evaluation of argumentation referring to consequences in legal decisions. For this author, argumentation referring to consequences is an argument that justifies a decision appealing to the consequences that adjusts to a desirable goal or that enable to reach that goal. That is, the positive or desirable consequences of an act are such to the extent that they satisfy a desirable or valuable goal.

In its basic formulation, consequentialist argument is structured as follows (Feteris 2002:355):

| | |
|---|---|
| point of view: | Act X is desirable |
| because: | Act X produces consequence Y (empirical statement) |
| and: | Consequence Y is desirable (normative statement) |

[14]In Wróblewski (1984) he distinguishes five levels of justification.

[15]One of the founding texts on pragma-dialectical theory is Van Eemeren, and Grootendorst (1992).

The point of view refers to a certain act X that can be a decision or an interpretation. The normative statement establishes that consequence Y is desirable, and the empirical statement holds that act X produces consequence Y. The important thing is to answer affirmatively the two critical questions that guide the evaluation of pragmatic argumentation: "Does application of rule X in interpretation X' lead to consequence Y?"[16]; "Is consequence Y indeed (un)desirable?". The first question is concerned with the existence of a causal relation between the act and the consequences, and evaluates the empirical statement; the second one asks for the justification of the normative statement, or in other words, for the reasons that support the statement affirming the desirability or acceptability of the consequences at stake.

It is in the subordinated level where these questions should be solved, the second one by demonstrating the compatibility of consequences Y' with a purpose P and justifying purpose P as intended by the historical legislator (e.g., through the study of parliamentary debate), or as objectively prescribed by the legal order (e.g., explaining to what extent purpose P underlies certain rules, principles or values).

However, these justifications are neither simple nor plain. Identification of the purpose intended by the historical legislator does not necessarily work when interpreting textural norms, such as constitutional clauses, because their vagueness was probably needed to reach an agreement that would enable different readings of them. In this sense, it would be difficult to identify "the" purpose of the historical legislator. In addition, it is frequently the case that the purpose of the legislator when enacting a norm can collide with other ends protected by different valid legal rules. Additionally, the purpose of a norm is not always clear, explicit or easy to detect. In the case of identifying the "purpose objectively prescribed by the legal order", similar problems arise.

As to the first critical question noted above, there is no further orientation of the elements that would help to answer it, because it refers to the causal relation between a decision or an act and the projected consequences, which is a factual problem relatively unsolved when arguing about possible future consequences.

Starting from the simple structure of consequentialist argument, Feteris proposes a pragma-dialectical framework for analysing and evaluating practical arguments in Law. The argument referring consequences on its own may be weak or insufficient, and it can be complemented redirecting the (un)desirability of consequences Y of act X to the (un)desirability of the end Z. This complex argumentation is structured in three levels – main, subordinated and sub-subordinated. The structure is represented as follows: (Feteris 2005:462ff)

---

[16]In a similar line of argument, Van Eemeren and Grootendorst point out that with instrumental argumentation, as a model of argumentation based on causality relation, the important questions are: "Is the announced effect of the proposed measure really so desirable? Will this effect indeed follow? Or could it be achieved more easily by way of another measure? Does the proposed measure not have any serious negative side-effects?" (1992:102).

1. Interpretation X is desirable; interpretation X leads to Y; T is desirable (consequentialist argument)
2. Y is desirable; Y satisfies principle, goal, directive or value Z; Z is desirable (teleological argument)
3. Z is desirable; Z is coherent and consistent with general legal principles, ends and values P underlying the legal system (argument from coherence or consistency)

As can be appreciated, this is not a simple model of consequentialist reasoning, but the coordination of three arguments – consequentialist argument, teleological argument and argument from coherence – provides a structure with more force than the sum of the individual argumentative weights. This type of justification is used when the judge is confronted with different possibilities of interpretation. In these cases, judicial argumentation should reflect the choice between the two rival points of views of the parties, and should show the balancing of these positions according to the desirable or undesirable consequences for the end of the rule.[17]

Feteris also emphasises the importance of reasonableness and equity as values for the judge to consider when balancing different competing interpretations of a rule, and that may be used in restricting or extending the sphere of application of a rule based on the absurd consequences that a too extensive or too restrictive application can produce with relation to the rule's goal (Feteris 2005:462ff).

In the pragma-dialectical model, as it has been shown, the determination of the goal or purpose of the norm applicable to the case plays a central role. However, legal systems contain a multiplicity of goals that can easily collide in a concrete case, so the decision to favour one and to leave aside the other should be also justified. A further problem could be those cases in which there are no explicit norms to adjudicate them. In such cases, the solution, according to this model, would be to recall the goals that inspire the legal order as a whole, even when they are not explicit ones. This type of technique has the known problems of how to "detect" or "read" the values that underlie a certain legal order, or else the problems of "assigning" meanings which implies several interpretative choices or definitions, with the result that the exercise of detection, reading or ascription of meaning can widely vary among different interpreters. A related point has to do with the argument referring to extra-legal consequences. Feteris' model does not differentiate among legal and extra-legal consequences, since the important point is that consequences are linked with the goal or purpose of the norm or of the legal order. In this regard, extra-legal consequences that cannot be easily related to a clear purpose of a norm or of the legal order would not fit in the proposed structure.

In this section, starting from an outline of the argument from consequences, I have briefly explained the main points of the theory of each scholar as to this type of argument. From the above description, some similarities and differences emerge,

---

[17]"If application of rule *R* in interpretation *X1* in the circumstances of the given case *C1*, *C2*, . . . *Cn* leads to *Y1*, and *Y1* is desirable, and if application of rule *R* in interpretation *X2* leads to *Y2* and *Y2* is undesirable, then application of rule *R* in interpretation *R1* is to be preferred to application of rule *R* in interpretation *X2*" (Feteris 2008:490).

which are interesting to highlight for the purpose of the following section. With regard to the similarities, all three scholars insist in one way or another that the decision, and therefore, the arguments from consequences that support it, has to respect the rule of law and the valid law of the legal system. Secondly, all three are concerned with the need of establishing criteria for evaluating the use of the argument from consequences. While MacCormick proposes general criteria and Wróblewski classifies consequences in three types, Feteris points out the critical question in terms of the desirability of the possible consequences to which a certain decision could lead, even though she does not define criteria for assessing them. Third, both MacCormick and Wróblewski make a distinction similar to the one given here between legal consequences – juridical and normative – and extra legal consequences – behavioural and factual. Finally, these same two authors consider that, in some cases, the use of the argument of extra legal consequences or the influence of no-law, to borrow Wróblewski's expression, is inevitable or, more precisely, it is a necessary condition for the rationality of the decision.

There are also divergent points among the proposals under analysis that come from the different ways of approaching consequentialist argumentation. MacCormick's normative view consists of including the argument from consequences in the wider picture of the two levels of justification and the requirement that the decision has to make sense both within the legal system and with the world. Wróblewski assumes an analytic style in treating this argument, since he distinguishes and classifies both the types of consequences relevant to the Law and the criteria for evaluation. Feteris, in turn, is mainly concerned with the structure of the argument from consequences or with how the different levels of argumentation are interconnected.

## 1.3 Judges on Consequences

This section will offer a synthesis of the main consequentialist arguments – both legal and extra-legal – given in a recent ruling of the Chilean Constitutional Court, and will analyse them in the light of the theoretical proposals described in the previous section, pointing out the arguments' strengths and weaknesses.[18]

The ruling chosen is one that declared unconstitutional an article of a statute that regulates the Previsional Health Institutions (PHI or "Isapres").[19] The article that was challenged through this legal proceeding regulated the faculty of the public institution that supervises the PHI (Superintendence) in fixing ranges for differentiating prices of the health insurance plans according to the age and gender of the insured (significantly more expensive for people of 60 or more years and for women of 20 years onwards). The Court considered this norm against the

[18]STC 1710-10-INC, 6th August 2010.

[19]The Chilean Health Systems combines, since 1981 reform, a public (National Health Fund or "Fonasa") and a private system. In 2011, 22% of the Chilean population has private health insurance.

constitutional principles of equality, protection of health and protection of social security (art.19 nº2, 9 and 18 of the Constitution).

The ruling, both in the majority and the dissenting opinions, includes arguments referring legal and extra-legal consequences. The Court argues early in its ruling that the convenience of the declaration of unconstitutionality for the constitutional order should be appreciated by means of "the determination of the consequences of the disappearance of the norm. If the result is more harmful or negative than the pre-existent to the annulment, the abolition of the norm is not convenient for the public interest and for the full validity of the Rule of Law".[20] Contrary to what it could be expected from introducing this argument as part of its reasoning, the majority opinion did not further develop it, and at the end decides to declare the challenged sections as contravening the Constitution.

Against the decision of the majority, more precise consequentialist arguments were given. For example, the German constitutional doctrine was cited to support the fact that the court should abstain itself from declaring the unconstitutionality of a statute if "(a) it avoids a normative gap on a certain matter in case of declaring it null; (b) it prevents that the ruling interferes in the liberty the legislator to enact norms (*Gestaltungsfreiheit*); (c) the declaration of voidness is not necessary to correct a partial omission of the legislator; (d) there is a technical impossibility in the Law, e.g., when the declaration of voidness does not permit to achieve the purpose of the ruling; and (e) the declaration of voidness cannot eliminate the damage that is trying to avoid".[21] Except for letter (c), the rest of the cases reveal the negative normative impacts that the elimination of a norm from the legal system would produce, such as the persistence of the damage that the ruling is trying to avoid – in this concrete case, the injury to fundamental rights –, the interference in the legislative sphere, the impossibility of re-establishing the legal order and the production of a legal vacuum.

In the same line of argument, the minority opinion argues that the constitutional ruling that derogates a norm produces a profound change in the system of sources of law. This means that the court should declare unconstitutional a norm only when there is no other possible interpretation harmonic with the Constitution. On the other hand, this opinion reproduces some of the considerations of the majority one, insisting that the exclusion of the norm from the legal order cannot generate more harmful effects than the ones produced by the existence of the norm being challenged. The legal vacuum and the legal uncertainty produced by the annulment, it is contended, leads to a state of "more unconstitutionality".

There is also extra-legal consequence-based reasoning in this case. Thus, the majority decision opposes to consider extra-legal consequences of the ruling as a factor of the decision, while the minority opinion stresses the need to include them in the reasoning to declare or not the unconstitutionality of the norm.

In a confusing paragraph, the majority opinion states that "It is possible, accordingly, that the decisions of the Constitutional Court produce an inevitable

---

[20]STC Rol 558, 5th June 2007, para. 18 y 19. Cited by STC 1710-10-INC, 6th August 2010, cons. 23.

[21]Presentation of the President Sebastián Piñera, 20th May 2010, p.37.

political, economic, social and cultural impact, but this does not mean that those decisions have been political, economic or cultural ones. All the decisions of the Constitutional Court are strictly legal, independent of the nature of the impact they produce, be it political, economic, social or cultural. From a different perspective, when adopting a decision the Court can be fully conscious of the extra-legal impact that it can produce, but that conviction cannot inhibit the court from solving the matter brought before it . . . ".

On the other hand, the minority opinion does not go into depth in the analysis of extra-legal consequences, but it only states that the declaration of unconstitutionality should balance all the effects that it could carry, being those legal or of a different type (i.e. social, economic and political ones).

Additionally, during the proceedings, several presentations were made in order to identify in a more concrete way which would these consequences be,[22] underscoring the need to establish: " . . . the constitutional effects that a possible derogation of the legal norm in question would cause in the affiliated and in the Previsional Health Institutions, especially in relation to the coverage of health plans, discrimination in prices and arbitrary injure to certain groups of the society, effects in the present and future health contracts, viability of the private health system constitutionally granted, among others". The final consequences of this legal proceeding, continues the argument, "could seriously impact the Chilean health system as a hole (public and private), including the coverage and benefits for the affiliated and the final price charged to them, the viability of the Previsional Health Institutions and, finally, the State that consequently, in case of derogation of the norm, should significantly increase its budget for health".

I will sum up the lines of consequentialist arguments alleged in this proceeding and reproduced above. On the one side, the ruling points out five cases where the declaration of unconstitutionality should be avoided for its negative or undesirable legal consequences. Thus, unconstitutionality should be avoided if: (a) it leads to a normative gap; (b) it produces legal uncertainty; (c) it results in a more harmful situation than that pre-existent to the declaration of unconstitutionality (*horror vacui*); (d) it is inconvenient for public interest or for the rule of law; or (e) it produces interference in the legislative sphere. On the other side, in the proceedings, arguments were given in order to demonstrate the possible negative extra-legal effects that the declaration of unconstitutionality could produce. Such a declaration could: (a) have negative effects on the contributors, such as a change in the coverage, benefits and price for their health insurance plans; (b) endanger the existence of the private health system; and (c) have deep negative economic repercussions in the public budget for Health, since the increase in the private insurance plans would generate a migration of people from the private to the public system.[23] However,

[22]Presentation of the Association of PHI, 30th April 2010.

[23]The latter is argued in the presentations of the governmental health institutions. These possible future consequences were backed by statistical data in the Report "Elimination of the Factors' Board", of the Superintendence of Health (30th May 2010).

despite these arguments – which are, at least in appearance, strong – to reject the petition of unconstitutionality of the challenged statute, the decision of the majority supported the declaration of unconstitutionality.

The analysis and evaluation of these arguments can be done using the different elements and tools reviewed in the former section.[24] Legal consequences, as it has been already suggested, are less problematic than extra-legal consequences since the former are linked with elements of the legal system, the existence of which is uncontroversial. In this sense, legal consequences such as avoiding legal gaps or ensuring legal certainty, from the perspective of the three theories above, cannot be understood in an isolated way but only in relation to other legal arguments such as the teleological argument and the argument from coherence. For example, the claim that the declaration of unconstitutionality would not be coherent with the rule of law could be understood as a mixed argumentation composed of consequentialist and coherence arguments.

On the other hand, the argument referring to extra-legal consequences appears as an expression of MacCormick's requirement that the decision should make sense with the world, viewing "making sense" as taking into account the decision's different effects in the extra-legal reality, such as the possible economic impact of declaring the statute unconstitutional. This economic impact could affect the beneficiaries of private health insurance, the State, and the private health system. Here, nevertheless, the questions of how to select *who*, within the different persons, groups or institutions that can be affected by these consequences, should be taken into account in the reasoning of the judge and the question of *how to balance* positive and negative consequences among those affected by a decision remains unanswered by the proposals of the scholars under study, even when those questions seem to contain decisive elements in the evaluation of the argument referring to extra-legal consequences.

Following MacCormick's proposal, the evaluation of consequences should be done through criteria such as substantive justice, public convenience and common sense. However, these criteria are insufficiently defined or, in other words, are soft directives for balancing positive and negative consequences of the alternative decisions, since they are based on contested concepts that need, in turn, to be delimited before being used as a parameter for the soundness or correctness of consequentialist arguments. For example, in the case under analysis, could it be said that the changes in coverage, benefits and price of the health insurance plans

[24] I will like to remark the fact that it could be contended to classify the propositions of letters (a) to (e) and (a) to (c), respectively, as proper arguments referring legal and extra-legal consequences, when they could be qualified as mere considerations that, together with other ones, push the decision in one direction. Therefore, if they are not arguments at all but only generic propositions which are found reasonable or of common sense within the legal practice, it would be problematic to treat them as proper arguments, and as such, to apply to them the theoretical proposals under review. Even assuming this last point of view, i.e., that there are argumentative deficiencies in the way the reasons are constructed, I think that some analysis of those propositions *qua* arguments is possible.

are unfavourable consequences of the declaration of unconstitutionality? And, is the correctness of this conclusion corroborated by the fact that those effects are against substantive justice? A similar problem arises with Wróblewski's criterion of acceptability: When should one conclude that the argument from consequences has complied with this criterion? Which is the particular audience that has to potentially accept the argument from consequences? In light of the extra-legal consequences of this proceeding, it is difficult to imagine to what extent a reference to the probability of being accepted by a social group or by the universal audience contributes to the soundness of an argument.

An additional difficulty is that these criteria are, on the one hand, multiple and there is uncertainty whether there is any order for applying them or if one of them alone is enough for assuring the proper construction of the argument from consequences. Moreover, if the solution that results from applying one criterion, e.g. substantive justice, is contrary to the solution that results from applying a different criterion, e.g. public interest or common sense, there are no meta-criteria that resolve the contradiction. On the other hand, these criteria do not account for the peculiarities and problems associated with each type of consequences.

A further issue in evaluating the argument referring to consequences is the test of universalisation, that is, to respond positively to the question "is it possible to use this same consequentialist argument in future similar cases and in this way, allow the decision to become a general norm of the system?". This test could be, nevertheless, problematic in the case of extra-legal consequences, because they are tightly interlinked with the particularities of the case. Additionally, in practice, in cases of abstract control of constitutionality as the one under study, the possibility of universalising the reasons would take place only when the challenged norm is the same one.

It is not necessary, in Wróblewski's vision, in apparent contrast to Feteris' proposal, to justify the introduction of extra-legal consequences as a factor in argumentation by trying to link them, sometimes in a forced way, with a certain norm or with values or purposes supposedly pursued by the legal order as a whole; instead, one should try to relate the argument to reliable data that supports the prediction of (un)favourable future consequences of the decision.

Feteris' pragma-dialectical approach makes explicit the different statements that are needed for producing a sound decision, including using justified premises and connecting and organising them in levels (main, subordinated, sub-subordinated). This approach properly points out the critical questions concerning the external justification of the empirical and normative statements, though it does not discuss in depth in how to achieve this. In the Chilean case study given above, the first critical question would be "does the unconstitutionality of the challenged statute leads to a legal gap?" It would then be necessary to rewrite this question with each of the effects alleged. The second critical question would be "is Y undesirable?", replacing Y with each of those effects (legal gaps, legal uncertainty, increase of the insurance plans, etc.) If the critical questions remain unanswered, or if it is detected that the attribution of (un)desirability of a possible consequence of a decision is unjustified, then the argument looses soundness and lacks force as a justificatory reason for the decision.

Applying the complex pragma-dialectical framework, which combines the argument from consequences, the teleological argument and the argument from coherence, to one of the arguments of the Chilean proceedings, one can reconstruct the framework as follows:

1. The declaration of unconstitutionality of the norm is undesirable; the declaration of unconstitutionality and the derogation of the norm generate a legal gap; this legal gap is undesirable.
2. This legal gap is undesirable; this legal gap violates the right to equality and leaves privately-insured people unprotected from PHI; violation of equality and leaving privately-insured people unprotected is undesirable.
3. Violation of equality and leaving privately-insured people unprotected is undesirable; violation of equality and leaving privately-insured people unprotected is incoherent with the legal system that grants equality and legal certainty as general principles of law.

According to this model, it is possible to say that the undesirability of producing a legal gap is linked with the violation of certain goals of the legal system, such as equality, and to the goal of the norm that regulates PHI, which is to protect the people affiliated to those health institutions. Nevertheless, a different interpretation is perfectly possible, considering other norms of the system and balancing diverse goals, which means that the selection of the goal has to also be justified, preventing reasonable counter-arguments.

Lastly, in these proceedings the arguments referring to extra-legal consequences are supported by empirical data, an element that is absent from the theoretical proposals.[25] For example, data are used by some parties to make a prospective picture of what the behaviour of privately-insured people would be if insurance plans increase their prices; there is also a calculation of the amount of money that the migration of the privately-insured to the public health system would cost the state. For this purpose, legal argumentation theory could bring in some of the methods and tools proposed by empirical jurisprudence and economic analysis of law; judicial practice could consider establishing mechanisms similar to those divisions that parliaments have for analysing the financial impact of legislation, so that higher and constitutional courts could evaluate the future economic effects of their rulings and that this information could be used as an argument in the decision.

In this section, I have applied three theoretical models to some consequentialist arguments that were put forward both by the court and the parties to the proceedings, and this has permitted me to identify some strong and weak points in each model. To sum them up, the strength of MacCormick's theory lies in distinguishing types

[25]With the consequences being hypothetical, there is no possibility of an empirical evaluation when those consequences are used as an argument, but their assessment is always made *a priori* and abstractly; empirical data, then, is only useful to give force to the claim to favourable or unfavourable future consequences by comparing with analogous past situation or attempting to predict the magnitude of the impact.

of consequences and being concerned with its problems and evaluation; the weak point refers mainly to the vagueness of the criteria for assessing consequences and the absence of specific elements for evaluating the argument from extra-legal consequences. Wróblewski's proposal of distinguishing types of criteria for evaluating consequences is useful because it includes different dimensions that can operate jointly; the problem is one of imprecision of the criteria of evaluation, as with MacCormick's theory, and the lack of a link between the types of consequences and the classification of criteria. Finally, Feteris' model has the strength of making visible the several argumentative steps to obtain a well-supported decision and of singling out the importance of the critical questions, though it fails to give criteria for evaluating consequences and purports to establish a strong link between argument referring to consequences and goals of the legal system, which is doubtful at least with respect to extra-legal consequences.

## 1.4 Conclusions

In this paper, I have examined three theoretical proposals concerning the argument referring to consequences and tried to show, with an example, to what extent they are helpful and sufficient for analysing and evaluating the use of this argument in judicial decisions.

The three proposals subscribe, in my view, to the original goal of argumentation theories: subjecting judicial decisions to criteria of rationality that constitutes a limit to judicial discretion. However, a way of enhancing the practical use of the argument to consequences would be to integrate elements of the three theories. The idea of universalising the reasons for making a decision, the identification of more precise formal and substantive criteria for its evaluation and a well-defined structure are features that contribute to a better framing and justification of the inclusion of the future possible consequences of a decision in judicial reasoning. Furthermore, the distinction between legal and extra-legal consequences is necessary because the latter are likely to produce more tensions than the former, especially if they are used to hide the judicial reading-in of political, economic and social considerations in cases of legal gaps or in the interpretation of open-texture legal norms. This may lead, therefore, to the need of increasing the standards of justification when extra-legal consequences arguments are at stake.

As to evaluation of the argument from consequences, concrete guidelines and a more accurate definition of the criteria should be given, so that they could stand as useful parameters to control the argument's soundness and correctness. On the other hand, empirical tools should be incorporated to evaluate extra-legal consequences in the argumentation. These last two suggestions could be the guiding questions of future research.

## References

Aarnio, A. 1987. *The rational as reasonable. A treatise on legal justification*. Dordrecht: Kluwer.

Bell, J. 1983. *Policy arguments in judicial decisions*. Oxford: Clarendon.

Bengoetxea, J. 1993a. *The legal reasoning of the European Court of Justice*. Oxford: Clarendon.

Bengoetxea, J. 1993b. Una defensa del consecuencialismo en el Derecho. *Telos (Revista latinoamericana de estudios utilitaristas)* II(2): 31–68.

Cserne, P. 2012. Consequence-based arguments in legal reasoning: A jurisprudential preface to law and economics. In *Efficiency, sustainability, and justice to future generations*, ed. K. Mathis, 31–54. Berlin: Springer.

Dworkin, R. 1986. *Law's empire*. Cambridge: Harvard University Press.

Feteris, E. 2002. A pragma-dialectical approach of the analysis and evaluation of pragmatic argumentation in a legal context. *Argumentation* 16: 349–367.

Feteris, E. 2005. The rational reconstruction of argumentation referring to consequences and purposes in the application of legal rules: A pragma-dialectical perspective. *Argumentation* 19: 459–470.

Feteris, E. 2008. The rational reconstruction of weighing and balancing on the basis of teleological-evaluative considerations in the justification of judicial decisions. *Ratio Juris* 21(4): 481–495.

García Amado, J.A. 1986. Del método jurídico a las teorías de la argumentación. *Anuario de Filosofía del Derecho* III: 151–182.

Gottlieb, G. 1968. *The logic of choice. An investigation of the concept of rule and rationality*. London: George Allen & Unwin Ltd.

MacCormick, N. 1983. On legal decisions and their consequences: From Dewey to Dworkin. *New York University Law Review* 58(2): 239–258.

MacCormick, N. 1997. *Legal reasoning and legal theory*. Oxford: Clarendon.

MacCormick, N. 2005. *Rhetoric and the rule of Law*. Oxford: Oxford University Press.

Perelman, Ch. 1974. *De la Justicia*. México: Universidad Nacional Autónoma de México.

Perelman, Ch. 1977. *The idea of justice and the problem of argument*. London: Routledge & Kegan Paul.

Perelman, Ch, and L. Olbrechts-Tyteca. 1969. *The new rhetoric. A treatise on argumentation*. Notre Dame: University of Notre Dame Press.

Rudden, B. 1979. Consequences. *Juridical Review* 24: 193–201.

Scheffler, S. (ed.). 1988. *Consequentialism and its critics*. Oxford: Oxford University Press.

Sinnot-Armstrong, W. 2006. Consequentialism. *Stanford Encyclopedia of Philosophy*. http://plato.stanford.edu/entries/consequentialism/. Accessed 20 Nov 2011.

Slote, M. 1992. Consequentialism. In *Encyclopedia of ethics*, ed. L.C. Becker and C.B. Becker, 211–214. New York/London: Garland.

van Eemeren, F.H., and R. Grootendorst. 1992. *Argumentation, communication and fallacies. A pragma-dialectical perspective*. Hillsdale: Lawrence Erlbaum.

Walton, D. 1999. Historical origins of *argumentum ad consequentiam*. *Argumentation* 13: 251–264.

Wróblewski, J. 1974. Legal syllogism and rationality of judicial decision. *Rechtstheorie* 1974: 33–46.

Wróblewski, J. 1984. Justification through principles and justification through consequences. In *Reason in law*, ed. C. Farrali and E. Pattaro, 129–161. Milano: Giuffrè.

Wróblewski, J. 1992. *The judicial application of the law*. Dordrecht: Kluwer.

# Chapter 2
# On the *Argumentum ad Absurdum* in Statutory Interpretation: Its Uses and Normative Significance

**Thomas Bustamante**

## 2.1 Introduction

In this chapter, I attempt to explain how the *argumentum ad absurdum* may be used in legal reasoning and to formulate a short set of directives to help lawyers justify their claims or decisions grounded in such argument. The main point of this effort is to define the essential *rules of interpretation* that can be derived from its structure and its underlying assumptions. By describing such rules, I believe that it is possible to understand the normative significance of that form of argument, i.e., the requirements that follow from this argument and the conditions under which one can rely on it as a solid basis for a legal decision.

In the recent literature on legal argumentation, there are two different versions of the *ad absurdum* argument that are accepted by scholars as being able to justify a particular legal opinion. Firstly, it can be understood in its strictly logical sense, that is, as a form of proof by contradiction. Nevertheless, as I will argue in the first section, this sense of the *argumentum ad absurdum* is of little use for ordinary legal argumentation, since it only makes explicit a logical fault that can be easily identified in the argument of the speaker. Secondly, in a less strict sense, which is the way in which lawyers usually refer to that kind of reasoning, the apagogic argument can be classified as a pragmatic argument or an argument about the desirability or undesirability of a certain proposition. Yet, as I intend to demonstrate, the current accounts of this latter version of the *argumentum ad absurdum* still have not developed an accurate understanding of that form of argument, since they fail to realize that the *reductio ad absurdum* is a special case of pragmatic argumentation whose strength is noticeably higher in comparison with the general

T. Bustamante (✉)
Department of Legal Theory and Labour Law (DIT), Federal University of Minas Gerais, Belo Horizonte, Minas Gerais, Brazil
e-mail: tbustamante@ufmg.br

C. Dahlman and E. Feteris (eds.), *Legal Argumentation Theory: Cross-Disciplinary Perspectives*, Law and Philosophy Library 102, DOI 10.1007/978-94-007-4670-1_2,

forms of pragmatic argumentation. Hence, in order to identify the conditions under which the *ad absurdum* argument can be correctly deployed in legal discourse, I will attempt to determine, in the second session of the chapter, (Sect. 2.3.1) the nature of the argument, (Sect. 2.3.2) how it can be distinguished from generic consequentialist arguments, (Sect. 2.3.3) its context, and (Sect. 2.3.4) the rules of interpretation which can be derived from it and that define its normative significance.

## 2.2 The Strictly Logical Sense of the *Argumentum ad Absurdum*

The first sense in which *ad absurdum* argument can be understood is in its strict logical formulation, which is its strongest form. In this sense, it is a formalized argumentative scheme which helps one to identify an unacceptable conclusion regardless of the plausibility of the contents of the premises, since the reasoning under consideration is internally flawed.

In this sense, the *reductio ad absurdum* "consists in deducing from a proposition or a complex of propositions consequences that are inconsistent with each other or with the original proposition" (Ryle 1945, p. 6). Hence, in its strict logical formulation, the reductio is founded on the principle that no contradiction can be admitted:

> Contradictions are absurd or *logically false* sentences. Any sentence which entails a contradiction or logical falsehood must itself be false; and it is exactly this fact which is exploited in any application of the reductio; if a contradiction can be shown to be derivable from a formula then, on that basis alone, we may validly assert the negation of that formula. Hence, reductio is often referred to as 'proof by contradiction' (Tomassi 1999, p. 102).

In short, one establishes a syllogism by showing the opponent's conclusion to be inconsistent with its premises.

This is not, however, the kind of *ad absurdum* argument that normally attracts the attention of lawyers and legal scholars, for in fact it does not say anything more than the general requirement of consistency in any sort of speech. In legal reasoning, unlike in mathematics, the premises and the conclusions are not unambiguously stated, and therefore lawyers tend to apply the apagogic argument in a "far less rigorous" way (Daube 1969, pp. 177–179).

## 2.3 The *Argumentum ad Absurdum* as a Special Case of Pragmatic Argument

While the strictly logical version of the *argumentum ad absurdum* points out an *internal* inconsistency of an argument, since the speaker demonstrates that her opponent is committed to contradictory views, the ordinary or *pragmatic* version of that argument consists in deducing from the opponent's claim a falsehood or a statement that leads to unacceptable consequences.

A pragmatic argument can be defined as "an argumentation defending the desirability or undesirability [or, we could add, the acceptability or the unacceptability] of a specific act or course of action" (Kloosterhuis 2007, p. 72). In this interpretation, which is the "most general construal" of the *ad absurdum* argument, one can define it as "a process of refutation on grounds that absurd – and patently untenable – consequences would ensue from accepting the item at issue" (Rescher 2005, 1).

This seems to be, indeed, the way in which jurists tend to use the *argumentum ad absurdum*. Golding, for instance, understands the "practical *reductio ad absurdum*" as the argument according to which "if a purported rule, judgment, or decision would have unacceptable consequences, then the rule, judgment or decision should be rejected" (Golding 2001, p. 38). And Alexy, in his famous Theory of Legal Argumentation, describes it as an argument employed to "support the thesis that a particular interpretation (I) of a rule (R) through a word usage (W) is inadmissible" on the ground that "it would result in unacceptable, meaningless, incomprehensible, or such like results" (Alexy 1989, p. 283). This last author describes the *ad absurdum* argument as an argument form – that is, as "a structure which comprises a proposition asserted by a speaker together with the propositions advanced or presupposed as directly supporting this proposition" (Alexy 1989, p. 92) – which could be expressed thus:

1. $O \neg Z$
2. $R' \rightarrow Z$
3. $\neg R'$

In this scheme, O is a deontic operator which expresses that it is obligatory to do something, $\neg$ stands for a negation, Z is a consequence considered forbidden by the interpreter of the norm, and $R'$ is a particular interpretation of a rule R. With the help of this formal scheme, Alexy describes the logical structure of the *argumentum ad absurdum* while emphasising the non-logical character of the process of determining the premises comprised in it (Alexy 1989, p. 280).

For Alexy, once premises (1) and (2) in the scheme above are given, it is possible to infer the conclusion (3) by a simple logical operation. Nevertheless, the hardest step in the process of justification of an argument is what Wróblewski calls "external justification" of a decision, which denotes the process of asserting and justifying the major premise (1), which needs to be based on general practical reasons, and the minor premise (2), which is based on empirical arguments (Alexy 1989, pp. 283–284).[1]

We can see, therefore, that Alexy portrays the *ad absurdum* argument as a conjunction of a practical argument in the major premise and an empirical argument in the minor premise. Whilst the former deals with an interpretative argument to settle the meaning of a norm, the latter deals with factual statements.

---

[1]Wróblewski distinguishes, in a famous paper, two stages of justification of a legal syllogism. While the *internal* justification is strictly logical and refers to the relation between the premises of an argument form, the *external* justification is not a logical process and consists in the justification of the premises themselves, on the basis of pragmatic or empirical considerations (Wróblewski 1974, p. 39).

To conclude this topic, the *ad absurdum* argument in legal interpretation is a special type of *pragmatic argumentation* where the main reason for the decision is a judgment about the desirability or undesirability of the proposed interpretation of a statute (Feteris 2005, p. 461).

### *2.3.1 The Problem of the Indeterminacy of Pragmatic Arguments and the Distinctive Feature of the ad Absurdum Argument*

There are, however, strong objections against the use of the *argumentum ad absurdum* once it is understood as a scheme for argumentation referring to the consequences or the desirability of a purported interpretation of a law.

The main problem is that there are multiple reasons that could be classified as "consequentialists." As MacCormick adverts,

> Judges often allude to justice, to public policy and/or common good of the community, to legal expediency or convenience and to common sense as ostensibly different grounds or criteria of evaluation which they apply to the juridical consequences and possible ulterior outcomes of possible rulings in contested cases (MacCormick 1983, p. 255).

By the same token, Maximiliano argues that the premises comprised in the *ad absurdum* argument can assume a vast range of meanings and configurations that can refer to "evident injustice", "incoherencies", "self-contradiction", "impossibilities", "inequity", incompatibility with "common sense" etc (Maximiliano 1992, p. 166).

In the light of these uncertainties over the contents of pragmatic and consequentialist reasons, many jurists are sceptical about the potency of the apagogic argument in legal discourses. Tarello, for instance, argues that the *ad absurdum* argument is both fragile and mistakable when applied as an independent argument for a legal decision. It is fragile because the notion of absurdity is historically biased and intrinsically changeable, and it is mistakable because of its natural ambiguity (Tarello 1980, p. 371). Guastini, on the same vein, holds that the idea of absurdity is indeed subjective, "and therefore always controversial." For this author, in the rare cases when a certain interpretation of a legal provision can indisputably be classified as "absurd", the *ad absurdum* argument would be completely useless, since it would "exclude only an interpretation which no one would ever dream to suggest" (Guastini 2004, p. 177).

Although it would be silly to simply dismiss the *argumentum ad absurdum* by classifying it as a mere rhetorical trick, these objections should lead us to give a narrower scope to that argument.

It is probable, therefore, that it is not enough to define the *argumentum ad absurdum* as a pragmatic argument. As Daube convincingly argues, if the apagogic argument is conceived "as propping up a decision by showing the alternative to be inconsistent with what is desirable, reasonable, fair, lawful", then "any reasoned decision is a *reductio ad absurdum*, at least by implication", for "any decision is chosen in preference to the opposite, less acceptable one" (Daube 1969, pp. 179–180). Therefore, according to the author, we should speak of the *reductio ad absurdum* as meaning that a conduct is not just inconvenient or undesirable, but "strikingly incongruous, in conflict with the conspicuous, professed purpose of the agent" (Daube 1969, p. 180). If this is the case, then we can say that the argument means something more than a sort of pragmatic incompatibility, as is visible in the following excerpt:

> Not if you simply go out without an umbrella, but if a valetudinarian who takes an umbrella in a drizzle goes without one in a downpour. Not if a buyer does not pay, but if a man who charitably buys from an impoverished friend in order to assist him does not pay. A particularly clear instance is self-defeating conduct, where by going to extreme lengths in one direction you land at the other end, achieving precisely the reverse of your plan (Daube 1969, p. 180).

As these examples show, Daube understands the *argumentum ad absurdum* as a normative standpoint which rules out the possibility of any manifestly incoherent legal decision, rather than regarding it always as a logical contradiction.

Compared to the other canons of interpretation, the apagogic argument should be characterized by the fact that it implies a *strong* evaluation against a proposed interpretation, which means much more than an ordinary pragmatic argument. Hence, the distinctive feature of the *ad absurdum* argument is that it implies a *strong evaluation* against the consequences of a certain interpretation, providing a *special degree* of certainty about the *untenability* of the opponent's point of view.

In English law, for example, there are two basic rules of statutory interpretation that can not be compatible with each other unless the *ad absurdum* argument is interpreted in this particular way.

The first rule of statutory interpretation is the so-called "Literal Rule", according to which "the judge is required to consider what the legislation actually says rather than considering what it might mean" (Slapper and Kelly 2006, p. 196). The point about the rule is that the judge should understand the words in legislation in "their literal meaning – that is, their plain, ordinary, everyday meaning – *even if the effect of this is to produce what might be considered an otherwise unjust or undesirable outcome*" (Slapper and Kelly 2006, p. 196).

The second rule, in turn, is the "Golden Rule", which is used to rule out an interpretation that is likely to result in "an *obviously absurd result*" (Slapper and Kelly 2006, p. 197). As Lord Blackburn has stated in *River Wear Commissioners v Adamson*, we must interpret the statutes in the ordinary meaning of the words used by the legislator, unless they lead to an inconsistency or to "*an absurdity or inconvenience so great as to convince the Court that the intention could not have been to use them in their ordinary signification.*"[2]

---

[2]*The River Wear Commissoners v William Adamson and Others*. [1876–77] L.R. 2 App. Cas. 743, at 764–765. The Golden Rule of statutory interpretation was originally stated by Lord Wensleydale

As it is clearly visible, the Golden Rule only can be compatible with the Literal Rule if the *ad absurdum* argument is understood in the sense described in this chapter, that is, as a strict form of pragmatic argument whose distinctive feature is the special degree of certainty about the absurdity or untenability of a particular conclusion.

In the remaining part of this paper, I will attempt to highlight the conditions under which the *ad absurdum* argument can acquire the sort of strength which distinguishes it from the ordinary type of pragmatic argumentation.

### 2.3.2 The Difference Between the Argumentum ad Absurdum and the Generic Consequentialist Arguments

Our first step is to distinguish the *argumentum ad absurdum* from generic consequentialist arguments. In effect, one can classify the apagogic argument not only as a type of pragmatic argument, but also as a special kind of consequentialist argument. Let us begin by an example that Dworkin made famous in his seminal work The Model of Rules. In *Henningsten v. Bloomfield Motors, Inc.*, a New Jersey court had to decide, in 1960, whether "an automobile manufacturer may limit his liability in case the automobile is defective."[3] As Dworkin summarizes, "Henningsten bought a car, and signed a contract which said that the manufacturer's liability for defects was limited to 'making good' defective parts. He argued that, at least in the circumstances of his case, the manufacturer ought not to be protected by this limitation, and ought to be liable for the medical and other expenses of persons injured in a crash" (Dworkin 1978, p. 23).

Dworkin uses this example to hold that the formal sources of law are not exhaustive of the concept of legality, since developed legal systems necessarily include principles of political morality that are binding in legal argumentation. In that judgment, in fact, the court relied on moral ideas such as the prohibition of inequity and injustice as grounds for the decision that the manufacturer was liable in spite of the wording of the contract (Dworkin 1978, p. 24 ff).

Nevertheless, we can use the same example for a different purpose. We can think, for instance, of hypothetical arguments for and against Henningsten's pretension. First, judge A might dismiss the case on the assumption that Henningsten's interpretation would turn against the interests of the community, since it would lead to an increase in prices of automobiles and transfer the costs of the liability from the manufacturer to the buyers. Second, judge B may accept Henningsten's argument on the assumption that the contractual limitation of liability was against the principles of justice and equality because it would place an excessive burden on the consumer and leave unprotected all the third parties.

---

in *Becke v Smith* [1836] 2 M. &W. 195 and restated with more precision in *Grey v. Pearson* [1857] 6 HL Cas 61, 106; 10 ER 1216.

[3] *Henningsten v. Bloomfield Motors, Inc.* 32 N. J. 358, 161 A.2d [1960].

In these two hypothetical opinions, only judge B would be deploying a genuine *argumentum ad absurdum*. In effect, one of the important clues to distinguish between a strong and a fallacious use of consequentialist argumentation is to analyse the nature of the consequences that are considered by the speaker. In the opinion of judge A, we are dealing with *probabilistic* consequences which do not follow logically from the acceptance of the interpretation under analysis (since the transfer of costs from the manufacturer to the consumer is an economical phenomenon that may never happen and is not a necessary implication of the decision), while in the opinion of judge B we are dealing with logical or hypothetical consequences that inevitably follow from the decision of the case, since the facts that "a burden on the consumer will be placed" and that "the decision will set a precedent that will leave the buyers unprotected" are consequences that necessarily follow from the decision discarded by the argument.

This is why MacCormick restricts the scope of his consequentialism in order to consider primarily relevant only the *juridical consequences* of a particular rule or proposed interpretation (MacCormick 1983, pp. 249–254), which can be defined as the facts that follow *logically* from a particular decision and their *legal implications*.[4]

We can assert, therefore, that the main criterion to distinguish a genuine use of the *argumentum ad absurdum* from the generic arguments from consequences is the hypothetical, rather than probabilistic, character of the former.[5,6]

### 2.3.3 *The Context of the ad Absurdum Argument*

A second step to determine the conditions under which the *ad absurdum* argument acquires its distinctive strength in legal argumentation is to identify the contexts where it can be deployed.

---

[4]If MacCormick is correct, then a consequentialist argumentation in law involves two stages. At the first stage, one must establish a factual premise stating that the course of action considered by the speaker implies the consequence C. Then, at the second stage, one must subsume C under a universal norm that is said to be part of the legal system. The argument is reliable only if the speaker can prove that C is prohibited by that norm.

[5]For a powerful argument against the account of legal consequentialism proposed by Dewey, who speaks about a "logic of consequences being a logic of probabilities rather than certainties", see MacCormick (1983, p. 251), where he claims that only hypothetical consequences seem to be relevant in legal argumentation.

[6]As Jansen explains, "the difference between the Argument from Consequences and the RAA concerns the kind of consequences that are being appealed to: causally induced consequences in the Argument from Consequences and logically implied consequences in the RAA" (Jansen 2007, p. 250). If we take up the scheme that Alexy uses to describe the structure of the *reductio ad absurdum* in legal reasoning (when he states: (1) $O \neg Z$; (2) $R' \rightarrow Z$; (3) $\neg R'$), we can see clearly that he distinction between the *reductio ad absurdum* and the generic argument from consequences lies only in the second premise (2). While in the RAA there is a strict logical implication between R' and Z, in a generic argument from consequences this is not the case.

Like every pragmatic argument, the *ad absurdum* argument finds its place "in the context of a *mixed dispute* in which one party argues that a particular rule should be applied in the concrete case and the other party argues that this rule should not be applied" (Feteris 2005, p. 462). The typical context of the argument, therefore, is the *comparison* of cases, conclusions and alternative interpretations of a statutory provision.

In this direction, Jansen recalls that many of the examples in the literature on the *reductio ad absurdum* "concern a specific use of the Argument from Comparison" which is known as *refutational analogy*. "The main line of reasoning followed in this argument," she notes, "is that if one accepts a certain way of thinking, one should also accept a comparable, but absurd way of thinking" (Jansen 2007, p. 253).

The Roman jurists from the classical period, for instance, were experts in Greek rhetoric and used the apagogic argument to compare alternative solutions to legal problems.[7] The *reductio ad absurdum* was a key methodological tool to choose between the alternatives that would follow form the analogical application of a legal rule or from its strict interpretation with support on the *e contrario* argument (Wacke 2008, p. 477).

Furthermore, the argument has been used since before the classical period of Roman law to overcome the ambiguity or the indeterminacy of the language used to express a normative statement. In an interesting historical review, Reggi has shown that in cases of *ambiguitas* Latin rhetoricians such as Cicerone and Roman jurists such as Celso (the son) would construct their arguments trying to demonstrate "the absurdity of the opponent's view" while "supporting their own thesis by showing that it escapes from that flaw (*vitium*)" and conforms with the principle of *aequitas* (Reggi 1974, p. 163).[8]

The context of the *argumentum ad absurdum*, therefore, is determined by the presence of different interpretations of a given provision, coupled with a strong evaluation against the consequences of one of the tentative solutions. It is always, therefore, a *comparative argument.*

### 2.3.4 The Foundation of the Argumentum ad Absurdum

The third step to build a model to determine the conditions under which the apagogic argument, understood as a special case of pragmatic argument, can be legitimately applied in legal reasoning is to identify the foundations of that argument.

[7]On the *argumentum ad absurdum* in Roman law see Wacke (2008), Reggi (1974), Capone (1997) and Daube (1969). This last author, for instance, claims that this form of argument had its hey-day in the early classical era of the Roman Empire (Daube 1969, p. 193).

[8]As the author explains, a *vitium* was a consequence absurd, against equity (*aequitas*), or contradictory (Reggi 1974, p. 363).

There is agreement among the majority of continental legal theorists that the foundation of the *argumentum ad absurdum* in legal reasoning lies in the *assumption of the rational legislator*, which rules out the possibility of accepting an overtly irrational interpretation of a legal norm because the legislator shall be considered as rational and reasonable (Tarello 1980, p. 369; Guastini 2004, p. 177; La Torre et al. 1991, p. 222; Maximiliano 1992, p. 166; Ezquiaga 1994, p. 97; Ziembinski 1978, p. 183).

None the less, it seems clear to me that the prohibition of absurdity in legal interpretation (the *ad absurdum* argument) and the exigency of rationality in the interpretation of the legislation (the assumption of the rational legislator) have an important common area and play a similar function in legal argumentation. They are both two strong versions of pragmatic arguments which repeal untenable interpretations of a statute.

In these matters, I believe that Bobbio is correct when he holds that the *essential rules of interpretation* that follow from the regulative ideal of the "reasonable legislator" are only those that can also be deduced from the prohibition of "absurdity" in legal reasoning (Bobbio 1971, p. 245).

The core of the *argumentum ad absurdum* is thus similar to that of the argument based on the general assumption of the rational legislator, what makes it odd to say that the latter can be at the foundation of the former. In effect, our analysis shows that it would not be very helpful to claim that the foundation of the apagogic argument lies in the assumption of the rational law-maker, since it would be equally plausible to change the direction of the argument by arguing that it is the latter that supports the former. As a matter of fact, what appears to be more plausible is the thesis that both of these standards of argumentation can be supported by the same principle.

Which is, then, this principle that can be used to vindicate both the *ad absurdum* argument and the "assumption of the rational legislator"?

Before we answer this question, we need to stop for a moment and inquire into the nature of the assumption of the rational legislator.

#### 2.3.4.1 The Nature of the Assumption of the Rational Legislator

Although the assumption of the "rational legislator" is ambiguous and may be interpreted in different ways, for the purposes of this essay we should understand it as a "normative standard which prescribes that jurists should interpret the law *as if* the legislator were rational" (Nino 1989, p. 90). The assumption of the rationality of the legislator, in this sense, is not an empirical hypothesis to be tested, but rather an assumption which is dogmatically settled and accepted without any empirical verification. In other words, it is a "methodological thesis" which is "admittedly counter-factual", but which is necessary to create a duty to shorten the distance between the "law as it is" and the "law that ought to be" (Iguartua Salaverría 1990, pp. 115–116).

The key point about the assumption of the rational legislator is to create a "model theory" the purpose of which is not epistemological, but *normative* or *critical* in the sense that it can help lawyers and legal scientists to "construct a system of norms that is well-adapted to play the role of a [rational] legal system" (Ziembinski 1978, p. 186). Instead of a factual statement about the psychological nature of the real law-maker, it is an "idealizational claim imposed upon the legislative body, i.e. a condition constituting the legislator's rationality" (Nowak 1987, p. 138). It is, thus, a model developed by legal dogmatics. As this author explains,

> The distinctive feature of the method of interpretation of legal texts provided by legal dogmatics is that it strives to optimize the statute, that is to say, to reconstruct from the statutes the best possible norms from the point of view of the requirements of the dominant moral and political doctrines (Nowak 1969, p. 82).

The assumption of the rational legislator, therefore, as a quasi-hypothesis dogmatically settled by legal dogmatics, is a normative ideal from which we can derive a set of *rules of legal interpretation* (Nowak 1969, p. 67) or meta-norms that may guide the process of interpretation and exclude all the tentative interpretations that are manifestly unreasonable or irrational. As such, the assumption of rationality of the legislator sets a standard by means of which a proposed interpretation of a legal provision can be evaluated: "that the legislator is rational means that he satisfies some criteria of rationality" (Nowak 1987, p. 138). Hence, we can define it as a normative structure (or a set of normative criteria) for legal argumentation.

#### 2.3.4.2 A Second Thought on the Nature of the *ad Absurdum* Argument: Absurdity as Unreasonableness

As I mentioned before, even in its non-strictly logical interpretation the *argumentum ad absurdum* is a strong type of argument form, since it presupposes a special degree of certainty about the untenability of a legal assertion. We can see, therefore, that the concept of absurdity can be understood similarly to the way that we describe the assumption of the rational legislator, i.e. as a *normative structure* for legal argumentation.

The apagogic argument is a normative requirement of a minimum degree of justifiability for any legal provision. Absurdity, here, is interpreted as what is contrary to the basic concept of "reasonableness" or "social acceptability." As Perelman persuasively argues, the "vague but indispensable" idea of reasonableness is always a normative standpoint for the correct interpretation of the law. The distinction between the "reasonable" and the absurd, he holds, has to do with the boundaries between what can be comprised within the margin of appreciation of the legal authorities and what falls out of this area, and can thus be considered "socially unacceptable" (Perelman 1978, p. 41). Whenever a legal agent is in a position in which she can claim that a certain norm or legal solution can be *universally* discarded for its striking injustice, she may count on the *argumentum ad absurdum* to reject the legal interpretation that leads to that norm. We can see, therefore, that for Perelman it is not possible to identify the "reasonable" without determining the "absurd."

Once again, one can find that Perelman's conception of reasonableness, although inspired by the use of the notion by Continental lawyers, fits perfectly well into the British case law concerning the judicial review of discretionary measures of the public authorities. In effect, in UK Administrative Law the general test for the acceptability of the use of discretion is the famous "Wednesbury test", stated by Lord Greene in *Associated Provincial Picture Houses, Limited v Wednesbury Corporation*, where he lays down that one is to avoid any decision that is "*so absurd that no sensible person could ever dream that it lay within the powers of the authority*."[9] As it is visible, this test connects the ideas of reasonableness and absurdity in the same way that Perelman does in his theoretical writings.

If the *ad absurdum* argument is interpreted in this strongly evaluative sense, as I believe it should, then it becomes a powerful normative standard that plays the very same discursive function of the assumption of the rational legislator.

#### 2.3.4.3 On the Foundations of the *ad Absurdum* Argument and the Assumption of the Rational Legislator

The analysis of the two arguments above has reinforced my point that there is an important common area between the *argumentum ad absurdum* and the assumption of the rational legislator. Both of them make reference to the same ideals – rationality and reasonableness – , are dogmatically settled, and intend to provide a normative structure for legal reasoning.

The foundation of the two forms of argumentation can be found in the principle of *reasonableness*, which can be vindicated with the help of the concept of performative contradictions.

As Alexy explains,

> A performative contradiction is contradiction in the classical sense. The performative character results from the fact that only one part of the contradiction stems from what is explicitly stated by performing the legal act, whereas the other part is implicit in the claim necessarily connected with the performance of this act. (...) It [a performative contradiction] is based on the classical concept of contradiction, which can be applied to law-making acts because those acts express and imply assertorial or propositional contents (Alexy 2000, p. 141).

There may be many types of performative contradictions, and all of them seem to lead to absurd conclusions or "self-defeating illocutionary acts."[10] With the help of this definition of performative contradictions, Alexy holds that the law necessarily

---

[9]*Associated Provincial Picture Houses, Limited v Wednesbury Corporation* [1948] 1 K.B 223, at 229, per Lord Greene, M.R. (Court of Appeal).

[10]In this sense, Searle and Vanderveken classify an illocution as self-defeating when "its conditions of success cannot possibly obtain" (Searle and Vanderveken 1985, p. 151). For these authors, "since a set of illocutionary acts is consistent if it is performable, no self-defeating illocutionary act is consistent" (Searle and Vanderveken 1985, p. 151).

raises a claim to correctness, for every norm-enacting speech act comprises an implicit assertion that such act is just and reasonable.

To make this point clear, we can recover Alexy's own examples. Let us imagine a constitutional assembly passing the constitution of a new state, with the following wording of its first article: "X is an unjust republic." Imagine, also, a judge who pronounced a sentence with the following contents: "I hereby convict Y to 10 years in prison, although this is an incorrect decision."

According to Alexy, that sort of provisions would incur on a performative contradiction because no legal official can perform a norm-enacting speech act without implicitly asserting that the provision created by the performance of such act is just and correct. By explicitly denying the correctness of the norms enacted through its own speech act, the assembly would be entering into a contradiction with the implicit claim it has raised while this act was being performed. Alexy believes, therefore, that every legal official necessarily raises a claim to correctness, and he uses the notion of performative contradiction to support this point.

If this is true, then it will not be very hard to vindicate the claim that the principle of reasonableness is implicitly asserted by all legal systems. The exigency of reasonableness, in fact, is always included in the idea of correctness and seems to be included in the claim to correctness that is necessarily evinced in every act of law-creation or law-application.[11] As a matter of fact, to deny the reasonableness of a law would be just as absurd as it would be to include an "injustice clause" in a statutory provision. The explicit assertion that the legal system is "unreasonable" would contradict the implicit part of the speech acts that are performed in the enactment of any legal norms. As Alexy shows in his writings, the claim to correctness includes a claim to reasonableness and justice (Alexy 1999a, p. 381), and this provides the foundation for the pragmatic interpretation of the *ad absurdum* argument and for the assumption of the rational legislator.

Since a performative contradiction is also a classical contradiction, it is analytically true that every legal system raises a claim to correctness.[12] We can see, therefore, that the binding force of the pragmatic version of the *ad absurdum* argument can be vindicated by the strictly logic version of the same argument, since it would be a performative contradiction to expressly deny the existence of a claim to correctness (which includes a claim to reasonableness).[13]

---

[11]According to Alexy, at the core of the claim to correctness there would be: (1) The *assertion* that the legal act is substantially and procedurally correct; (2) The claim (which generates a *guarantee*) of justifiability of this assertion; and (3) The *expectation* of acceptance of correctness by all addressees of the legal norm (Alexy 1998, p. 208). Furthermore, he argues that the claim to correctness is not only a moral claim, but also a legal claim. And this legal claim "corresponds with a legal obligation necessarily connected with judicial judgments to hand down correct decisions" (Alexy 1998, p. 216).

[12]According to Alexy, his examples "show that participants in a legal system necessarily, on all sorts of levels, lay claim to correctness (Alexy 2003, p. 39)."

[13]For a complete description of the many kinds of performative contradictions in norm-enacting speech acts and a defence of Alexy's thesis of the claim to correctness, see Rotolo and Roversi (2009).

### 2.3.5 The Practical Requirements of the Pragmatic Version of the ad Absurdum Argument

The final challenge for this chapter is to provide a proper account of the practical requirements or rules of interpretation that can be associated with the *argumentum ad absurdum*. If we try to find a catalogue of such rules in the legal literature about the apagogic argument, the results probably will be disappointing, since very little is said about these rules in the legal writings on the *argumentum ad absurdum*. The biggest part of the literature on this subject is either empirical, analysing the kind of uses of the argument that one can find in legal practice, or purely analytical, dealing with the structure of such argument.[14] Not very much is said about its normative significance.[15] The main reason for this is that the dominant position among legal theorists is to classify the *argumentum ad absurdum* either as a formal argument scheme, which is able to accommodate any premises that one can think of, or as a generic pragmatic argument which appeals to generic undesirable consequences. In both cases, not enough attention is paid to the *normative* significance of the idea of absurdity and to its relationship to the ideas of rationality and reasonableness. This relationship only becomes clear once the identities between the *ad absurdum* argument and the assumption of the rational legislator are established, and both of these forms of argumentation are recognized as deriving from the claim to reasonableness which is entrenched in the norm-enacting speech acts that produce valid legal norms.

1. The first rule of interpretation that we can establish requires the interpreter to avoid any interpretation that would undermine the *authority* of the law. In effect, such interpretation would lead to a self-defeating speech act of the legislator, for one of its preparatory conditions would lack, and can obviously be qualified as absurd. In effect, one of the most interesting contributions of contemporary Anglo-Saxon jurisprudence was to demonstrate the authoritative dimension of law and the conditions under which a legal system can acquire the kind of effective authority that maintains its normativity.

As Raz has shown since his earliest writings, "the law has authority if the existence of a law requiring a certain action is a protective reason for performing that action; i.e. a law is authoritative if its existence is a reason for conforming action and for excluding conflicting considerations" (Raz 2009, p. 29). Hence, if one proposes a certain legal claim or statement that would lead to threat the authority of a law or

[14]For empirical approaches, which consider particular legal systems, see Lazzaro (1970), Wacke (2008), Reggi (1974), Capone (1997) and Daube (1969). For analytical studies see Alexy (1989), Klug (1990), Tarello (1980), Guastini (2004), Golding (2001) and Jansen (2007).

[15]When it comes to the assumption of the rational legislator the juristic literature tends to be a bit more helpful in its normative dimension. See, for instance, Bobbio (1971), Ziembinski (1978), Nowak (1969; 1987), Iguartua Salaverría (1990) and Nino (1989).

to reject the protective or "pre-emptive" nature of the legal reasons, such claim or statement shall be considered unacceptable in a strong way.

· The authoritative character of the law provides the basis for the kind of reasoning that is found in some of the most significant uses of the *argumentum ad absurdum*. To quote an example, we can mention the most famous judicial opinion in the History of Constitutional Law, issued when Chief Justice Marshall ruled that the Supreme Court of the United States of America was competent to refuse implementation of unconstitutional acts of Congress. As MacCormick (1983, p. 240) points out, this is a typical case of argument from absurd or unacceptable consequences, as one can see in the following quote from Marshall's opinion:

> Those... who controvert the principle that the constitution is to be considered, in court, as a permanent law, are reduced to the necessity of maintaining that courts must close their eyes to the constitution, and see only the law.
>
> This doctrine would subvert the very foundation of all written constitutions. It would declare that an act which, according to the principles and theory of our government, is entirely void, is yet, in practice completely obligatory.[16]

We can see, thus, that the main reason why the interpretation rejected by Marshal is considered absurd is that it would pose a threat to the authority of the constitution. This seems to be, indeed, a general standard of argumentation which is accepted across very different legal cultures. It is clear, therefore, that the following rule of interpretation may be defined as a directive for the *ad absurdum* argument:

RI-1: *When determining the meaning of a statute, one ought to reject any interpretation that can compromise the authority of the legal system.*

2. The second rule of interpretation that can be deduced from the prohibition of absurdity is the so-called "rule of justice", according to which we should treat equally those that are on the same situation and unequally those that are not. This rule can be traced back to the principle of equal concern and respect for persons, which is considered by Dworkin as the sovereign virtue in a democratic society (Dworkin 2002). The most classical formulation of the principle can be found in Justianian's Digest [D.I,1,10,1], as the obligation of "giving to each his/her own" (*'suum cuique tribuere'*) (MacCormick 2005, p. 115).

We can find a paradigmatic example of that use of the *ad absurdum* argument in the case law of the German Constitutional Court concerning whether or not Nazi decrees that withdrew the nationality of Jews and confiscated their property could be considered legally valid. Since no post-war law had been issued to deal with this specific problem, the authorities assumed that Decree 11 in regards of the Reich's Citizenship Law of 25 November 1941 was still valid, and that the property lost by a Jewish lawyer on the basis of that decree could not be recovered. On the basis of Radbruch's post-war papers which denied legal validity to whatever laws achieved a horrible or "insupportable" degree of injustice, the court decided that the

---

[16] *Marbury v. Madison* 5 US (1 Cranch) 137 (1803), p. 178.

lawyer had not lost its property because the Nazi decrees under consideration were from the outset void, since they "so evidently contradict fundamental principles of justice that the judge who applied them or recognised their legal consequences would pronounce injustice instead of law."[17]

The absurdity here would even affect the legality of appropriately enacted statutes, since their validity was repealed on the ground that to act in accordance with them would mean to enter into a "contradiction" in an "intolerable level" with the rule of justice (Alexy 1999b, p. 18).[18]

We can see that in the example above the argument from injustice is pushed to the extreme, since the court deployed it to deny validity and applicability to a properly enacted statute without being able to point any constitutional provision that would lead to the unconstitutionality of such statute.

This is not, however, the normal use of the *argumentum ad absurdum* as prohibition of injustice, since in ordinary cases we do not need to go that far.

In effect, we can also mention another example from Roman Law, when Pomponius held that the only acceptable interpretation of the *lex commisoria* in a contract of sale – a clause stating that "if the price is not paid on time the sale can be rescinded" – is that which benefits exclusively the vendor, since otherwise the buyer would be able to frustrate the contract at her own pleasure, even if the object of the contract is damaged or destroyed, as it would be the case if a building constructed in the piece of land were hit by fire or natural disaster.[19] As pointed out by Long,

> The *lex commissoria* did not make the transaction a conditional purchase; for in that case, if the property were damaged or destroyed, the loss would be the loss of the vendor, inasmuch as the purchaser, by non-payment of the money at the time agreed on, would fail to perform the condition, but it was an absolute sale, subject to be rescinded at the sole pleasure of the vendor, if the money was not paid at the time agreed on; and consequently if after this agreement the property was lost or destroyed before the day agreed on for payment, the loss fell on the purchaser (Long 1870, p. 240).

As we can see, Pomponius' reasoning to classify the *lex commisoria* as a privilege of the vendor, rather than a conditional purchase, is the only way to

---

[17]BVerfGE 3, 58 (119); 6, 132 (198). I quote the example from Alexy (1999b), whose translation was used above. Alexy quotes the example in defence of Radbruch's Formula, who asserts that a statute loses its legal validity whenever it expressly disavows the idea of justice or reaches an intolerable degree of substantive injustice. On Radbruch's arguments, see Radbruch (2006), Paulson (2006) and Alexy (1999b, 2003).

[18]Alexy obviously presents this argument as a criticism against positivism. Nevertheless, a positivist would normally claim that it is wrong to conclude that the argument from injustice works in legal adjudication only if you dismiss positivism. In Hart's debates with Radbruch on the validity of Nazi Laws, for instance, he makes it very clear that positivism is merely a theory about legal validity, ant not a theory about how difficult cases should be decided. For Hart it would be perfectly possible to decide cases involving Nazi legislation without dismissing positivism, as long as retrospective effects were attributed to the post-war legislation (Hart 1977).

[19]See D.18,3,2–3 (Pomponius). Classifying this reasoning as an instance of the *reductio ad absurdum*, see Wacke (2008, pp. 456–457).

achieve a balance in the contract and to avoid the flagrant injustices that could eventually occur in case the buyer could benefit from her own wrong. In this case, the interpretation criticized on the basis of the *ad absurdum* argument is indeed flawed from the point of view of distributive justice, since it fails to treat differently subjects in very different situations, allowing the buyer to take advantage from the fact that she did not comply with her obligation.

As a matter of fact, both cases (the German cases on the validity of Nazi laws and Pomponius' reasoning on the interpretation of the clause of the *lex commissoria*) applied the Rule of Justice to dismiss an interpretation that would lead to severely unjust results.

The following two rules of interpretation seem to be implied by Radbruch's formulation of the Rule of Justice, and they are generally accepted in all developed legal systems:

RI-2: *No legal norm should be interpreted in such a way that would bring insupportable injustice into the legal system.*

RI-2′: *No legal norm should be interpreted in a way that would lead to the conclusion that the legislator explicitly or impliedly disavows the idea of justice*

Nevertheless, these rules may be interpreted in different senses. When we compare the German decisions on the validity of Nazi laws with Pomponius reasoning on the *lex commissoria*, we can see that they differ in an important sense, for the former decision implies the lack of validity for formally enacted laws, while the latter merely selects one of the interpretations compatible with the ordinary meaning of the clause.

In their strong interpretation, the rules RI-2 and RI-2′ affect the *validity* of a statutory provision, since no statute can be accepted as legally valid if it reaches the utmost level of injustice. In their weak interpretation, in turn, they help one to choose among the interpretations of a statute that are permitted by the literal wording of the legal texts, but they do not go as far as to claim that a statute is void because of its unjust contents.

In British law, for instance, it seems that the judges tend to accept the weak version while rejecting the strong, since the famous Golden Rule of statutory interpretation, is limited to the "construction of statutes".[20]

Nevertheless, there are strong arguments for both versions of the *argumentum ad absurdum* as Rule of Justice, and we may leave open the question of which of its interpretations shall prevail in legal adjudication. For the moment it is enough to hold that the weak interpretation of the rules RI-2 and RI-2′ tend to be generally accepted in developed legal systems.

3. The third rule of interpretation that follows from the prohibition of absurdity requires one to avoid an interpretation that would lead one norm to come into conflict with another norm of the system.

[20] *Grey v. Pearson* [1857] 6 HL Cas 61, 106; 10 ER 1216, 1234.

Perhaps one of the most interesting accounts of this interpretation of the *ad absurdum* argument is that of Kloosterhuis (2007), who distinguishes two forms of the apagogic argument. While the weakest form is that of a generic pragmatic argument, the strongest form (or the *ad absurdum* argument in strict sense) makes reference to an undisputed norm or a hypothetical set of juridical consequences that are logically derived from it. A Dutch judicial decision about the scope of the locution "wilful act", in Section 5:23 of the Dutch civil code, is given as a paradigmatic example of use of the *ad absurdum* argument in its strict sense. In that case, a hot-air balloon landed in the adjacencies of two properties, causing damage to their owners due to the fact that a number of farmed animals fled or died of suffocation. The farmers sued the owners of the balloon and threatened to prevent its removal from their property until they received compensation for the loss caused by its landing. In defence, the owners of the balloon argued that since the event was not a wilful act in the sense of the article 5:23 of the Dutch Civil Code there was no right of retention concerning the balloon. The farmers, in turn, argued that the landing of the balloon was a wilful act in the sense of article 5:23. This article states that an object (or animal) that finds its way onto another person's property other than through the wilful or negligent act of the owner may be traced back and removed by the owner if and when he so requests. If a landing of a balloon is considered to be a wilful act, there was a right of retention for the farmers; if not, the balloon could be removed without previous payment for the damage caused by it (Kloosterhuis 2007, p. 68).

In the light of these facts, and taking into consideration another norm whose meaning is uncontroversial (a statutory rule expressly authorizing the landing of a balloon everywhere except in densely populated areas), the court ruled that:

> The interpretation that a 'wilful act' as defined in Section 5:23 of the Dutch civil code must be assumed to have been performed if a decision for a specific landing site is made in the last phase of the flight is false;
>
> Because: If this interpretation is true, each successful landing will be a wilful act;
>
> And: The assumption that each successful landing is a wilful act is at odds with the provision in Dutch aviation law that allows untethered balloons to land everywhere except on public roads in high-density developed, industrial and port areas (Kloosterhuis 2007, p. 71).

Here, the court is not referring to a generic pragmatic form of reasoning, but rather to a *systematic argument*. According to MacCormick and Summer's classification of interpretative arguments,[21] the case could be an instance of a

[21]By referring to MacCormick and Summers' classification of interpretative arguments – see note below – Kloosterhuis holds that the *ad absurdum* argument may express on the one hand a *systematic* argument that involves a "contradiction or inconsistency between a proposed interpretation of a rule of law and an undisputed, generally accepted legal interpretation or assumption" (Kloosterhuis 2007, p. 72), or, on the other hand, an argument from *substantive* reasons in which the strength of the argumentation "does not depend on the authoritativeness that the reasons may have" (Kloosterhuis 2007, p. 73). The former is called the strict sense of the *argumentum ad absurdum*, while the latter the broad sense of that argument.

*systematic argument* from the group of "contextual-harmonization arguments."[22] The argument is at stake in order to preserve the consistency of the legislation. The *ad absurdum* argument in strict sense expresses a contradiction between the content of a norm the meaning of which is presupposed by the participants of the discourse and the content of an interpretative proposition hypothetically tested by the speaker.[23]

As it is visible, this strict version of the argument depicts it as equivalent to the general requirement of consistency in adjudication. In deciding a legal problem, the judge should discard any interpretation that leads to a contradiction in the legal system.[24]

The following rule of interpretation, therefore, can be asserted:

RI-3: *No legal rule should be interpreted in a sense that comes into conflict with a norm whose meaning and validity is undisputed in a legal system.*

4. Another standard of argumentation that is associated with the *argumentum ad absurdum* is that which does not admit one to interpret a statute in any way that renders its prescriptions inefficient from the point of view of instrumental rationality (Nowak 1969, p. 68). In this sense, the assumption of the rational legislator – and the same could be said about the *ad absurdum* argument – supposes that the law-maker has a "critical sense" and an "adequate knowledge of the reality" (Ziembinski 1978, p. 180), so one cannot interpret a particular statutory provision in such a way that would dismiss that assumption.

Furthermore, from the point of view of instrumental rationality, one cannot admit an interpretation that would lead to an empirically failed norm according to the available knowledge (Nowak 1987, p. 141), since the statutes under consideration must be constructed in such a way that preserves their efficacy (Lazzaro 1970, p. 96). In short, the interpreter "must base his interpretation on the idea that the norm is the most adequate means that a reasonable person can find to achieve the goals of the legislator in a given situation" (Bobbio 1971, p. 245).

---

[22]The eleven argument types proposed by MacCormick and Summers (1991, pp. 512–516) are these: (1) Linguistic Arguments: (i) argument from the ordinary meaning and (ii) argument from technical meaning; (2) Systemic Arguments: (iii) argument from contextual-harmonization, (iv) argument from precedent, (v) argument from analogy, (vi) logical-conceptual argument, (vii) argument from the general principles of law and (viii) argument from history; (3) Teleological/Evaluative Arguments: (ix) argument from purpose and (x) argument from substantive reasons; (4) Transcategorial Argument: (xi) argument from intention.

[23]The difference between the *ad absurdum* argument in this sense and the strictly logical version of the argument, analysed above (see supra, n. 1) is that while the latter presupposes an internal contradiction of the speaker, the former applies when the proposed interpretation is not consistent with another norm belonging to the legal system.

[24]In the same sense, see Bobbio (1971, pp. 244–245) and Lazzaro (1970, p. 96). The difference between Kloosterhuis' use of the *argumentum ad absurdum* and the strictly logical version of the *reductio ad absurdum* is that in the former the norm which contradicts the proposed interpretation is not a premise adopted by the speaker, so there is no "internal contradiction" in the reasoning under consideration.

In a relatively recent case, for instance, the Brazilian Supreme Court had to decide on the meaning of the word "glebe" (from Latin *gleba*) in article 243 of the Constitution, whose wording is as follows:

> Art. 243. The glebes used to cultivate psychotropic plants will be immediately confiscated and specifically destined to settlements of workers, who will be entitled use them for growing groceries or medicinal plants, with no compensation to the former owner and regardless of any other sanctions established by ordinary laws.

The problem here was to define the meaning of the word "glebe", which in the Portuguese language (*gleba*) is as ambiguous and archaic as it is in English. The 1st Federal Court of Justice had ruled that a "glebe" (*gleba*) was just the portion of a rural property were psychotropic plants (in the case, cannabis) were grown, rather than the entire property. On extraordinary appeal to the Federal Supreme Court, however, a different interpretation prevailed. After stating that "the law, as Carlos Maximiliano has taught, must be interpreted 'intelligently, in such a way that there is no absurdity in the legal system and does not allow it to prescribe inconveniencies or lead to inconsistent or impossible conclusions,'" the court decided that the interpretation proposed by the lower court "cannot be accepted, since it leads to the absurd" conclusion that 150 square metres or rural land should be expropriated in order to "settle workers to grow groceries and medical plants" in this insignificant piece of land.[25] The court decided, by unanimous opinions of its 11 members, to follow Min. Eros Grau's opinion and to consider that the whole property (in that case, a farm with 28.000 square metres) should be expropriated as a sanction for growing psychotropic and illegal drugs, since otherwise the law would lack its coercive force and would not gain the required social efficacy.

As the case illustrates, the following rule of interpretation can be also associated with the *ad absurdum* argument:

RI-4: *When interpreting a statutory provision, one must construct the norm in a way that the means adopted by the legislator are adequate to the goals that the norm intends to achieve.*

5. Finally, the last directive of argumentation that seems to be connected to the *argumentum ad absurdum* forbids one to interpret a norm N in a sense that its application would lead to an impossibility or to a state of affairs that can easily be dismissed by empirical observation.

In *Maclennan v. Maclennan*, for instance, the Scottish Court of Session relied on the *ad absurdum* argument to determine the meaning of the word "adultery" in the Scottish family laws.[26] In this case, a man brought an action against his wife on ground of her adultery, since she had given birth to a child more than a year after the last meeting of the couple. In defence, however, the wife argued that the child was conceived by means of artificial insemination with an anonymous donor,

---

[25] STF, Pleno, RE 543974/MG, Rel. Min. Eros Grau, j. 26/03/2009, p. DJe-099, 28/05/2009.

[26] *Maclennan v. Maclennan* (1958) S. C. 105, per Lord Wheatley.

and hence no adulterous act of sexual intercourse had taken place. The key problem was to decide whether a pregnancy with genetic material from an anonymous donor should count as adultery for the purposes of justifying a divorce. The court ruled according to the opinion of Lord Wheatley, who argued that artificial insemination by a donor does not constitute adultery according to the Scottish law. Although it "constitutes a grievous material offence against a non-consenting husband," he says, the law cannot accept it amongst the grounds on which divorce may be granted, since otherwise a wife might be found to commit adultery with a dead man, which would amount to an absurdity.[27]

It can be said, therefore, the *ad absurdum* argument implies that no rule should be interpreted in such a way that it would require impossible actions or factual assertions against empirical evidence.

Hence, the following rule of interpretation can be established:

RI-5. *When interpreting a statutory provision, one must construct the norm in a way that no impossible actions or factual assertions that can be easily falsified by empirical evidence would follow from such norm.*

## 2.4 Final Considerations

Our analysis has brought us to the following theses.

1. The *argumentum ad absurdum* can be understood in two senses. As a strictly logical argument, it can be described as a classical *reductio ad absurdum*, according to which a conclusion shall be rejected whenever its proponent is committed to contradictory views. In this case, the argument is internally flawed, in the sense that the conclusion cannot be supported by its premises. The *reductio ad absurdum* is a valid logical argument that can lead to an indirect demonstration of that flaw.
2. Furthermore, the *ad absurdum* argument can be understood also as a pragmatic argument. A pragmatic argument is an argument about the desirability or the undesirability of a given consequence. In legal reasoning, however, the *argumentum ad absurdum* is a special case of pragmatic reason the distinctive feature of which is that it presupposes a *strong evaluation* against the interpretation rejected by such argument. In legal argumentation, lawyers tend to understand the *argumentum ad absurdum* in this second sense, since the classic *reductio ad absurdum* becomes trivial and unnecessary, for the elementary rules of logic suffice to reject the conclusion considered by the speaker.
3. To understand the special force of the pragmatic version of the *ad absurdum* argument, which seems to be the sort of argument adopted by lawyers in support of their claims and decisions, one must consider the following factors.

[27](1958) S. C., at 114.

4. First, the *ad absurdum* argument is not the same as a generic form of consequentialist reasoning. While the former deals only with hypothetical facts and its juridical consequences, the latter may include probabilistic consequences that cannot be demonstrated by the speaker. Hence, only the former has a relevant argumentative strength.
5. The context in which the *ad absurdum* argument is deployed is that of a disputable argumentation over the proper interpretation of a statute. The speaker analyses her own interpretation in the light of an alternative, which is deemed to be untenable. The *argumentum ad absurdum*, thus, is always a comparative argument.
6. The *argumentum ad absurdum* has an important common area to the assumption of the rational legislator. They are both normative standards that require the interpreter to fix the meaning of a norm in a sense that is rational and reasonable. The basic principle that supports both of them is the principle of reasonableness. In effect, as Perelman has shown, one cannot know what is reasonable without determining what is absurd, for these predicates are correlatives in the sense that whenever one is present, the other will be absent.
7. The validity of the principle of reasonableness can be demonstrated with the help of the concept of performative contradictions. When Alexy shows that the law officials necessarily raise a claim to correctness when they perform a norm-enacting speech act, that demonstration is also useful to provide the foundation for the requirement of reasonableness in legal argumentation. The claim to correctness includes a claim to reasonableness and a prohibition of absurdity and irrationality.
8. In the uses of the pragmatic version of the argumentum ad absurdum, the following rules of interpretation seem to bind lawyers across different legal systems: **RI-1**: When determining the meaning of a statute, one ought to reject any interpretation that can compromise the authority of the legal system. **RI-2**: No legal norm should be interpreted in such a way that would bring insupportable injustice into the legal system. **RI-2′**: No legal norm can be interpreted in a way that would lead to the conclusion that the legislator explicitly or impliedly disavows the idea of justice. **RI-3**: No legal rule should be interpreted in a sense that comes into conflict with a norm whose meaning and validity is undisputed in a legal system. **RI-4**: When interpreting a statutory provision, one must construct the norm in a way that the means adopted by the legislator are adequate to the goals that the norm intends to achieve. **RI-5.** When interpreting a statutory provision, one must construct the norm in a way that no impossible actions or factual assertions against empirical evidence would follow from such norm.

These theses are relevant and achieve the scope of this paper because, taken together, the rules of interpretation stated above define the normative significance of the *argumentum ad absurdum* in statutory interpretation. They can be relied on and classified as a reliable set or directives for legal argumentation, allowing us to distinguish between correct and incorrect uses of that type of argument in a way that clarifies the specific role played by the apagogic argument in the context of legal discourses.

**Acknowledgments** The author would like to thank Carlos Bernal Pulido, Matyas Bodig, Christian Dahlman, Eveline Feteris, Antonino Rotolo, Humberto Ávila and Henrike Jansen for the helpful comments and suggestions on a previous draft of this paper. Furthermore, he is indebted to the Foundation for the Development of the Research of the State of Minas Gerais (FAPEMIG – *Fundação de Amparo à Pesquisa do Estado de Minas Gerais*), for funding part of the research that led to this paper.

## References

Alexy, Robert. 1989. *A theory of legal argumentation*. Oxford: Clarendon.

Alexy, Robert. 1998. Law and correctness. *Current Legal Problems* 51: 205–221.

Alexy, Robert. 1999a. A defence of Radbruch's formula. In *Recrafting the rule of law: The limits of the legal order*, ed. David Dyzenhaus, 15–39. Oxford: Hart Publishing.

Alexy, Robert. 1999b. The special case thesis. *Ratio Juris* 12: 374–384.

Alexy, Robert. 2000. On the thesis of a necessary connection between law and morality: Bulygin's critique. *Ratio Juris* 13: 138–147.

Alexy, Robert. 2003. *The argument from injustice: A reply to legal positivism* (trans: Bonnie L. Paulson and Stanley L. Paulson). Oxford: Oxford University Press.

Bobbio, Norberto. 1971. Le bon législateur. In *Le Raisonnement juridique – Actes du Congrés Mondial de Philosophie du Droit et de Philosophie Sociale*, ed. Hubert Hubien. Brussels: Bruylant.

Capone, Piera. 1997. Valore ed uso giurisprudenziale di *absurdus/e*. *Studia et documenta historiae et iuris* 63: 197–257.

Daube, David. 1969. Reductio ad absurdum. In *Roman law: Linguistic, social and philosophical aspects (The Gray Lectures 1966)*, 176–194. Edinburgh: Edinburgh University Press.

Dworkin, Ronald. 1978. *Taking rights seriously*, 2nd ed. Cambridge: Harvard University Press.

Dworkin, Ronald. 2002. *Sovereign virtue: Theory and practice of equality*. Cambridge: Harvard University Press.

Ezquiaga, Francisco Javier. 1994. Argumentos interpretativos y postulado del legislador racional. *Isonomía* 1: 69–98.

Feteris, Eveline. 2005. The rational reconstruction of argumentation referring to consequences and purposes in the application of legal rules: A pragma-dialectical perspective. *Argumentation* 19: 459–470.

Golding, Martin. 2001. *Legal reasoning*. Toronto: Encore.

Guastini, Riccardo. 2004. *L'Interpretazione dei documenti normativi*. Milan: Giuffrè.

Hart, H.L.A. 1977. Positivism and the separation of law and morals. In *The philosophy of law*, ed. Dworkin Ronald, 17–37. Oxford: Oxford University Press.

Iguartua Salaverría, Juan. 1990. El postulado del legislador racional. *Revista Vasca de Administración Pública* 28: 113–125.

Jansen, Henrike. 2007. Refuting a standpoint by appealing to its outcomes: *Reductio ad absurdum* vs Argument from Consequences. *Informal Logic* 27: 249–266.

Kloosterhuis, Harm. 2007. *Ad absurdum* arguments in legal decisions. In *Logic, argumentation and interpretation – Proceedings of the 22nd IVR World Congress Granada 2005*, vol. V, ed. Josep Aguiló-Regla, 68–74. ARSP-Beihet 110.

Klug, Ulrich. 1990. *Lógica Jurídica* (trans: Gardella, J.C.). Bogotá: Temis.

Lazzaro, Giorgio. 1970. *Argomenti dei giudici – Estratto dai lavori della ricerca sulla "Argomentazione Giuridica" patrocinata dal C.N.R.* Turim: Emilio Bono.

La Torre, Massimo, Enrico Pattaro, and Michele Taruffo. 1991. Statutory interpretation in Italy. In *Interpreting statutes – A comparative study*, ed. Neil MacCormick and Robert Summers, 213–256. Aldershot: Dartmouth.

Long, George. 1870. Commissaria lex. In *Dictionary of Greek and Roman antiquities*, ed. Sir. William Smith, 340. Boston: C. Little and J. Brown. There is a scanned online edition at http://www.ancientlibrary.com/smith-dgra/index.html. Consulted on 28 July 2011.
MacCormick, Neil. 1983. On legal decisions and their consequences: From Dewey to Dworkin. *New York University Law Review* 58: 239–258.
MacCormick, Neil. 2005. *Rhetoric and the rule of law*. Oxford: Oxford University Press.
MacCormick, Neil, and Robert Summers. 1991. Interpretation and justification. In *Interpreting statutes – A comparative study*, ed. Neil MacCormick and Robert Summers, 511–544. Aldershot: Dartmouth.
Maximiliano, Carlos. 1992. *Hermenêutica e Aplicação do Direito*, 12th ed. Rio de Janeiro: Forense.
Nino, Carlos Santiago. 1989. El modelo dogmático del legislador racional. In *Consideraciones sobre la dogmática jurídica (con referencia particular a la dogmática penal)*, ed. Carlos Santiago Nino, 85–110. Mexico: Universidad Nacional Autónoma de Mexico.
Nowak, Leszek. 1969. De la rationalité du législateur comme élément de l'interprétation juridique. In *Études de Logique Juridique*, vol. III, ed. Chaïm Perelman, 65–86. Brussels: Bruylant.
Nowak, Leszek. 1987. A concept of rational legislator. In *Polish contributions to the theory and philosophy of law*, ed. Zygmunt Ziembinski, 137–145. Amsterdam: Rodopi.
Paulson, Stanley L. 2006. On the background and significance of Gustav Radbruch's post-war papers. *Oxford Journal of Legal Studies* 26: 17–40.
Perelman, Chaïm. 1978. Le raisonnable et le déraisonnable en droit. *Archives de Philosophie du Droit* 23: 35–42.
Radbruch, Gustav. 2006. Statutory lawlessness and supra-statutory law (trans: Paulson, Stanley L. and Paulson, Bonnie L.). *Oxford Journal of Legal Studies* 26: 1–11.
Raz, Joseph. 2009. *The authority of law*, 2nd ed. Oxford: Oxford University Press.
Reggi, Roberto. 1974. L'argomentazione per assurdo e Celso Figlio. In *Studi in onore di Giuseppe Grosso*, 145–172. Turim: Giappichelli.
Rescher, Nicholas. 2005. Reductio ad absurdum. In *The internet encyclopedia of philosophy*. Available at http://www.iep.utm.edu/reductio. Accessed on 28 July 2011.
Rotolo, Antonino, and Corrado Roversi. 2009. Norm enactment and performative contradictions. *Ratio Juris* 22: 455–482.
Ryle, Gilbert. 1945. *Philosophical arguments*. Oxford: Clarendon Press.
Searle, John R., and Daniel Vanderveken. 1985. *Foundations of illocutionary logic*. Cambridge: Cambridge University Press.
Slapper, Gary, and David Kelly. 2006. *The English legal system*. Oxon: Routledge-Cavendish.
Tarello, Giovanni. 1980. *L'Interpretazione della Legge*. Milan: Giuffrè.
Tomassi, Paul. 1999. *Logic*, 8th ed. London: Routledge.
Wacke, Andreas. 2008. La consideración de las consecuencias de las decisiones jurídicas mediante *deductio ad absurdum* (en Derecho romano y en derecho moderno). *Seminarios Complutenses de Derecho Romano* 20–21: 451–480.
Wróblewski, Jerzy. 1974. Legal syllogism and rationality of judicial decisions. *Rechtstheorie* 5: 33–46.
Ziembinski, Zygmunt. 1978. La notion de rationalité du législateur. *Archives de Philosophie du Droit* 23: 175–187.

# Chapter 3
# Why Precedent in Law (and Elsewhere) Is Not Totally (or Even Substantially) About Analogy*

**Frederick Schauer**

Reasoning by analogy is a central and domain-general characteristic of human cognition (Forbus 2001; Hofstadter 2001; Holyoak et al. 2001; Holyoak and Thagard 1997), as well as being a key component of expert and professional decision making (Blanchette and Dunbar 2000; Holyoak 1982, 2005; Khong 1992; Spellman and Holyoak 1992; Tetlock 1999). Politicians, physicians, scientists, and countless others reason analogically, and there is much to be learned about how people think by understanding how analogies work and are used in ordinary and professional life.

Yet although analogical reasoning is a key component of human thought, claims about the importance of analogy research become more open to challenge when psychologists maintain that reasoning by analogy is what lawyers do when they argue from the legally pervasive phenomenon of *precedent* (Holyoak and Thagard 1995; Kokinov and French 2003), or what judges do when they use precedent as an essential component of their reasoning and decision making (Hofstadter 2001). Thus, a recent survey of analogy research asserts that the use of legal precedents "is a formalized application of analogical reasoning" (Holyoak 1995), and another overview (Ellsworth 2005) points to the pervasiveness of precedent in law as a reason for lawyers and judges to study analogy. One series of studies suggests that we can learn about judicial reasoning and decision making generally from studying how ordinary people construct analogies (Holyoak and Simon 1999; Simon et al. 2004), while (Hunt 2006) describes the analogical reasoning that psychologists study as "typical of the law." And clearest is the claim by one cognitive psychologist that "the principle of precedent [in] the common law" is "totally about analogy" (Spellman 2004).

*This chapter first appeared in *Perspectives on Psychological Science*, vol. 3 (2008), pp. 454–460.

F. Schauer (✉)
School of Law, University of Virginia, 580 Massie Road, Charlottesville, VA 22903, USA
e-mail: fred_schauer@harvard.edu

C. Dahlman and E. Feteris (eds.), *Legal Argumentation Theory: Cross-Disciplinary Perspectives*, Law and Philosophy Library 102, DOI 10.1007/978-94-007-4670-1_3,

Legal scholars have written extensively about analogy (Ashley 1990; Brewer 1996; Hunter 1997; Levi 1949; Sunstein 1993; Weinreb 2005), because the use of analogies to past cases is indeed a common feature of legal argument. But the frequent use of analogical reasoning in law does not entail the conclusion that making decisions by following precedent is the same thing (Alexander and Sherwin 2001; Lamond 2006; Posner 2008).[1] Rather, following precedent is a form of decision making, almost as common outside the legal system as within, in which judges and other decision makers are expected to adhere to prior decisions addressing the *same* issue regardless of their own views about how the issue *ought* to be decided (Wasserstrom 1961). Precedent-bound decision makers are thus obliged to answer the same question in the same way as others have answered it earlier, even if they would prefer to answer it differently. Precedential constraint is precisely this obligation to follow earlier decisions just because of their existence and not because of their perceived (by the current decision maker) correctness, and this counter-intuitive form of reasoning, ubiquitous in legal reasoning and widespread elsewhere, is importantly different from the typical form of analogical reasoning, whether in law or outside it. Although lawyers use analogies frequently, the use of analogies by lawyers does not support the view (Hofstadter 1995) that analogical reasoning is all or even most of legal reasoning, precisely because the obligatory following of earlier decisions is substantially different from the selection of an analogy to illuminate or inform a current decision. An argument from precedent does require an initial determination of relevant similarity, but from there the paths diverge, especially when the question of relevant similarity admits of only one plausible answer, and the typical use of precedent, especially but not only by judges, bears far less affinity to analogical reasoning than most psychologists and even some lawyers appear to believe. Or so I argue here.

My goal is not (only) to demonstrate that a common claim in the psychological literature is mistaken. That alone might be useful, but even more is showing how following or obeying a precedent – something that ordinary people, and not just lawyers and judges, do all the time – represents a distinct but rarely studied form of decision making. If this conclusion is sound, then recognizing the distinctiveness of precedential reasoning may open the door for psychological research on precedent that can be as rich and useful as the psychological research on analogy has been.

Consider, for example, the contemporary criticism (Editorial 2007) of the Supreme Court for failing to follow precedents from previous Courts.[2] When critics chastise the Supreme Court for disregarding precedent on issues like abortion, defendants' rights, or affirmative action, they are not suggesting that the Court

[1]"There is no word which is used more loosely, or in a greater variety of senses, than Analogy" (Mill 1861).

[2]Technically, the obligation of a court to follow previous decisions of the same court is referred to as *stare decisis* ("stand by what has been decided"), and the more encompassing term *precedent* is used to refer both to *stare decisis* and the obligation of a lower court to follow decisions of a higher one. What I say here applies to both kinds of precedent, although *stare decisis* is to many non-lawyers more counter-intuitive.

employed the wrong analogy, or identified as analogous a prior case with only superficial but not structural similarities to the current case, or failed to map the proper features of the earlier (source) case onto the features of the current (target) case. Rather, they insist that when presented with a situation in which the very *same* issue was decided previously by the same (even if differently staffed) Supreme Court, the current Court is obliged to reach the same conclusion about the same issue, even if a majority of the current members of the Court believed the earlier decision mistaken.

It is open to argument whether the Supreme Court is now doing what its critics charge, just as it is open to argument whether it is wise to require judges (and not only the Justices of the Supreme Court) or other decision makers to make decisions contrary to their own best judgment solely because someone else has made what appears to them to be a mistake in the past. What is less open to question, however, is that a form of reasoning in which past decisions are taken as binding just because of their existence and not because of their wisdom is quite different from a form of reasoning in which current decision makers retrieve from an array of previous decisions the one that will be most helpful to them, or most persuasive to others. Following precedent, I maintain, is a central component of legal argument and legal reasoning, as the recent criticisms of the Supreme Court make plain, but it is a component whose features will remain misunderstood and unstudied as long as psychologists and others mistakenly equate it with reasoning by analogy.

But following precedent is by no means restricted to law. What makes understanding and studying reasoning from precedent even more important is that its use is hardly unique to the legal system. This is well understood by parents of more than one child, for when a younger child claims the right to be given permission to do at a given age what his or her older sibling was permitted to do at the same age, the child is making an argument from precedent and demanding that a previous decision be followed regardless of the current views of the decision maker about the wisdom of the earlier decision (Alexander 1989; Schauer 1987). Like judges, children do reason analogically (Brown 1989) at times, but children also make arguments from precedent, so understanding the difference between the two will help in understanding the thinking and reasoning of children just as it will help do the same for lawyers and judges. So too with administrative decisions in government and universities, for example, for here again it is commonly argued that administrators should follow previous decisions and practices solely for the sake of consistency, without regard to whether those administrators have good reasons for believing the previous decisions or practices wise. Indeed, the frequency with which people argue against a proposal or course of action because it will "set a precedent," or constitute a "dangerous precedent," show that people have a superficial understanding of the way in which previous decisions can *constrain* and not just guide or inform. Even the consumer who demands the same deal from a retailer as one that had been offered in the past is relying on precedent for precedent's sake, again underscoring the pervasiveness of the phenomenon whose mistaken equation with analogical reasoning has unfortunately precluded the psychological research that would facilitate knowing whether and under what circumstances reasoning from precedent is possible, what kinds of mental processes it involves, and whether some reasoners, by virtue of natural inclination or specialized training, can do it better than others. My goal here is thus not principally to focus on the law, but instead to use the law to show that psychologists, because of a mistaken view about the law, have let a pervasive feature of human decision making go largely unresearched. If psychologists can understand that following a precedent is different from using an analogy, they may see that the cognitive processes of following precedent can be a target of scientific research in their own right.

## 3.1 Analogy as a Friend

Albeit with some disagreement (Hofstadter 2001; Forbus et al. 1998), there is broad consensus among psychologists about the basic structure of analogical thought. So it is more or less common ground that analogical reasoning involves a three-stage process in which the first stage is *retrieval*, where a decision maker seeking guidance or an advocate looking to persuade initially identifies the source analog to which to compare some aspect of a target situation. The second stage is *mapping*, in which the relevant similarities between source and target are located; and the third is *transfer*, where the structural elements of the source are used to reach a conclusion or make an argument with respect to the target (Gick and Holyoak 1980, 1983).

One implicit but rarely analyzed assumption in the standard account of the framework of analogical reasoning is that the analogical reasoner typically has a choice of source analogs, and that the source analog actually retrieved from among the logically available candidates is one that is "potentially useful" (Holyoak 2005) either in making a decision or in persuading someone else of the wisdom of a chosen course of action (Spellman and Holyoak 1996). We use analogies, therefore, because they are helpful. They assist us in making decisions, they help us to persuade others of the correctness of our decisions, and they illuminate aspects of a current situation that may otherwise have been obscured. And at their best they enable us to identify or construct generalizations that connect the source and the target, thereby facilitating the development of new theories that in turn might help in predicting future events. So when President George H.W. Bush analogized Saddam Hussein to Adolph Hitler in order to garner support for the first Iraq war (Spellman and Holyoak 1992), and when opponents of the second Iraq war analogized that war to the American misadventure in Vietnam, they both selected their source analogs (or exemplars) – Hitler and Vietnam respectively – from among multiple potential candidates, and they selected the ones they did because of the power of the ensuing analogy to persuade those who might otherwise have disagreed with the position offered by the user of the analogy.

Consistent with the foregoing account, one searches in vain in the psychological literature for examples of constraining (or frustrating) analogies. Although analogies are often used to argue against rather than for some course of action – cigarettes should not be banned because of the lessons of Prohibition – and although people often retrieve mistaken analogs (Khong 1992; Spiro et al. 1989), it remains the case that source analogs are retrieved because of the guidance they are perceived to offer, the illumination they are believed to provide, or the persuasion they are thought to facilitate. The intentional retrieval of an analogy that prevents the analogical reasoner from doing what would otherwise be (to the reasoner) a good idea is a stranger in the psychological literature, with the implicit message being that decision-makers never (or rarely) see or retrieve the analogies that would impede a course of action that, but for the analogy, would have much to recommend it. And this is not surprising. Analogical reasoning is a type of reasoning, and those who wish to engage in successful reasoning are seeking, as the psychological literature correctly understands, ways of making better decisions and methods of supporting most effectively the decisions that have already been made.

## 3.2 Precedent as a Foe

With this simplified sketch of analogical reasoning in mind, we can turn to the concept of precedent. More particularly, we turn to the situation in which an obligation to follow a previous decision will impede an otherwise preferred current decision. The legal system, like reasoning generally, does frequently use analogies with previous decisions to inform or assist current decisions. But the legal system, again like decision making generally, often also uses a method of decision making in which the decision makers are expected not just to use past decisions to help them make better ones now, but also to follow past decisions even when the decision makers believe those decisions are mistaken. The child who relies on precedent to demand that she be treated as her sister was treated at the same age is insisting that a previous decision be taken as binding, regardless of the parent's current views, and regardless of any distinction that the parents might now see between the two cases. So too with the consumer who claims an entitlement to the same terms offered to a previous customer, and so too, perhaps most prominently, in the legal system. Thus, Lord Mansfield noted more than two centuries ago in *Roe v. Griffits* (1766) that a legal rule "must be adhered to; although it is not founded upon truly rational grounds and principles," and contemporary commentators agree that "a genuine theory of *stare decisis* requires giving decision altering weight to a prior judicial decision just because it was a prior judicial decision, and not because of its merit . . ." (Paulsen 2005; and see also Alexander 1989; Lamond 2006; Schauer 1987). As an American court put it in 1955, "Stare decisis has no bite when it means merely that a court adheres to a precedent it considers correct. It is significant only when a court feels constrained to stick to a former ruling although the court has come to regard it as unwise or unjust." (United States ex rel. Fong Foo 1955).

Because law is such a common site for precedential constraint, we can illuminate the differences between analogical and precedential decision making by examining a legal example. So consider the opinion of Supreme Court Justice Potter Stewart in the 1973 abortion case of *Roe v. Wade*. The central issue was whether a right to privacy, not explicitly recognized as such in the text of the Constitution, could support a woman's right to choose, just as it had supported the right to purchase contraceptives in the 1965 case of *Griswold v. Connecticut*. For the Justices who agreed with the outcome in *Griswold*, the result in *Roe* was unexceptional. From their perspective, they were merely extending slightly the broad principle of privacy set forth in the earlier case. But Justice Stewart did not fit this mold, for he had been one of the dissenters in *Griswold*. For Justice Stewart in *Griswold*, the lack of textual embodiment of a right to privacy was conclusive as to its non-existence. Yet although Justice Stewart so believed in *Griswold*, and by all accounts had not abandoned this view 8 years later, he did not dissent in *Roe*, believing that the obligation to follow even those precedents he believed mistaken mandated that he follow *Griswold* even as he continued to believe its outcome erroneous.

Although such crisp deference to precedent is rare in the Supreme Court (Segal and Spaeth 1996), it is hardly absent. In the 1950s and 1960s Justice John Marshall Harlan would often join the majority in criminal procedure decisions from whose basic principles he had dissented in previous cases, just as Justice Byron White in 1981 in *Edwards v. Arizona* felt obliged faithfully to follow the Supreme Court's earlier decision in *Miranda v. Arizona* (1966), a case in which he had been among the dissenters. And in *Ring v. Arizona* in 2002, which dealt with the requirement that a jury (and not the judge) determine any fact necessary to support the punishment in a criminal case, Justice Anthony Kennedy stated explicitly that "[t]hough it is still my view that [the earlier case of] *Apprendi* was wrongly decided, *Apprendi* is now the law, and its holding must be implemented in a principled way."

These examples from the Supreme Court of the United States are highlighted not only because of their prominence, but also because the Supreme Court is where we are *least* likely to find genuine precedential constraint. Because the Supreme Court hears and decides barely more than 70 cases a year out of the more than 9,000 petitions for review presented to it, and because even the 9,000 represent cases far along in the judicial system, the Supreme Court would be the last place to look for cases whose outcomes are plainly dictated by a previous decision. But when we examine the Federal Courts of Appeals, for example, where hearing a case is compulsory and not discretionary, and where more than 80% of the decisions are not only unanimous but are also not even thought deserving of a published written opinion (Judicial Business, 2005), we see a much larger proportion of cases in which an existing decision of that or an equivalent (or higher) court is understood to mandate a particular outcome regardless of what the judges believe would otherwise be the just result. So although genuine precedential constraint does occasional surface in the Supreme Court, it is far more ubiquitous in state and lower federal court decisions, and in common law jurisdictions outside the United States. When we take account all of these courts and their decisions, therefore, the point should now be clear: The legal system's use of precedent is not about retrieving one from among numerous candidates for the source analog, nor about using analogy to help a decision maker reach a better decision now. Rather, it is about a decision maker's felt (or imposed) obligation to follow a mistaken (to her) earlier decision solely because of its existence. It is, to put it bluntly, about a decision maker's obligation to make what she believes is the wrong decision.

## 3.3 On the Differences Between Analogy and Precedent

Because precedential decision making is thus about constraining and not assisting a decision maker, it operates only under conditions in which the constraining precedent presents itself as inescapable. It is thus in the retrieval process that the differences between analogy and precedent are most apparent. Although an analogical reasoner will refuse to retrieve a source analog she perceives not be helpful, a decision maker constrained by precedent will have no such choice. Perhaps the most striking difference between precedential constraint and the classic case of reasoning by analogy is therefore the typical lack of freedom a precedential reasoner perceives in the retrieval of the precedent example. Whereas analogical reasoners are commonly understood to have a choice among which of various candidate source analogs to retrieve, and whereas it is often argued that experts can be distinguished from novices by the way in which they retrieve their source analogs on the basis of structural rather than superficial similarities to the target (Gentner 1983; Gentner et al. 1993; Holyoak and Koh 1987), the choice is ordinarily highly constrained with respect to constraint by precedent. Justice Stewart would have thought bizarre the suggestion that finding another earlier case could let him avoid the constraints of *Griswold*, just as Justice White would surely have laughed at the idea that feeling constrained by *Miranda* was simply a function of not having recognized or retrieved the best source case. Although on occasion creative and effective advocates can persuade a court to see a case or an issue in an entirely new light, far more often a previous decision about issue *X* looms so large that it is implausible for a judge to avoid that decision by maintaining that the current case is about *Y* and not about *X*.

Thus, it is characteristic of the ordinary instance of precedential constraint that the current question is so widely perceived to be the same as answered in a previous decision that it is not open – politically or professionally – for the current decision-maker to maintain that there is a relevant difference. A foreign policy decision-maker in 1990 might have been able with roughly equivalent plausibility to analogize Saddam to Hitler and war against Iraq to Vietnam, but a Supreme Court Justice asked in 2008 to rule on the constitutionality of a state law totally prohibiting abortion would find it virtually impossible – logically, linguistically, psychologically, professionally, and politically – to distinguish that case from *Roe v. Wade*. It may be logically possible to say that the question whether total bans on abortion are constitutionally permissible in 2008 is different from the question whether total bans on abortion are constitutionally permissible in 1973, but just barely. For all practical purposes they are the *same* question. Analogical reasoning is about similarities – whether structural or surface – between acts or events or examples that are in some respects different, but being bound by precedent is to be bound by a previous answer to what is now in virtually all respects the same question.

So too with precedent outside of law. The child who demands to be able to stay up until ten because her older sister was allowed to stay up until ten at the same age will not be persuaded by arguments about different circumstances, just as the bureaucrat who justifies an action by reliance on past practice will rarely be convinced that this case is relevantly different. For past practice – precedent – to determine an outcome solely because of the past practice's existence and not because of its perceived correctness, the similarity between the past practice and current issue must be seen as inescapable, but legal and non-legal decision-making appear to furnish numerous examples of just this kind of perceived inescapable similarity – verging on identity – between the source and the target.

Once we see that that the retrieval of source decisions is in the case of precedent typically not seen as a choice at all, we can understand the most dramatic difference between analogy and precedent. Whereas in the case of analogy the reasoner is looking for assistance in reaching the best decision (or in persuading someone else of the best decision), in the case of precedent the effect is just the opposite. The unavoidable similarity between the source and the target, when combined with a norm of deciding the target case in the same way that the source case was decided, causes the decision-maker operating under a norm of precedent at least sometimes to feel constrained to reach what she believes to be the wrong result. Whereas in the case of analogy the decision-maker is looking for a source decision (or event) in order to help her make the right decision now, in the case of precedent the decision-maker feels constrained and compelled to make what she now believes to be the wrong decision. And thus precedent-based decision making differs from analogical reasoning not only because retrieval is so much more and differently constrained in the former than in the latter, but also because in the case of precedential reasoning the essential identity between source and target renders the process of transfer – the third step in analogical reasoning – essentially redundant.

## 3.4 Does Precedential Constraint Make Sense?

As just described, it is hardly self-evident that precedential constraint is a desirable approach to thinking, reasoning, and decision making. Why, after all, would anyone want to make the wrong decision, and why would a society want decision makers to make what those decision makers believe to be the wrong decision, and which often may in fact be the wrong decision?

One answer to this question is that usually society does not. Once we appreciate that reasoning from precedent typically requires the decision maker to make what she believes to be the wrong decision,[3] we can see why reliance on precedent is the

---

[3]Of course it is often the case that the precedent case or event or decision is consistent with what the decision-maker now wishes to do. In such instances, however, the existence of the precedent actually has no effect. Only when the existence of a precedent constrains a decision-maker to do what she would otherwise not do does the precedent in fact make a difference, and that is what distinguishes a precedent as make-weight from a precedent that has some causal effect on the decision.

exception and not the rule. Citizens did not expect President Bush to follow the lead of President Clinton just because Clinton had dealt with the same issue, just as we do not expect scientists to reach the conclusions reached by their predecessors for that reason alone. Indeed, introductory logic texts often describe arguments from precedent as logical fallacies. But although denial of the value of the constraint by precedent is the rule, there are noteworthy exceptions. When we expect parents or bureaucrats or retailers to do what they have done before even if they now think it mistaken, or to do what their predecessors have done even if they think their predecessors misguided, we recognize the Aristotelian mandate to treat like cases alike, and we recognize as well, as Justice Brandeis famously expressed it, that "sometimes it is more important that things be decided than that they be decided correctly." In other words, it is sometimes desirable to recognize the values of settlement for settlement's sake, or consistency for consistency's sake.

It is, arguably, the special responsibility of law to pursue these values of settlement, stability, and consistency. While these values do have their place in other decision making domains, and are seen throughout our decision making lives, the greater centrality of precedent in law may reflect a certain role that the legal system is expected to play more than, say, a legislature enacting a law, an executive administering the law, a physician diagnosing an illness, or a therapist counseling a patient. Reasoning from precedent, and the constraints that precedent imposes, may exist in numerous places, but may exist somewhat more in law than elsewhere because of the particular function that legal systems are expected to fulfill.

## 3.5 Towards a Research Program on Precedent

Two conclusions emerge from the foregoing. First is that the structure of an argument from precedent is very different from the structure of an argument by analogy. And second is that making decisions constrained by precedent – doing the wrong thing just because it has been done before – is highly counter-intuitive, possibly making it something difficult for many or even most people to do.

But if reaching the wrong (first-order) decision because of the (second-order) constraints of precedent is both difficult yet expected, there are important questions about how often decision makers can make what they believe to be wrong decisions, whether some people are better at it than others, whether some people – prospective lawyers and judges, most obviously – can be trained to do what they might have otherwise have thought difficult or impossible, and whether skill at subjugating one's outcome preferences for *this* case, like the skill at generalizing from the particular context (Stanovich and West 2000), correlates with common measures of general intelligence. Thus, one hypothesis might be that there can be experts in precedential constraint, and, indeed, it is part of the traditional claim of law schools that they are able to train students in the special facility for subjugating their own sense of the best decision to the rule-based and precedent-based demands of the legal system. But an alternative hypothesis might be that the greater the degree of expertise someone has in some field, the *less* they will be able to suppress their own expert judgments to the constraints of precedent. Yet in part because of the erroneous assumption that reasoning from precedent is the same as reasoning by analogy, there has been virtually no research on any of these important questions or hypotheses.

Merely by way of preliminary suggestion, therefore, one can imagine experiments aimed at determining, for example, whether those who self-select for legal training (or are selected for legal training) are superior, prior to receiving that training, at subjugating their preferences for the right answer to a norm of precedent; whether those who are trained in the constraints of precedent (recent graduates of law school, for example) are better at following uncomfortable (to them) precedents than those who have, controlling for self-selection, yet to receive such training; or whether those who self-select for judging, or who are selected to be judges, are better at following precedent than practicing lawyers of similar experience.

All of the this is by way of trying to determine if there are experts at following precedent, what characteristics these experts possess that non-experts do not, and what skills these experts have that novices do not. Perhaps, for example, creativity would be positively correlated with facility at analogical reasoning, but negatively correlated with the intrinsically non-creative act of following a precedent. If being constrained by precedent is largely dependent on a reasoning process in which the decision makers sees (and thus retrieves) only one source exemplar, then we might expect that those whose vision is narrower will be more likely to be constrained by precedent than those whose broader scope of imagination and creativity will enable them to see analogical opportunities where others see only precedential constraint.

As the recent discourse about the Supreme Court makes clear, many people expect judges to follow precedents with which they disagree, but we have little research on the extent to which such a task is possible, and if so who is likely to be good at it, and how people might be trained to perform it. This is a research task for psychologists and not lawyers, and it is unfortunate that the mistaken equation of precedent and analogy has prevented psychologists from addressing this issue. Moreover, if following precedents even when they seem wrong to the decision maker is not only a large part of law, but a substantial even if not as large a part of much of personal, family, administrative, bureaucratic and commercial decision-making, then psychological research about following precedent in law may tell us much about following precedent in these even more pervasive decision making domains.

**Acknowledgements** This paper emerged out of a series of illuminating conversations and exchanges with Dan Simon and Barbara Spellman, and I thank both of them for serving as involuntary foils and for extensive comments on an earlier draft. Larry Alexander, Michelle Cowley, and David Lynch also provided helpful comments, and Henry Monaghan, Matt Stephenson, Carol Steiker, Bill Stuntz, Larry Tribe, Mark Tushnet, and Lloyd Weinreb furnished useful legal references. Research support was provided by the Harvard Law School, the Joan Shorenstein Center on the Press, Politics and Public Policy, Harvard University, and the University of Oxford.

## References


Alexander, L. 1989. Constrained by precedent. *Southern California Law Review* 63: 1–64.

Alexander, L., and E. Sherwin. 2001. *The rule of rules: Morality, rules, and the dilemmas of law*. Durham: Duke University Press.

Ashley, K.D. 1990. *Modeling legal arguments: Reasoning with cases and hypotheticals*. Cambridge: MIT Press.

Blanchette, I., and K. Dunbar. 2000. Analogy use in naturalistic settings: The place of audience, emotion and goals. *Memory and Cognition* 29: 330–335.

Brewer, S. 1996. Exemplary reasoning: Semantics, pragmatics, and the rational force of legal argument. *Harvard Law Review* 109: 923–1028.

Brown, A.L. 1989. Analogical learning and transfer: What develops? In *Similarity and analogical reasoning*, ed. S. Vosniadou and A. Ortony, 396–412. New York: Cambridge University Press.

*Burnet v. Coronado Oil. & Gas Co.*, 285 U.S. 393, 406 (1932) (Brandeis, J., dissenting). Editorial – Justice Denied. 2007. *New York Times*, July 5, 2007, p. 12

*Edwards v. Arizona*. 1981. 451 U.S. 477.

Ellsworth, P. 2005. Legal reasoning. In *The Cambridge handbook of thinking and reasoning*, ed. K.J. Holyoak and R.G. Morison, 685–704. Cambridge: Cambridge University Press.

Forbus, K.D. 2001. Exploring analogy in the large. In *The analogical mind: Perspectives from cognitive science*, ed. D. Gentner, K.J. Holyoak, and B.N. Kokinov, 23–58. Cambridge: MIT Press.

Forbus, K.D., D. Gentner, A.B. Markman, and R.W. Ferguson. 1998. Analogy just looks like high level perception: Why a domain general approach to analogical mapping is right. *Journal of Experimental and Theoretical Artificial Intelligence* 10: 231–257.

Gentner, D. 1983. Structure mapping: A theoretical framework for analogy. *Cognitive Science* 7: 155–170.

Gentner, D., M.J. Rattermann, and K.D. Forbus. 1993. The role of similarity in transfer: Separating retrievability from inferential soundness. *Cognitive Psychology* 25: 524–575.

Gick, M.L., and K.J. Holyoak. 1980. Analogical problem solving. *Cognitive Psychology* 12:306–355.

Gick, M.L., and K.J. Holyoak. 1983. Schema induction and analogical transfer. *Cognitive Psychology* 15: 1–38.

*Griswold v. Connecticut*. 1965. 381 U.S. 479.

Hofstadter, D.R. 1995. A review of *mental leaps: Analogy in creative thought*. *AI Magazine, Fall* 1995: 75–81.

Hofstadter, D.R. 2001. Analogy as the core of cognition. In *The analogical mind: Perspectives from cognitive science*, ed. D. Gentner, K.J. Holyoak, and B.N. Kokinov, 499–538. Cambridge: MIT Press.

Holyoak, K.J. 1982. An analogical framework for literary interpretation. *Poetics* 11: 105–126.

Holyoak, K.J. 2005. Analogy. In *The Cambridge handbook of thinking and reasoning*, ed. K.J. Holyoak and R.G. Morison, 117–142. Cambridge: Cambridge University Press.

Holyoak, K.J., and K. Koh. 1987. Surface and structural similarity in analogical transfer. *Memory and Cognition* 15: 323–340.

Holyoak, K.J., and D. Simon. 1999. Bidirectional reasoning in decision making by constraint satisfaction. *Journal of Experimental Psychology. General* 128: 3–31.

Holyoak, K.J., and P. Thagard. 1995. *Mental leaps: Analogy in creative thought*. Cambridge: MIT Press.

Holyoak, K.J., and P. Thagard. 1997. The analogical mind. *American Psychologist* 52: 35–44.

Holyoak, K.J., D. Gentner, and B.N. Kokinov. 2001. Introduction: The place of analogy in cognition. In *The analogical mind: Perspectives from cognitive science*, ed. D. Gentner, K.J. Holyoak, and B.N. Kokinov, 1–19. Cambridge: MIT Press.

Hunt, E. 2006. Expertise, talent, and social encouragement. In *The Cambridge handbook of expertise and expert performance*, ed. K.A. Ericsson, N. Charness, P.J. Feltovich, and R.R. Hoffman, 31–40. Cambridge: Cambridge University Press.
Hunter, D. 1997. Reason is too large: Analogy and precedent in law. *Emory Law Journal* 50: 1197–1243.
Judicial Business of the United States Courts (Administrative Office of the United States Courts), Table S-3. 2005. http://www.uscourts.gov/judbus2005/tables/s3.pdf.
Khong, Y.F. 1992. *Analogies at war: Korea, Munich, Dien Bien Phu, and the Vietnam decisions of 1965*. Princeton: Princeton University Press.
Kokinov, B.N., and R.M. French. 2003. Computational models of analogy-making. In *Encyclopedia of cognitive science*, vol. 1, ed. L. Nadel, 113–118. London: Nature Publishing Group.
Lamond, G. 2006. Precedent and analogy in legal reasoning. In *Stanford encyclopedia of philosophy*, ed. N. Zalta. http://plato.stanford.edu/archives/sum2006/entries/legal-reas-prec/.
Levi, E. 1949. *Introduction to legal reasoning*. Chicago: University of Chicago Press.
Mill, J.S. 1861. Considerations on representative government. In J.M. Robson (Ed.), *Collected works of John Stuart Mill, 29*, 371–577 (1963). Toronto: University of Toronto Press.
*Miranda v. Arizona*. 1966. 384 U.S. 436.
Paulsen, M.S. 2005. The intrinsically corrupting influence of precedent. *Constitutional Commentary* 22: 289–298.
Posner, R.A. 2008. *How judges think*. Cambridge: Harvard University Press.
*Ring v. Arizona*. 2002. 536 U.S. 584, 613 (Kennedy, J., concurring).
*Roe v. Griffits*. 1766. 98 Eng. Rep. 17.
*Roe v. Wade*. 1973. 410 U.S. 113.
Schauer, F. 1987. Precedent. *Stanford Law Review* 39: 571–605.
Segal, J., and H. Spaeth. 1996. The influence of stare decisis on the votes of Supreme Court justices. *American Journal of Political Science* 40: 971–1004.
Simon, D., D.C. Krawczyk, and K.J. Holyoak. 2004. Construction of preferences by constraint satisfaction. *Psychological Science* 15: 331–336.
Spellman, B.A. 2004. Reflections of a recovering lawyer: How becoming a cognitive psychologist – and (in particular) studying analogical and causal reasoning – changed my views about the field of law and psychology. *Chicago-Kent Law Review* 79: 1187–1214.
Spellman, B.A., and K.J. Holyoak. 1992. If Saddam is Hitler then who is George Bush?: Analogical mapping between systems of social roles. *Journal of Personality and Social Psychology* 62: 913–933.
Spellman, B.A., and K.J. Holyoak. 1996. Pragmatics in analogical mapping. *Cognitive Psychology* 31: 307–346.
Spiro, R.J., P.J. Feltovich, R.L. Coulson, and D.K. Anderson. 1989. Multiple analogies for complex concepts: Antidotes for analogy-induced misconception in advanced knowledge acquisition. In *Similarity and analogical reasoning*, ed. S. Vosniadou and A. Ortony, 498–531. New York: Cambridge University Press.
Stanovich, K.E., and R.E. West. 2000. Individual differences in reasoning: Implications for the rationality debate. *The Behavioral and Brain Sciences* 23: 645–665.
Sunstein, C.R. 1993. On analogical reasoning. *Harvard Law Review* 106: 741–791.
Tetlock, P.E. 1999. Theory driven reasoning about possible pasts and probable futures: Are we prisoners of our perceptions? *American Journal of Political Science* 43: 335–366.
*United States ex rel. Fong Foo v. Shaughnessy*, 234 F.2d 715 (2d Cir. 1955).
Wasserstrom, R. 1961. *The judicial decision: Toward a theory of legal justification*. Stanford: Stanford University Press.
Weinreb, L.L. 2005. *Legal reason: The use of analogy in legal argument*. Cambridge: Cambridge University Press.

# Chapter 4
# Fallacies in *Ad Hominem* Arguments*

**Christian Dahlman, David Reidhav, and Lena Wahlberg**

## 4.1 Introduction

One of the most common ways to argue against a claim is to attack it indirectly, by attacking the person who makes the claim. Examples are easy to find in political debates, courtrooms and dinner conversations. A politician who claims that the government should cut taxes is countered with the argument that he endorses tax cuts because it would benefit him personally. The testimony of an eye witness in a murder trial is attacked by the defense attorney, with the argument that the witness is unreliable because he is a drug addict. A guest at a dinner party who says that people in rich countries should do more for the people in poor countries is met with the argument that she does not do much for poor people herself.

Counter arguments of this kind are usually dismissed as bad arguments. They are rejected as unfair and irrelevant, and it is said that they commit the *ad hominem* fallacy. This reaction gives rise to questions. Are these arguments always fallacious? Is the attack always aimed at the opposing arguer in the discussion? Are all arguments that commit the *ad hominem* fallacy fallacious in the same way? Our answer to each of these three questions is negative. An *ad hominem* argument is not always fallacious. Some *ad hominem* arguments attack a person who is not a

*The research presented in this article was funded by Torsten och Ragnar Söderbergs Stiftelser. We owe thanks to Niklas Arvidsson, Roberta Colonna Dahlman, Eveline Feteris, Åke Frändberg, Tobias Hansson Wahlberg, Patricia Mindus, Antonino Rotolo, Stefan Schubert, Torben Spaak, Lennart Åqvist and two anonymous referees for helpful comments on earlier drafts.

C. Dahlman (✉) • D. Reidhav • L. Wahlberg
Faculty of Law, Lund University, Lund, Sweden
e-mail: Christian.Dahlman@jur.lu.se; David.Reidhav@jur.lu.se; Lena.Wahlberg@jur.lu.se

C. Dahlman and E. Feteris (eds.), *Legal Argumentation Theory: Cross-Disciplinary Perspectives*, Law and Philosophy Library 102, DOI 10.1007/978-94-007-4670-1_4,

participant in the discussion. And the *ad hominem* arguments that are fallacious can commit a number of different fallacies. This article will explain and develop these views.

That an argument which seeks to undermine a claim by attacking the person who makes the claim is not always fallacious has been pointed out by many other scholars. It can, for example, make good sense to challenge the testimony of an eye-witness with the observation that the witness is almost blind. If a speaker claims that she should be relied on, it becomes relevant to challenge that claim with an argument that attacks her reliability. Some authors, including John Woods (2010, xxv), Douglas Walton (1998, 125), Alan Brinton (1995, 215) and Bruce Waller (2005, 180–192), say that this shows that an argument *ad hominem* is not always fallacious. In their treatment of *ad hominem* arguments, there are *ad hominem* arguments that are legitimate and *ad hominem* arguments that commit the *ad hominem* fallacy. Others, notably Irving Copi and Carl Cohen (2002, 143–145), prefer to reserve the term *ad hominem* for arguments that commit the *ad hominem* fallacy: If an argument is not fallacious it is not an *ad hominem* argument. This difference in terminology can be confusing, and it is important to bear in mind that it does not reflect a substantial disagreement over legitimacy. Like Woods, Walton, Brinton and Waller we prefer to distinguish between *ad hominem* argument and *ad hominem* fallacy. We therefore begin our investigation by developing a general definition of *ad hominem* argument. We then move on to investigate the conditions under which these arguments are fallacious.

Our approach to *ad hominem* arguments differs from the standard approach taken in textbooks on fallacies. The main structure in the standard approach is the division of *ad hominem* arguments in the subtypes known as abusive *ad hominem* and circumstantial *ad hominem*, along with the additional subtype known as *tu quoque*. Our approach is structured around a general definition: an argument *ad hominem* is an argument that points out that a person has a certain attribute and claims that this affects the reliability of the person with regard to the performance of a certain function. In the following, we will relate our framework to the standard classification at appropriate points.

In our account, an *ad hominem* argument does not necessarily attack the opposing arguer in the discussion. A personal attack on someone who does not participate in the discussion is also an *ad hominem* argument. Such attacks are often used as counter arguments against an authority argument. Think, for example, of a discussion where one of the participants backs up his claim by referring to Professor X as an authority, and the other participant replies with a personal attack against Professor X, intended to undermine the Professor's reliability as an authority. In our understanding this is clearly an argument *ad hominem*, but there are scholars who have a different view. According to Frans van Eemeren, Rob Grootendorst and other members of the pragma-dialectical school this kind of argument does not count as an argument *ad hominem*, as it attacks a person outside the discussion. According to their definition, an argument *ad hominem* is an argument that violates the first rule of discussion, that "parties must not prevent each other from advancing standpoints or casting doubt on standpoints" (see, e.g., van Eemeren and Grootendorst 1992, 153–155). In our view, this makes the analysis of *ad hominem* arguments too narrow. As we understand it, the soundness of a personal attack depends on a number of factors, but participation in the discussion is not one of them. It makes no difference for the soundness of the argument whether the person under attack is a participant in the discussion or not.

In our analysis, an argument that commits the *ad hominem* fallacy can be fallacious in seven different ways. We will identify each of these errors and analyze them as seven separate *ad hominem* fallacies. This means that our account of how *ad hominem* arguments can be fallacious is broader than the exposition you would find in most textbooks. It is often said that *ad hominem* arguments are fallacious because they try to attack a claim by attacking the reliability of the person who makes the claim, in spite of the fact that this is irrelevant to the correctness of the claim (see, e.g., Hamblin 1970, 41; Walton 1987, 317; Copi and Cohen 2002, 143). In our account, this is just one of the seven ways in which an *ad hominem* argument can be fallacious. It will be analyzed in Sect. 4.3 as "the fallacy of reliability irrelevance".

At the outset, our approach is similar in some ways to Brinton's treatment of *ad hominem* arguments. Like Brinton we seek to identify different ways in which *ad hominem* arguments can go wrong. An important difference between our approach and Brinton's is that we analyze all these errors as false premises. As we shall see, we represent *ad hominem* arguments as deductively valid arguments and understand every *ad hominem* fallacy in terms of a false premise. This approach is somewhat unorthodox. The *ad hominem* fallacy is normally assumed to involve an illegitimate move from premise to conclusion. It is important to understand, however, that this difference is a matter of presentation. To describe an *ad hominem* fallacy as a false premise instead of an illegitimate move from premise to conclusion is just a different way of describing the same thing. To see this, consider the following reasoning: "What the witness says is not true. He is an alcoholic." This might be held to commit an *ad hominem* fallacy because it makes an illegitimate move from premise to conclusion: the conclusion (what the witness says is not true) cannot be derived from the premise (the witness is an alcoholic). A different way to say the same thing is to say that the argument is fallacious because the premise that would make it legitimate (what an alcoholic says is not true) is false. It is exactly because this premise is false that some scholars say that we are dealing with an illegitimate move from premise to conclusion.

We believe our approach has several advantages. By conceptualizing every *ad hominem* error as the result of a false premise we are able to give a uniform treatment of the various ways in which *ad hominem* arguments can go wrong. We are also in a position to classify these errors not only on basis of which premise of the argument is false, but also in terms of the grounds on which the premise is false. This makes it possible to give a comprehensive and detailed description of the various forms of error.

## 4.2 Definition of Argument *Ad Hominem*

We propose the following general definition: an argument *ad hominem* is an argument that makes a claim about the *reliability* of a *person*, P, based on an *attribute*, A, of P. The argument points out that P has A, and it claims that, because P has A, P's *reliability* in the performance of a certain *function*, F, amounts to the degree D. *Ad hominem* argumentation, in its basic form, can be represented as follows.

Argument *ad hominem* (basic form):

(i) *P has A*
(ii) *If P has A, the reliability of P in the performance of F is D*
(iii) *The reliability of P in the performance of F is D*

We will speak of the first premise as the *attribution premise* and the second premise as the *effect premise*.

As is indicated by the term "*ad hominem*" P is a person. However, traditionally, arguments in which P is a group of people or an organization have been categorized as *ad hominem* as well, and we see no reason to break with this tradition. By "attribute" we mean a property, in the widest sense of the term, which can be ascribed to the person P. An attribute can, for example, consist in having bad eyesight, being a compulsive liar or being in Lund. Some of the things we here call attributes are normally referred to, not as attributes or properties, but rather as "circumstances". For example, the fact that a witness was in Lund at a certain time would be described by lawyers as a "circumstance". However, in order to maintain a coherent terminology, we will treat any fact that can be ascribed to a person as an attribute.

An argument *ad hominem* is an argument about reliability. It is an argument claiming that a certain attribute has a certain effect on a person's reliability. This is not always apparent when one looks at the way *ad hominem* arguments are described, but a number of other scholars who describe the effect of *ad hominem* arguments regard them broadly in these terms. Thus Brinton (1985, 56) says *ad hominem* arguments typically question someone's credentials as a speaker, and Walton (1998, 273–278) observes that they seek to affect the opponent's "credibility".[1]

Reliability depends on *ability* as well as *motivation*. That a person is reliable in the performance of a function means that he or she is able to perform the function and motivated to do so. A witness, for example, is reliable when he or she has the cognitive ability to observe and remember events correctly as well as the motivation to tell the truth. As we shall see, some *ad hominem* arguments are aimed at ability while others are aimed at motivation.

---

[1]That the arguments we are interested in are fundamentally about reliability was detected by Bentham. He does not use the term *ad hominem* at all. Instead he speaks of arguments that commit this kind of fallacy as modifications of the "fallacy of distrust" (1824/1952, 83–92, 100–102).

According to our definition *ad hominem* arguments target P's reliability with respect to a certain *function*, F. In this formulation F can stand for any function that a person can be relied upon to fulfill. It can stand for the function of serving as an eyewitness in a court of law, but it can just as well stand for the function of being Prime Minister. This makes our account of *ad hominem* argument broader than Brinton's. Brinton (1995, 213–215) describes an argument *ad hominem* as an argument that attacks someone's reliability as an advocate. In our account, F can stand for the function of advocating a certain proposition, but it can also stand for other functions that can be related to reliability. When F is the Prime Ministerial function, it stands for confidence in P to exercise good judgment on political issues. When F is the function of serving as an eye witness, it stands for reliability to give an accurate account of certain events. In our account "credibility" (i.e. reliability as a source of information) is thus a sub-class of reliability in the performance of function.[2]

An argument that is not about reliability is not an argument *ad hominem*. The argument that Pedro is older than me because he was born in 1956 is not an argument *ad hominem*. Being older than someone is not a question of reliability. In some cases, it is a matter of interpretation whether an argument is an argument about reliability. Consider the argument "Alfred can't run fast. He has a bad leg". This is not necessarily an argument about reliability, but it can be interpreted as such. It can be interpreted as an argument to the effect that Alfred cannot be relied on to run fast. We could, for example, imagine that Alfred is being considered for the position of courier. Someone is needed to deliver an important message before a certain time. As we all know, interpretation is difficult. For present purposes this need not worry us. That an argument *ad hominem* is an argument about reliability simply means that an argument that is interpreted as an argument *ad hominem* is an argument that is interpreted as an argument about reliability.

The effect that A has on P's reliability can be positive or negative: it can improve P's reliability, or it can reduce it. We will talk about arguments where the effect is positive as *positive ad hominem arguments* and arguments where the effect is negative as *negative ad hominem arguments*.

*Ad hominem* arguments are often used as counter-arguments to claims about P's reliability. They are therefore often defined as counter-arguments. In our view, this makes the analysis too narrow. Given our definition, an *ad hominem* argument does not need to be a counter-argument. As we have seen above, the *ad hominem* argument in its basic form is an argument in its own right. The claim that it makes about P's reliability need not stand in opposition to some other claim about P's reliability.

[2]According to Brinton arguments directed at functions which are merely accidentally associated with human beings are not *ad hominem*. He concludes (1995, 213–214) that only arguments directed at advocacy qualify as *ad hominem* arguments. Given the structural similarities of arguments about reliability in the performance of functions of all kinds, an account which is applicable to any of these functions is in our view methodologically preferable. Besides, we are not convinced that advocacy is an essential attribute for being a person, as Brinton assumes.

An *ad hominem* argument that targets a particular claim, and which draws the conclusion that the effect that A has on P's reliability makes this *target claim* false, can be represented as an extension of the *ad hominem* argument in its basic form.

Argument *ad Hominem* (extended form):

(i) *P has A*
(ii) *If P has A, the reliability of P in the performance of F is D*
(iii) *If the reliability of P in the performance of F is D, the target claim is false*
(iv) *The target claim is false*

The *ad hominem* argument in its extended form has three premises: the attribution premise and the effect premise from the basic form, plus a third premise that we shall label the *rebuttal premise*.

The following dialogue serves as an example.

X: "Mrs. Borg is very reliable as an eyewitness."
Y: "No, she is not. She has poor eyesight."

The argument advanced by Y is an *ad hominem* in the extended form. It is a counter-argument to the claim that Mrs. Borg is very reliable, and it draws the conclusion that the target claim is false. In full, the argument of Y in the dialogue is:

(i) Mrs. Borg has poor eyesight.
(ii) If Mrs. Borg has poor eyesight, the reliability of Mrs. Borg as an eye witness is low.
(iii) If the reliability of Mrs. Borg as an eye witness is low, the claim "Mrs. Borg is very reliable as an eye witness" is false.
(iv) The claim "Mrs. Borg is very reliable as an eye witness" is false.

## 4.3 *Ad Hominem* Fallacies

An argument *ad hominem* can go wrong in many different ways. We shall now identify seven kinds of error. We talk about these errors as *ad hominem* fallacies, and we refer to them by the following names.

1. the fallacy of false attribution
2. the fallacy of irrelevant attribute
3. the fallacy of overrated effect
4. the fallacy of reliability irrelevance
5. the fallacy of irrelevant person
6. the fallacy of insufficient degree
7. the fallacy of irrelevant function

Each fallacy results from the presence of a false premise in the *ad hominem* argument. An argument that commits the fallacy of false attribution is unsound because the attribution premise is false. In arguments committing the fallacy of irrelevant attribute or overrated effect the effect premise is false. Arguments that commit the fallacy of reliability irrelevance, irrelevant person, insufficient degree or irrelevant function have a false rebuttal premise. In its basic form *ad hominem* argumentation can commit only the first three fallacies. Since the last four fallacies consist in a false rebuttal premise, they cannot be committed by arguments in the basic form. *Ad hominem* arguments in the extended form, on the other hand, can commit any of the seven fallacies.

The *fallacy of false attribution* is committed when the argument claims that P has an attribute P in fact lacks. Here is an example.

> Barack Obama shouldn't be trusted as Commander in Chief. He is a Muslim, you know.

The *fallacy of irrelevant attribute* is committed in cases when A has no effect on P's reliability in the performance of F. Here is an obvious example.

> You cannot take him seriously as an expert on foreign policy. He looks like an aardvark.

This kind of error in *ad hominem* arguments is also identified by Woods (2010, 98, 105). As the example shows, sometimes a negative *ad hominem* argument that commits the fallacy of irrelevant attribute is not only a bad argument, but a downright insult. And indeed arguments of this kind are classified as "abusive" *ad hominem* arguments by Copi and Cohen (2002, 143). However, the fallacy of irrelevant attribute is not always abusive. It is not abusive in positive *ad hominem* arguments, of course, and there are cases where a negative *ad hominem* argument commits the fallacy of irrelevant attribute without being abusive. Consider the following example.

> It is true that Mr. Berg has testified that the plaintiff was bleeding, but we should not rely too much on this testimony, since Mr. Berg is not a medical expert.

This argument commits the fallacy of irrelevant attribute (you do not need to be a medical expert to recognize that someone is bleeding), but it is not abusive. The mere observation that someone is not a doctor is not an insult.

The effect of an attribute depends on the context (see, e.g., Walton 1987, 323). In this article, we treat context as a bundle of attributes. An *ad hominem* argument must be understood as being made relative to an assumption about a certain bundle of attributes that includes A. This bundle determines the effect that the attribute is assumed to have on P's reliability. We propose to label this bundle $B_{AH}$. Note that this is the *assumed* context, and that it may not correspond with the actual context. For example, the argument might be made on the mistaken assumption that a person has poor eyesight. Given this mistaken assumption, the effect of the circumstance that the eyewitness was not close to the scene of the crime (A) is likely to be overrated.

We use the label $B_A$ for the bundle of attributes that *actually* holds for P. On our account this actual context determines the real effect of A on P's reliability. It is against the background of $B_A$ that an *ad hominem* argument should ideally be assessed. In other words, a fallacy can occur because reliability is assessed on the basis of a non-actual bundle of attributes, or because the relevance of A in the actual bundle is estimated inaccurately by the arguer.

The following sets of relationships – between A, the degree of reliability in a particular function F, and a particular person P with his or her actual bundle of attributes ($B_A$) including A – are conceivable.

(a) The attribute A never affects the reliability of a person in the performance of F and therefore does not affect the reliability of the particular person P in the actual context $B_A$.
(b) The attribute A sometimes affects the reliability of a person in the performance of F, but does not affect the reliability of the particular person P in the actual context $B_A$.
(c) The attribute A sometimes affects the reliability of a person in the performance of F, and the particular person P in the actual context $B_A$ represents a case where A has such an effect.
(d) The attribute A always affects the reliability of a person in the performance of F and therefore affects the reliability of the particular person P in the actual context $B_A$.

It can be questioned whether there really are attributes that never affect the reliability of P in performing F. If, however, A never is relevant, it will be irrelevant irrespective of other attributes that P has. For example, if the color of the clothes of the person testifying is never relevant to the assessment of that person's reliability as a source of information, it does not matter what other attributes the person has. In any situation of the sort described in (a) an *ad hominem* argument to the effect that A is relevant will commit the fallacy of irrelevant attribute.

The fact that a fallacy is being committed is easy to spot in cases where it is unthinkable, or at least highly implausible, that the attribute that is pointed out could ever affect a certain kind of reliability: an example would be the attribute of an expert on foreign policy looking like an aardvark. It is more difficult to spot when the argument points to an attribute that is relevant in some contexts but not in the one at hand (situation (b) above). For example, not wearing one's glasses normally affects a person's reliability as an eyewitness. However, the fact that P was not wearing her glasses is an irrelevant attribute for her reliability as an eye witness if she has perfect vision and wears glasses as a fashion accessory.

The *fallacy of overrated effect* is committed in cases where A has an effect on P's reliability in performing F but this effect is less than the effect premise claims. The argument does not commit the fallacy of irrelevant attribute, as it points to an attribute that is relevant to the reliability issue at hand. What is wrong in the argument is simply that it exaggerates the effect of the attribute. This error has also been identified by Brinton as one of the ways that *ad hominem* arguments can go wrong. Brinton describes it as a "failure in degree of support" (1995, 218).

An example of the fallacy of overrated effect in legal argumentation occurs in the Swedish case NJA 1986 s. 358. A man, TS, reported to his insurance company that his car had been stolen and claimed compensation for his loss in accordance with the insurance policy. The company did not believe his story and refused to pay. TS sued. The company argued, before the court, that TS should be considered unreliable because he had a criminal record: TS had previously been convicted for several crimes, including attempted insurance fraud. This argument is clearly *ad hominem*. The company claimed that the conviction for insurance fraud had a strong negative effect on TS's reliability to give accurate testimony. This negative *ad hominem* was not accepted by the appellate court. Confirming that TS's criminal record did indeed have a negative effect on his reliability, but emphasizing that many years had passed since the last conviction, the court held that the effect was less significant than the insurance company had argued. The appellate judges were, in effect, insisting that the *ad hominem* argument presented by the insurance company committed the fallacy of overrated effect.

The fallacy of overrated effect can occur in situations (c) and (d) above. This fallacy – like the fallacy of irrelevant attribute – can be the result of the reliability being assessed relative to an non-actual bundle of attributes or an inaccurate estimate of the effect of the bundle by the arguer. Thus, in the example from the Swedish Supreme Court the insurance company based their reliability assessment on an incompletely specified (and in this sense non-actual) bundle in which the time-span between the conviction and the compensation claim was not included.

Some *ad hominem* arguments claim that the attribute they invoke categorically disqualifies P from reliable performance of F. Consider, for example, the following argument.

> There is just one thing you need to know about the next witness. She is the mother of the accused. As we all know, a mother would say anything to protect her son. You should therefore disregard everything she has to say. No other thing that you learn about her could ever change that.

This kind of argumentation is sometimes referred to as *poisoning the well* (see, e.g., Walton 2006, 289). Where it is claimed that A renders P completely unreliable, no matter what other attributes P has, the situation is of kind (d). Plainly, any claim imputing complete unreliability will be a very strong one, and even when the situation indeed is of kind (d) this kind of argumentation often involves the fallacy of overrated effect.

An attribute's effect on reliability depends, not just on the bundle, but also on the function at issue. The fallacies of irrelevant attribute and overrated effect can therefore occur if information about an attribute's effect on reliability in the performance of one function is unwarrantedly generalized or extrapolated to another function. This mistake is not uncommon in assessments of the credibility of expert witnesses.

The *fallacy of reliability irrelevance* is committed when the effect that A has on P's reliability does not make the target claim false, because the target claim is not about reliability. Consider the following example.

X: "The government should cut taxes. It would be good for the economy."
Y: "You're just saying that because you would benefit from tax cuts."

The argument advanced by X has an unstated major premise to the effect that the government should cut taxes if tax cuts would be good for the economy, a minor premise affirming that tax cuts would be good for the economy, and the conclusion that the government should cut taxes. None of these three claims are about X's reliability. Y may well be right when he says that X is making the argument because tax cuts would benefit him personally, but that does not falsify any claim in X's argument, and therefore does not affect its soundness.

The fallacy of reliability irrelevance is a special case of the fallacy known as *ignoratio elenchi* (cf. Walton 1998, 65). It presents an argument on an issue as a counter-argument to a claim on a different issue. This fallacy is sometimes used deliberately, with rhetorical intent, to divert attention from the main argument and shift discussion to a different issue (van Eemeren and Grootendorst 1992, 152–153). The latter is sometimes referred to as a *red herring*.

It should be noted that an argument that is not about reliability can be backed up by an argument about reliability. This means that an *ad hominem* argument that commits the fallacy of reliability irrelevance in relation to a certain argument could be a legitimate counter-argument against a backing argument. Consider the following dialogue.

X: "The government should cut taxes. It would be good for the economy."
Y: "I'm not sure. I don't understand that much about economics."
X: "You can trust me. I have a PhD in economics. That should make me reliable as an expert on the economic impact of tax cuts."
Y: "Sorry. You would also benefit from tax cuts, and therefore you're not reliable as an expert on the economic impact of tax cuts."

X is now backing up the main argument with an authority argument. He says he is a reliable expert on the economic impact of tax cuts because he has a PhD in economics. This is a positive *ad hominem* argument. The argument advanced by Y is also an *ad hominem* argument – a negative one that stands as a counter-argument to the positive argument advanced by X. This second argument targets the conclusion in X's *ad hominem* argument and says that this conclusion makes a false claim. In this way, the counter-argument adds another attribute, X's personal interest in tax cuts, to the bundle and claims that X's credibility, given his doctoral qualification *and* this additional attribute, differs considerably from his credibility given the doctoral qualification alone. Since the negative *ad hominem* argument invoked by Y draws the conclusion that X's claim about his own reliability is false, Y's argument is an *ad hominem* argument in the extended form. This argument does not commit the fallacy of reliability irrelevance.

Here lies the crucial difference between Y's response that X would benefit personally from tax cuts when we regard it as a counter-argument to X's backing argument and the same response when we regard it as a counter-argument to X's main argument. As we saw above, the response commits the fallacy of reliability irrelevance against the main argument. This shows the importance of picking the right target claim. An *ad hominem* argument committing the fallacy of reliability irrelevance vis-à-vis one claim can be perfectly sound as a counter-argument to another claim.

Notice that this makes it difficult to assess *ad hominem* arguments in many of their applications to actual events and issues. In real life it is often unclear what the target claim is. If the rebuttal premise is such that it would come out false if the argument is taken to target one claim and true if it is taken to target another, the soundness of the argument may be equally unclear. This only goes to show that if we are to determine whether an argument is successful, it must be clear what the argument is meant to target.

Some scholars have suggested that *ad hominem* arguments do not commit a fallacy of irrelevance when there is doubt about the truth of a premise invoked by the opposing arguer. Lawrence Hinman (1982, 339) presented this idea in the early 1980s, and a similar argument has recently been made by Christopher Johnson (2009, 256–259). When there is doubt about the truth of a premise invoked by the opposing arguer it is not irrelevant, their argument goes, to question whether the opposing arguer should be relied on in his claim that the premise is true. There is some truth in this observation, but it overlooks the fact that a counter-argument will always have a specific target, and it fails to separate counter-arguments that target a claim in the main argument from counter-arguments to a claim in the backing argument. That an *ad hominem* argument is relevant as a falsifier against a claim in a backing argument does not mean that it is relevant as a falsifier against a claim in the main argument. The *ad hominem* argument will still commit the fallacy of reliability irrelevance against the main argument if the main argument is not about reliability.

One type of argument that commits the fallacy of reliability irrelevance is the argument known as *tu quoque*. The standard treatment of *ad hominem* arguments identifies *tu quoque* as a special kind of *ad hominem* fallacy. *Tu quoque* is a counter-argument to the argument that a certain way of acting is wrong which attacks the opposing arguer by pointing out that he has acted in that very way.

An interesting example can be taken from the Nuremberg Trials (see, Yee 2004, 103–116; Heise 2009, 10–14). The German Admiral Karl Dönitz was accused of unrestricted submarine warfare in violation of the London Naval Treaty of 1936, to which Germany was a party. Dönitz had ordered his submarines to attack British merchant vessels without warning. Before the court, Dönitz made the counter-argument that allied submarines had done the same thing. For example, the American Admiral Chester Nimitz had torpedoed Japanese merchant vessels without warning. This is an argument *ad hominem*, although in this case the opposing arguer being responded to is not a person but rather a group of people that he represents. The argument challenges the reliability of the allies to pass judgment on the unrestricted submarine warfare ordered by Dönitz.

The tribunal found Dönitz guilty on the charge of illegal submarine warfare. This can be taken to show that the tribunal recognized the *tu quoque* argument as fallacious. It should be mentioned, however, that no sentence was imposed on Dönitz for this crime, in addition to his sentence for other crimes. This strange decision suggests that the tribunal was, to some degree, taken in by the argument.

The *fallacy of irrelevant person* is committed when the target argument is about someone's reliability, but that person is not P. An argument that commits the fallacy of irrelevant person presents an argument against P's reliability as a counter-argument to a claim about P*s reliability. Here is an example.

X: "Miss Limpany is highly reliable as an expert witness. She has a PhD in fire engineering."
Y: "With all due respect, let me just remind the court that every argument that X makes is biased. As we all know, he is paid by the plaintiff to argue this case."

Since Y's argument is about the reliability of the opposing advocate (X), it does not falsify X's claim about Miss Limpany's reliability. Waller (2005, 188) has called attention to this kind of fallacy in legal argumentation. As is probably already apparent, the fallacy of irrelevant person is similar to the fallacy of reliability irrelevance. It is also a special case of *ignoratio elenchi.*

The *fallacy of insufficient degree* is committed when the target argument is about P's reliability, but the effect that A has on P's degree of reliability is insufficient to falsify the target claim. The fallacy can be illustrated by the following counter-argument.

X: "I don't think that Jane Jetson is less qualified than the average politician to be Prime Minister."
Y: "Well, she never took a PhD . . . "

The fact that a politician does not have a PhD may have a small negative effect on the degree to which she can be relied upon to serve as Prime Minister, but the effect of not having a PhD does not make her less qualified than the average politician. After all, the average politician does not have a PhD. The fallacy of insufficient degree is also a special case of *ignoratio elenchi.* It involves presenting an argument that is unable to falsify the target claim.

Lastly, an error occurs if the effect premise in the extended ad hominem argument concerns a function other than the one in the target claim. The following exchange illustrates this *fallacy of irrelevant function*:

X: "I would rather trust Bill Clinton than Barack Obama to handle the economic crisis."
Y: "No way! I wouldn't trust Bill Clinton to date my daughter."

## 4.4 Talking About Errors as Fallacies

As we have seen, *ad hominem* arguments can go wrong in seven different ways. We have referred to these errors as seven different *ad hominem* fallacies. Some scholars object to our analysis and claim that some of the errors that we have identified should not be called "fallacies". They accept that we have identified seven different ways in which *ad hominem* arguments can go wrong, but deny that all of them qualify as "fallacies".

There are different opinions among scholars on how the term fallacy should be used. Some scholars argue, for instance, that an error must be deceptive to qualify as a fallacy (see, e.g., Hitchcock 2006; Woods 2007, 110). We prefer not to employ this psychological criterion. Perhaps some of the errors that we have identified are not very deceptive, but this makes no difference in our analysis. When we talk about an argument as fallacious we make no claim about its psychological effect. It has also been insisted that a fallacious error must occur with some frequency in real arguments (see, e.g., Hitchcock 2006; Woods 2007, 110). Some of the errors that we have identified are perhaps not common enough to qualify as fallacies on this view. However, we do not subscribe to this kind of empirical criterion either.

Brinton has identified some ways that *ad hominem* arguments can go wrong, but he is only prepared to talk about one of them as a fallacy. For Brinton (1995, 216–217), only the kind of error that we have classified as the fallacy of reliability irrelevance comes close to qualifying as a fallacy. When he identifies the kind of error that we have called the fallacy of false attribution he says that this error should not be called a fallacy, as it is not a "logical failure", but merely consists in a false premise (1995, 217–218). This reflects a fundamental difference between Brinton and us. In our approach, where the *ad hominem argument* is given a deductively valid form, all errors in this argument will manifest themselves as false premises.

## 4.5 Conclusions

In this paper we have elaborated a framework which can be summarized as follows. Arguments *ad hominem* note that a person P has a certain attribute and claim that this attribute affects P's reliability in performing a certain function. P can be another participant in the discussion, but this is not necessarily the case.

Arguments *ad hominem* are often used as counter-arguments, but they need not be counter-arguments. In its basic form, an *ad hominem* argument merely makes a claim about someone's reliability. It need not stand in opposition to some other claim. When an *ad hominem* argument says that some other claim about the person's reliability is false it becomes an ad *hominem* argument in the extended form.

By including all kinds of function that a person can be relied upon to fulfill, this framework can be used to analyze and explain a wide range of arguments about reliability. It is not limited to the subcategory of arguments about credibility.

As we have seen, our understanding of *ad hominem* arguments covers positive as well as negative variants. An argument where the attribute pointed out is said to increase reliability is a positive *ad hominem*, and an argument where the attribute is said to decrease reliability is a negative *ad hominem*.

Once we give the *ad hominem* argument a deductively valid form, all errors manifest themselves as false premises. Every possible error either involves a false attribution premise, or a false effect premise, or (in the extended form of the argument) a false rebuttal premise. As we have seen, these premises can be false for various, rather different reasons. We have identified seven grounds of falsity here, and we have suggested that these grounds create, in effect, seven distinct *ad hominem* fallacies: false attribution, irrelevant attribute, overrated effect, reliability irrelevance, irrelevant person, insufficient degree and irrelevant function.

The presented framework allows questions about when, and to what extent, different kinds of error occur to be addressed rigorously. It also helps to explain why such errors occur. Thus we have seen that the falsity of the effect premise, whether it consists in the fallacy of irrelevant attribute or the fallacy of overrated effect, can be due to a misjudgment of some kind about the function. And when we discussed the relevance of the assumed bundle of attributes we saw that this error can result either from a mistaken assumption about the actual bundle or from a faulty estimate of the effect of an attribute in that bundle.

The framework that has been presented in this article provides a widely applicable tool for approaching and analyzing *ad hominem* arguments. We recommend that judges use it in their assessment of legal argumentation. As we have seen, *ad hominem* arguments are often used to attack witness testimony, and we believe that our framework would help judges to identify the various fallacies that are committed in such arguments.

We also hope, of course, that our framework will be used for assessing political argumentation and everyday conversation. We believe, in general, that our framework makes it easier to spot *ad hominem* fallacies, and easier to avoid them.

## References

Bentham, Jeremy. 1824/1952. *The handbook of political fallacies*. New York: Harper & Brothers.

Brinton, Alan. 1985. A rhetorical view of the *Ad Hominem*. *Australasian Journal of Philosophy* 63(1): 50–63.

Brinton, Alan. 1995. The *Ad Hominem*. In *Fallacies – Classical and contemporary readings*, ed. Hans Hansen and Robert Pinto, 213–222. University Park: Pennsylvania State University Press.

Copi, Irving, and Carl Cohen. 2002. *Introduction to logic*, 11th ed. Upper Saddle River: Prentice Hall.

Hamblin, Charles L. 1970. *Fallacies*. London: Methuen.

Heise, Nicole. 2009. Deciding not to decide: Nuremberg and the ambiguous history of the *Tu Quoque* defense. Social Science Research Network. Social Science Electronic Publishing, Inc., http://ssrn.com/abstract=1354048.

Hinman, Lawrence. 1982. The case for *Ad Hominem* arguments. *Australasian Journal of Philosophy* 60(4): 338–345.

Hitchcock, David. 2006. Why there is no *Argumentum ad Hominem* fallacy. McMaster University, http://www.humanities.mcmaster.ca/~hitchckd/adhominemissa.htm.

Johnson, Christopher. 2009. Reconsidering the *Ad Hominem*. *Philosophy* 84(2): 251–266.

van Eemeren, Frans, and Rob Grootendorst. 1992. Relevance reviewed: The case of argumentum ad Hominem. *Argumentation* 6(2): 141–159.

Waller, Bruce. 2005. *Critical thinking – Consider the verdict*, 5th ed. Upper Saddle River: Prentice Hall.

Walton, Douglas. 1987. The Ad Hominem argument as an informal fallacy. *Argumentation* 1(3): 317–331.

Walton, Douglas. 1998. *Ad Hominem arguments*. Tuscaloosa: University of Alabama Press.

Walton, Douglas. 2006. Poisoning the well. *Argumentation* 20(3): 273–307.

Woods, John. 2007. Lightening up on the *Ad Hominem*. *Informal Logic* 27(1): 109–134.

Woods, John. 2010. *The death of argument*. Dordrecht: Kluwer Academic Publishers.

Yee, Sienho. 2004. The *Tu Quoque* argument as a defence to international crimes, prosecution or punishment. *Chinese Journal of International Law* 3(1): 87–134.

# Chapter 5
# The Rule of Law and the Ideal of a Critical Discussion

**Harm Kloosterhuis**

## 5.1 Introduction

In *Rhetoric and the Rule of Law* (2005) Neil MacCormick argues that modern legal systems are characterized by a tension between two commonplaces: the arguable character of law on the one hand and the rule of law on the other. According to MacCormick (and many others), law is an *argumentative* discipline. This means that legal argumentation is not characterized by the certainty of demonstrative arguments with undisputed premises and deductive proof: legal questions are answered in terms of acceptable argumentation and in the process of pro- and contra-argumentation there is always room for *rational disagreement.*

The antithetical commonplace is the *rule of law* with legal certainty and predictability as central values. Where the rule of law is observed, people can have reasonable certainty in advance concerning the rules and standards by which their conduct will be judged. The central thesis of *Rhetoric and the Rule of Law* is that reconciliation is possible between the rule of law and the arguable character of legal decisions. According to MacCormick, achieving such reconciliation is the task of a theory about of rational argumentation, a theory of how we can draw non-deductive, yet rationally supported conclusions.

I agree with MacCormick's view on the important function of argumentation in the context of the rule of law. One of the main incentives for the growing interest in legal argumentation has to do with changing views on judicial tasks within the context of the rule of law. In modern legal systems a judge not only applies legal rules but also resolves interpretation problems and justifies his doing so in a reasoned decision. Although it is a part of the rule of law that legal decisions

H. Kloosterhuis (✉)
Erasmus School of Law, Erasmus University Rotterdam, Burgemeester Oudlaan,
503062 PA, Rotterdam
e-mail: kloosterhuis@law.eur.nl

C. Dahlman and E. Feteris (eds.), *Legal Argumentation Theory: Cross-Disciplinary Perspectives*, Law and Philosophy Library 102, DOI 10.1007/978-94-007-4670-1_5,

must be justified, explicit legal norms for this justification can hardly be found. Therefore, one of the important problems in the study of legal argumentation is the question *which standards of soundness the argumentation should meet*. Is it enough that the judge mentions the facts of the case and the legal rules, or does he also have to explain why the legal rules are applicable to the concrete case? How can the interpretation of a legal rule be acceptably justified? What, in the context of legal justification, is the relation between legal rules, legal principles and general moral norms and values (Feteris: 1999 and Feteris and Kloosterhuis: 2009)?[1]

A second important problem in the study of legal argumentation is the question how to reconstruct *real life* argumentation in legal decisions in order to evaluate the justification. For instance when a judge resolves an interpretation problem in deciding a case, he can choose different types of *interpretative arguments* to justify his decision. Ideally, these arguments are recognizable in the justification of the legal decision. But in practice these arguments are not always presented in an explicitly, clear and well ordered way. The critical reader who wants to evaluate the argumentation must therefore solve a number of reconstruction problems in order to evaluate the argumentation.

Within the framework of legal theory, argumentation in legal decisions is traditionally reconstructed from a logical or a rhetorical perspective. In the *logical* approach legal argumentation is reconstructed with the aim to check whether the conclusion is justified on formal grounds.[2] Legal argumentation is analyzed as a form of reasoning consisting of premises, which lead to a certain conclusion. The evaluation concentrates on the question whether there is a formally valid argument underlying the argumentation.

In the *rhetorical* approach to legal argumentation not the formal, but the material aspects of legal argumentation are the focus of analysis and evaluation. In this approach the acceptability of argumentation is dependent on the effectiveness of the argumentation for the audience to which it is addressed.[3]

As a reaction to the shortcomings of the logical and rhetorical approaches Aarnio (1987), Aarnio et al. (1981), Alexy (1989), and Peczenik (1989) developed *dialogical* theories of legal argumentation. In the dialogical approach legal argumentation is considered from the perspective of a critical discussion. The rationality of the argumentation depends on whether the procedure meets certain formal and material standards of acceptability.

In line with this dialogical tradition, the *pragma-dialectical* approach to legal argumentation conceives the justification of a legal standpoint as part of a critical

[1] As MacCormick points out in his *Legal Reasoning and Legal Theory* (1978), one of the central questions in these different approaches is the search for criteria of soundness of legal argumentation. According to MacCormick, legal reasoning is an activity conducted within more or less vague or clear, implicit or explicit, normative criteria. Any study of legal interpretation and argumentation – he argues – is an attempt to explicate and explain these criteria as to what constitutes an acceptable or an unacceptable type of argument in law.

[2] Cf. Feteris (1999).

[3] Cf. Feteris (1999).

discussion in which a protagonist defends a standpoint against the anticipated or actual reactions of an antagonist. In the pragma-dialectical reconstruction of legal decisions, argumentation is analyzed as an exchange of arguments and counter-arguments. This analysis aims to give a better account of real life argumentation than the abstract *logical* reconstructions.[4]

Analyzing argumentation in judicial decisions from the perspective of a rational discussion is sometimes criticized. One of the main objections is that a judge does not have a standpoint in a critical discussion, but simply decides a case. As a result the critical norms for evaluating argumentation are not applicable to a legal decision. In this contribution I will try to refute these two objections by showing how the ideals of a critical discussion relate to the ideals of the *Rule of Law* and how these ideals function as starting points in analyzing and evaluating legal decisions, focusing on reconstructing standpoints. I start with a sketch of the pragma-dialectical perspective to legal argumentation.

## 5.2 The Pragma-Dialectical Approach to Legal Argumentation

### *5.2.1 Methodological Starting-Points*

In the pragma-dialectical approach it is assumed that a legal argumentation theory should integrate descriptive and normative perspectives on argumentation. Legal discourse should be studied as a sample of normal verbal communication and interaction and it should, at the same time, be measured against certain standards of reasonableness. This implies first a philosophical ideal of reasonableness, second a theoretical model for acceptable argumentation and third tools to analyze actual legal argumentation from the perspective of the model.

In the pragma-dialectical theory, the study of argumentation is approached with four basic premises each of which represents a point of departure from other perspectives on argumentation. It is characteristic of the pragma-dialectical approach that argumentation is socialized, functionalized, externalized and dialectified (van Eemeren and Grootendorst: 1992, 2004).

According to the first starting point – socialization – argumentation is put in the social context of a problem-solving process. Argumentation is part of an interactional process between two or more language users instead of a reasoning product of just one language user. In the analysis of legal argumentation attention

[4]Characteristic of the logical approach is the abstraction from the communicative and interactional context in which the legal argumentation is used. The argumentation is reconstructed as an abstract argumentative product of just one language user, usually a judge. As a consequence this approach cannot adequately describe and explain the structural complexity of argumentation in legal decisions.

can be paid to the claims and counterclaims of the different parties in a legal discussion. Specific attention can be paid to one party in the discussion: the judge. In a juridical discussion it is the task of the judge to apply rules to certain facts. In doing this, the judge uses the law as a system of primary and secondary rules and principles. These rules and principles indicate in what way juridical problems can be solved. For a proper description and evaluation of argumentation in legal decisions, it is important to relate this argumentation to these secondary rules and principles. These rules and principles – to be found in or outside legislation – are the discussion rules that regulate the way in which a judge can, should or should not solve interpretation problems.

According to the second starting point – functionalization – an adequate description and evaluation of argumentation can only be given if the purpose for which the argumentation is put forward in the interaction is duly taken into account. The pragma-dialectical approach to argumentation concentrates on its function in managing the resolution of disagreements. In solving a legal problem, a judge uses argumentation in order to convince implicit or explicit antagonists of the correctness of his decision.

According to the third starting point – externalization – we have to focus on the positions to which the parties can be committed in the discourse, instead of speculation about 'real motives' parties could have for defending a certain standpoint. For a proper description and evaluation of interpretative argumentation it is necessary to focus on the positions to which the judge can be committed, whether these positions have been expressed explicitly or implicitly in the judicial decision.

According to the last starting point – dialectification – argumentation is appropriate only if it is capable of accommodating the critical reactions of a *reasonable* judge. In order to determine whether this is the case, the argumentation must be viewed as part of a discussion conducted in accordance with the criteria for a critical discussion. Besides the substantive question of the acceptability of the premises and the formal question of the logical validity of the derivation in the interpretative reasoning, also procedural standards of judgment are relevant, for instance standards about the question of whether in a concrete case a specific interpretative argument is the best way to solve a certain interpretation problem.

### 5.2.2 Reasonableness and the Ideal Model of a Critical Discussion

In the pragma-dialectical approach argumentation, the conception of reasonableness is associated with a critical testing procedure. This critical and dialectical conception of reasonableness is associated with a 'critical rationalist' philosophy of reasonableness which claims that, ultimately, we cannot be certain of anything and takes as its guiding principle the idea of critically testing all claims that are made to acceptability (van Eemeren 2010).

This concept of reasonableness is the basis of a model of a critical discussion that gives substance to the idea of resolving differences of opinion on the merits by means of dialectically regulated critical exchanges in which the acceptability of the standpoints at issue is put to the test. The outcome of the discussion between the protagonist and the antagonist depends on the critical questions asked by the antagonist and the adequacy of the protagonist's responses to these critical questions. The systematic account of the interaction that takes place between the speech acts performed by the protagonist to defend the standpoint and those performed by the antagonist to respond critically is characteristic of the pragma-dialectical resolution procedure. It combines a dialectical view of argumentative reasonableness with a pragmatic view of the verbal moves made in argumentative discourse as contextualized speech acts.

The model of a critical discussion provides an overview of the argumentative moves. Analytically, in a critical discussion four stages can be distinguished. First, there is the *confrontation stage* in which the difference of opinion is externalized. Next there is the *opening stage* in which the protagonist and the antagonist of a standpoint at issue in the difference of opinion determine their zone of agreement as far as common procedural and material starting points are concerned. In the *argumentation stage* both parties try to establish whether, given the point of departure acknowledged by the parties, the protagonist's standpoint is tenable in the light of the antagonist's critical responses. Finally, in the *concluding stage*, the result of the critical discussion is established. This *ideal model* of a critical discussion is used as a heuristic instrument for the reconstruction of the standpoints and argumentation and as a critical instrument to evaluate argumentation.

## 5.3 The Ideal of the Rule of Law

Analyzing argumentation in judicial decisions from the ideal perspective of a rational discussion is sometimes criticized. One of the main objections is that a judge does not have a standpoint in a critical discussion, but simply decides a case. As a result the norms for evaluating the reasonableness of the argumentation are not applicable to a legal decision. I think that the first claim is a consequence of an inadequate analysis of a legal decision and its function in a legal discussion. The second claim is a misunderstanding of the status of ideal norms for argumentation and the relation with *argumentation in action.* In my opinion there are good grounds – as is shown in recent publications on the rule of law – to claim that the ideal norms of a critical discussion and the ideal of the rule of law are closely connected and that there is only an apparent opposition between the two. As Cohen (2010), MacCormick (2005), Waldron (2008, 2010) and others show, the concept of the rule of law has become inseparable from the idea that legal decision-makers should give reasons to justify their decisions.

Let us – as a start – have a look at the traditional ideals of the rule of law and some recent developments in rule of law research. According to the traditional *thin* ideal of the rule of law government officials and citizens are bound by and act consistent with the law. These requirements entail a set of minimal *formal* characteristics: law must be set forth in advance (be prospective), be made public, be general, be clear, be stable and certain, and be applied to everyone according to its terms. According to the more *substantive* or *thicker* ideal of the rule of law these formal characteristics should be completed by fundamental rights, democracy, and criteria of justice or right.

In several recent publications Jeremy Waldron argues for a 'third layer' in the rule of law: the procedural aspects relating to 'natural Justice' or 'procedural due process'. According to Waldron (2010) these aspects have been neglected in the jurisprudential literature devoted specifically to the idea of the rule of law and they deserve much greater emphasis. Waldron argues that procedural values go beyond elementary principles like the guarantee of an unbiased tribunal or the opportunity to present and confront evidence. They include the right to argue in a court about what the law is and what its bearing should be on one's situation. As a preliminary sketch, Waldron proposes the following procedural aspects of rule of law:

1. A hearing by an impartial tribunal that is required to act on the basis of evidence and argument presented formally before it in relation to legal norms that govern the imposition of penalty, stigma, loss etc.
2. A legally-trained judicial officer, whose independence of other agencies of government is assured.
3. A right to representation by counsel and to the time and opportunity required to prepare a case.
4. A right to be present at all critical stages of the proceeding.
5. A right to confront witnesses against the detainee.
6. A right to an assurance that the evidence presented by the government has been gathered in a properly supervised way.
7. A right to present evidence in one's own behalf;
8. A right to make legal argument about the bearing of the evidence and about the bearing of the various legal norms relevant to the case.
9. A right to hear reasons from the tribunal when it reaches its decision, which are responsive to the evidence and arguments presented before it;
10. Some right of appeal to a higher tribunal of a similar character.

According to Waldron these requirements are important parts of the rule of law. Waldron argues that a procedural understanding of the rule of law does not just require that officials apply the rules as they are set out; it requires that they apply them in accordance with ideals such as natural justice and procedural due process. And here the role of reasonable argumentation is central.

Waldron is of the opinion that there is no opposition between the classical conception and the procedural – argumentative – conception of the rule of law. The classical view emphasizes the importance of predictability, determinacy and settlement. This view on the rule of law is closely connected to a classic positivistic *concept of law*. It highlights the role of rules rather than standards, literal meanings rather than systemic inferences, direct applications rather than arguments. In this positivistic conception it is obvious that there is a tension between the rule of law and the uncertainty that arises out of law's argumentative character. Waldron claims that in a non-positivistic concept of law there is no such tension. Waldron concludes that there is a natural correlation between a conceptual account of law that emphasizes rules and a rule of law ideal that concentrates on their characteristics, their generality and determinacy. And there is a natural correlation between, on the one hand, a conceptual account of law that focuses not just on the general norms established but on the distinctive procedural features of the institutions that administer them, and on the other hand, an account of the rule of law that is less fixated on predictability and more insistent on the opportunities for argumentation.

Another recent publication on this subject is Mathilda Cohen's 'The Rule of Law as the Rule of Reasons' (2010). Cohen examines whether reason giving is necessarily connected with the rule of law in the sense that a legal system would not conform to the rule of law if its decisions were not supported by publicly articulated reasons. According to Cohen reason giving vindicates both *procedural* and *substantive* conceptions of the rule of law. Reason giving is an essential element of the procedural conception because all the procedural account seems to require is that the state does whatever it does in a predictable and consistent way and justify it by reasons. Reason giving also characterizes the core of the substantive conceptions of the rule of law. These conceptions claim that the rule of law's central purpose is to ensure certain just outcomes. In that perspective, requiring that legal decision-makers give reasons is more apt to protect us against abuse than other forms of decision-making. Cohen argues that theoretical reflections on the rule of law should pay more attention to the legal duty to give reasons than has been done in the past, thereby leading to a context-sensitive assessment of the rule of law and its virtue(s). Understanding the rule of law from the point of view of reason giving enables us to view the rule of law not as an all-or-nothing matter, but rather as a matter of degree. The rule of law may obtain more or less and the extent to which a legal system provides reasons is a good indicator of this sensitivity to context.

## 5.4 Reconstructing Judicial Standpoints in Legal Decisions

As I have shown in the last section, recent publications on the rule of law imply that MacCormick's claim that there is a tension between the rule of law and the commonplace that law is an argumentative practice leans heavily on which concept of the rule of law is taken as starting point. Once you abandon the idea that the rule of law is connected with legal certainty and predictability in the *strict sense*, there is no opposition at all. As a result there is no conceptual problem in reconstructing a legal decision as complex of standpoints and argumentation and that the norms for a critical discussion can be used for the evaluation of a legal decision. As I said in the introduction, one of the main objections against the pragma-dialectical approach to argumentation in legal decisions is that a judge does not have a standpoint in a critical discussion, but simply decides a case. I want to refute this claim by solving the apparent contradiction between the judicial ruling as a *decision* and as a *standpoint* with help of the pragma-dialectical model of a discussion and the conception of a standpoint in a discussion.

In his study *The Concept of Law* (1961) Hart says that decisions of a court are statements with a certain authority making them final but not also infallible. To clarify this, Hart uses the example of an umpire in a game. In a game the judgments of an umpire – for instance about the scoring – have a certain authority. His judgments are given, by the *secondary rules* of the game, a status which renders them unchallengeable. In this sense it is true, says Hart, that for the purposes of the game 'the score is what the scorer says it is'. But it is important to see that there is a scoring *rule* and it is the scorer's duty to apply this rule as best he can.[5] It is this scoring rule which makes decisions of the umpire, though final, not infallible, for this scoring rule offers reasons for criticizing the decision. According to Hart the same is true in the law. Like the umpire's decision in a game, the decisions of a judge like 'X is guilty' or 'X has a right' are – up to a certain point – final. But, like the umpire in a game, the judge has an obligation to apply the rules correctly according to the *secondary rules* in a legal system. As a result judicial decisions are fallible.

Both in argumentation theory and in legal theory these observations about finality and fallibility of judicial decisions give rise to the question what type of speech act is involved. It is posed as a problem whether these speech acts are, or are to be reconstructed, as a *declarative*, or as an *assertive* speech act. For on the one hand the judge declares that somebody is guilty, but one the other hand the judge gives a justification for his decision that somebody is guilty according to the law. And this justification is a reason to reconstruct the decision as an assertive, or to be more precise: as a standpoint in a context of a discussion.[6]

My starting point is that it is a misunderstanding to treat speech acts in judicial decisions as *either* an assertive *or* a declarative – or, as some authors as a directive. I think that for an adequate analysis of the speech act, in the context in which it occurs, one has to make a distinction between different discussions in a legal process and related this distinction, different functions of the speech act in a decision like 'you are guilty'.

---

[5]Cf. Hart (1961:142): '"The score is what the scorer says it is" would be false if it meant that there was no rule for scoring save what the scorer in his discretion chose to apply. There might indeed be a game with such a rule, and some amusement might be found in playing it if the scorer's discretion were exercised with some regularity; but it would be a different game. We may call such a game the game of 'scorer's discretion'.'

[6]Already in his first publications in 1962 about Speech Acts J.L. Austin made observations about the nature of judicial decisions. He argues that if it is established that a performative utterance is performed happily and in all sincerity, that still does not suffice it beyond the reach of all criticism. It may always be criticized in a different dimension, a dimension comparable with the true/false criterium used to evaluate constative utterances: 'Allowing that, in declaring the accused guilty, you have reached your verdict properly and in good faith, it still remains to ask whether the verdict was just, or fair' (1974:21).

Let me start with the analysis proposed by Feteris (1989). Following the pragma-dialectical model of a discussion, she gives a reconstruction of judicial decisions. Feteris locates the judicial decision in the *concluding stage* of the discussion between two parties in a process. If the facts stated can be considered as established facts and the judge has decided that there is a legal rule which connect the claim to these facts, the judge will grant the claim. But the judge has not only an obligation to give a *decision* in the dispute, he also has a legal obligation to give a *justification*. The parties have a right to know which considerations underlie the decision. When a party does not agree with the decision, he can appeal the decision on the basis of the argumentation given in the justification.

On the basis of this analysis, Feteris concludes that a final decision of a judge can be seen as an *assertive-declarative* speech act. And she proposes to reconstruct this speech act as an assertive speech act because the judge is bound to the acceptability of the propositional content of the speech act.

I think that relating the question of speech act character of a final decision to a stage in a legal discussion is an important step forward, but it leaves a few questions unanswered.

The first question is: how can we conceive the final decision both as a standpoint of the judge – an assertive – *and* as a part of the concluding stage of the discussion between the parties? For in the concluding stage it is established whether the dispute has been resolved. Why should a standpoint and argumentation be part of a concluding stage?

For an answer to this question I think we must make a distinction between at least two discussions in legal decision making. The *first* discussion is the discussion between the parties. In this discussion the two parties defend and criticize a standpoint and the judge is a third party to the dispute. In this discussion the decision of the judge is part of the *concluding* stage where the discussion is brought to an end. The judge has the extra linguistic position to *declare* that somebody is guilty.

I think that this utterance of the judge can be reconstructed as a declarative speech act, for the fact that the judges says that 'X is guilty' brings about the state of affairs that 'X is guilty'. This reconstruction is I think in line with the pragma-dialectical theory about a critical discussion and the difference that is made between resolving a difference of opinion on the one hand and settling a dispute on the other. The declaration of the judge is, seen from the perspective of the discussion between parties, not a part of a critical discussion but a form of dispute settlement. So, the declarative is legal according to the rules.

But as Feteris has pointed out, a judge does not only *declare* that somebody is guilty, the judge also justifies why he is guilty according to established facts and legal rules. In other words, the judge defends the standpoint that the decision is acceptable. This standpoint is not a part of the discussion between the parties, but a part of the discussion between the judge and the parties, or between the judge and other explicit or implicit antagonists. In this discussion the standpoint of the judge is part of the confrontation stage. And since the argumentation the judge gives, is meant to convince the parties that his standpoint is right according to the law, his standpoint and argumentation are part of a critical discussion aimed at resolving a difference of opinion. When a party does not agree with the decision, he can appeal the decision on the basis of the argumentation given in the justification. And then, there is an explicit discussion between a party and the judge.

So, when we reconstruct the final decision of the judge both as a part of a concluding stage in the discussion between parties and as a part of a confrontation stage in the discussion between the judge and one or more parties, another judge or the legal audience, the decision can be reconstructed both as a declarative and as an assertive. The judge's decision that somebody is guilty constitutes the institutional fact of his being guilty in the concluding stage of the discussion between parties. The decision has of course success of fit on the assertive illocutionary point only if he really is guilty according to the law. But if X is not guilty, he will nevertheless institutionally be guilty as long as the judge's decision is not redressed. Though the falsity of assertion 'X is guilty' may offer a *reason* for invalidating it, it remains valid unless it is invalidated. In this way a false representation of a state of affairs counts legally as a state of affairs notwithstanding its lack of correspondence with reality.

In answering the question whether the decision is a declarative or an assertive, I have said that it is a declarative from one point of view and a standpoint from another point of view. Until now it was understood that the speech act 'advancing a standpoint' is an assertive speech act. But the next question is: what type of assertive is involved? I will now discuss some implications of the pragma-dialectical characterization of the assertive speech act 'advancing a standpoint' as given by Houtlosser (1994), for the standpoint character of legal decisions. Houtlosser characterizes the speech act advancing a standpoint as a complex assertive that is at a higher textual level than the sentence connected to an expressed opinion that is confronted (or assumed to be confronted) with doubt or contradiction on the part of a critical listener.

### *5.4.1 Houtlosser Defines the Speech Act 'Advancing a Standpoint' with the following conditions*

Essential Condition

> Advancing a standpoint counts as taking the responsibility for a positive or negative position in respect of an expressed opinion, i.e. as assuming an obligation to defend this position in respect of the expressed opinion if called upon to do so.

Propositional Content Condition

1. The expressed opinion to which the standpoint pertains expresses that the speech act S, or the constellation of speech acts S (1,2,...,n) is (not) acceptable.
2. The expressed opinion is the propositional content of the standpoint.

According to the *essential* condition, advancing a standpoint counts as taking the responsibility for a positive or negative position in respect of an expressed opinion, i.e. as assuming an obligation to defend this position in respect of the expressed opinion if called upon to do so. In principle, Houtlosser explains, the assertive speech act advancing a standpoint is related to *assertive* speech acts, but it can also be related to *non-assertive* speech acts. In the latter case, the expressed opinion consists of an assumption concerning the acceptability of a speech act that has become the object of contention in a debate or a text.

What are the consequences of this characterization of a standpoint for the discussion between the judge and a party in a legal discussion? Let us look at the example where the judge finds X guilty of murder and one of the arguments is that X had the intention to murder his wife. According to Houtlosser we can analyze this example as follows. The judge *asserts* that X is guilty of murder. This assertive presupposes its own acceptability. In his argument 'X had the intention to murder his wife' the judge reacts to or anticipates on the criticism of the accused ('it was self-defense') by supporting the disputed presupposition that his assertive is acceptable. In doing so, he makes it function as a standpoint. He supports his standpoint with an argument supporting the propositional content of the assertive. According to Houtlosser we can reconstruct the standpoint as follows: 'It is my standpoint that the *assertion* that X is guilty of murder is acceptable'.

This example shows how we can reconstruct the *assertive* of the judge as a standpoint in the discussion between the judge and one of the parties in a process or other antagonists. What about a *declarative* of the judge in the concluding stage of the discussion between parties? Is it possible that this speech act – so to say – develops into a standpoint? I think that is possible. As I have said, Houtlosser explains that the assertive speech act advancing a standpoint can be related to *non-assertive* speech acts. In these cases, the acceptability of the non-assertive speech act has become the object of discussion. Let us look at the example where the judge finds X guilty of murder and one of the arguments is that X murdered his wife *in London*. How can we reconstruct this argumentation? Let us start by analyzing the utterance 'X is guilty of murder' as a *declaration* in the concluding stage of the discussion between the parties. As we have seen, it is a necessary condition for a successful performance of this speech act that the judge has the extra linguistic position to declare something. Let us assume that it was this aspect of the speech act, that was (or was expected to be) criticized by the accused in saying that the judge has no jurisdiction in this case. By criticizing the acceptability of the judge's (expected) declarative, the accused turns the presupposition that the declarative could be successfully performed into an issue for discussion.[7] The judge reacts to or anticipates on this criticism supporting the disputed presupposition that he *could* perform the declarative because he had jurisdiction. He supports his standpoint with an argument relating to the conditions for performing a declarative. The standpoint of the judge can be reconstructed as 'It is my standpoint that the *declaration* that X is guilty of murder is acceptable'.

---

[7]Cf. Austin (1974:14) '[...] Our performative, like any other ritual or ceremony, may be, as the lawyers say, "nul and void". If for example, the speaker is not in a position to perform an act of that kind, or if the object with respect to which he purports to perform is not suitable for the purpose, then he doesn't manage simply by issuing his utterance, to carry out the purported act.'

## 5.5 Conclusion

In this contribution I argued that rational argumentation is vital for solving problems resulting from the tension between the rule of law and the arguable character of law. I tried to answer some questions concerning two related central problems in legal argumentation theory. The first problem is which standards of soundness the argumentation should meet and the second is how to reconstruct real life argumentation in legal decisions in order to evaluate the justification. I showed that the pragma-dialectical approach to legal argumentation conceives the justification of a judicial decision as part of a critical discussion. In this approach legal argumentation is studied as a sample of normal verbal communication and interaction and at the same time, measured against standards of a critical discussion. Analyzing argumentation in judicial decisions from the ideal-perspective of a critical discussion is sometimes criticized. One of the main objections is that a judge does not have a standpoint in a critical discussion, but simply decides a case. As a result the critical norms for evaluating argumentation are not applicable to a legal decision. In this contribution I tried to refute these two objections by showing how the ideals of a critical discussion relate to the ideals of the rule of law and how these ideals function as starting points in analyzing and evaluating legal decisions, focusing on reconstructing standpoints. I showed that there is no conceptual problem in reconstructing a decision as complex of standpoints and argumentation. I illustrated this claim by solving the apparent contradiction between the judicial ruling as a *decision* and as a *standpoint* with help of the pragma-dialectical model of a discussion and the conception of a standpoint in a discussion. In doing this I tried to refute one important critical comment on the applicability of the pragma-dialectical theory of a critical discussion on judicial decisions. I have argued that the ideal norms of a critical discussion and the ideal of the rule of law are closely connected and that there is only an apparent opposition between the two. I agree with Waldron that there is only a real opposition within the framework of a positivistic rule-based concept of law.

## References


Aarnio, A. 1987. *The rational as reasonable. A treatise of legal justification.* Dordrecht: Reidel.

Aarnio, A., R. Alexy., and A. Peczenik. 1981. The foundation of legal reasoning. *Rechtstheorie*, Band 21, No. 2, pp. 133–158, No. 3, pp. 257–279, No. 4, pp. 423–448.

Alexy, R. 1989. *A theory of legal argumentation. The theory of rational discourse as theory of legal justification.* Oxford: Clarendon press (Translation of: *Theorie der juristischen Argumentation. Die Theorie des rationalen Diskurses als Theorie der juristischen Begründung*. Frankfurt a.M.: Suhrkamp, 1978).

Austin, J.L. 1974. Performative-constative. In *The philosophy of language*, ed. J.R. Searle, 13–22. Oxford: Oxford University Press [Transl. of Austin, J.L. (1962). 'Performatif- Constatif'. Cahiers de Royaumont, Philosophie IV: La Philosophie analytique. Paris: Les Éditions de Minuit, 271–304.].

Cohen, Mathilde. 2010. The rule of law as the rule of reasons. *Archiv für Rechts – und Sozialphilosophie* 96(1): 1–16. http://ssrn.com/abstract=1518006.

Feteris, E.T. 1989. *Discussieregels in het recht. Een pragma-dialectische analyse van het burgerlijk proces en het strafproces. (Discussion rules in law. A pragma-dialectical analysis of the Dutch civil process and criminal process).* Dordrecht: Foris.

Feteris, E.T. 1999. *Fundamentals of legal argumentation. A survey of theories on the justification of judicial decisions.* Dordrecht: Kluwer.

Feteris, E.T.H., and H.J. Plug Kloosterhuis (eds.). 2009. *Argumentation and the application of legal rules.* Amsterdam: Sic Sat.

Hart, H.L.A. 1961. *The concept of law.* Oxford: Oxford University Press.

Houtlosser, P. 1994. The speech act 'advancing a standpoint'. In *Studies in pragma-dialectics*, ed. F.H. van Eemeren and R. Grootendorst, 166–171. Amsterdam: Sic Sat.

MacCormick, N. 1978. *Legal reasoning and legal theory.* Oxford: Oxford University Press.

MacCormick, N. 2005. *Rhetoric and the rule of Law. A theory of legal reasoning.* Oxford: Oxford University Press.

Peczenik, A. 1989. *On law and reason.* Dordrecht: Reidel.

van Eemeren, F.H. 2010. *Strategic manoeuvering in argumentative discourse. Extending the pragma-dialectical theory of argumentation.* Amsterdam: John Benjamins.

van Eemeren, F.H., and R. Grootendorst. 1992. *Argumentation, communication and fallacies.* Hillsdale: Erlbaum.

van Eemeren, F.H., and R. Grootendorst. 2004. *A systematic theory of argumentation. The pragma-dialectical approach.* Cambridge: Cambridge University Press.

Waldron, Jeremy. 2008. The concept and the rule of law. *Georgia Law Review, Forthcoming.* NYU School of Law, Public Law Research Paper No. 08–50. http://papers.ssrn.com/sol3/papers.cfm?abstract_id=1273005.

Waldron, Jeremy. 2010. The rule of law and the importance of procedure. http://ssrn.com/abstract=1688491.

# Chapter 6
# Strategic Maneuvering with the Argumentative Role of Legal Principles in the Case of the "Unworthy Spouse"

**Eveline T. Feteris**

## 6.1 Introduction

When courts must decide whether certain legal principles can be used to make an exception to a legal rule this implies that they must decide also about the argumentative role of the legal principles. They must determine whether the principles can be used as independent arguments justifying the decision or whether they can only be considered as arguments that play a role in combination with other arguments. From the perspective of legal certainty and from the perspective of the rationality of legal decision-making the question arises under which conditions such a decision about the argumentative role of legal principles is correct. When courts make use of their discretionary power to make an exception to a legal rule, it is important that they give insight in the considerations underlying such a decision. This implies that they must account for the way in which they have used their discretionary power by making explicit what the argumentative role of the legal principles should be.

An example of a case in which a court had to answer such a question was the famous Dutch case of the 'Unworthy Spouse' (HR 1991/593 07-12-1990) in which the Dutch Supreme Court had to decide whether an exception to the existing law regarding the matrimonial community of property (article 1:100 of the Dutch Civil Code) on the basis of certain legal principles is acceptable in a case in which a spouse has murdered his wife. At the moment this case had to be decided there was no legal rule regarding unworthiness and there was no general rule on the basis of which a judge could make an exception on the basis of reasonableness and fairness. The district court and the court of appeal were of the opinion that an exception could be justified on the basis of two legal principles that could be summarized as

E.T. Feteris (✉)
Department of Speech Communication, Argumentation Theory and Rhetoric, International Learned Institute for Argumentation Studies (ILIAS), University of Amsterdam, Spuistraat 134, 1012 VB, Amsterdam, Netherlands
e-mail: e.t.feteris@uva.nl

C. Dahlman and E. Feteris (eds.), *Legal Argumentation Theory: Cross-Disciplinary Perspectives*, Law and Philosophy Library 102, DOI 10.1007/978-94-007-4670-1_6,

'crime does not pay', pointing in an 'obiter dictum' at a justification on the basis of reasonableness and fairness.[1] In its evaluation, the Supreme Court acknowledges that an exception can be made but gives the legal principles a different argumentative role in the justification: the Supreme Court states that the exception can be justified on the basis of reasonableness and fairness in the specific case, which is, in its turn, based on the two legal principles.[2] To reach a result that would be acceptable from the perspective of the development of family law, the Supreme Court decides that the legal principles have the role of arguments supporting the exception on the basis of reasonableness and fairness in the specific case instead of independent arguments directly supporting the decision.[3]

Although the Supreme Court does not agree with the argumentative role of the legal principles in the decision of the court of appeal, in its justification, the Supreme Court does not explicitly say so. An explicit statement regarding the difference of opinion about the argumentative role of the legal principles as a support for the decision would have implied that the decision of the court of appeal had to be corrected. Instead, the Supreme Court gives an implicit signal to the legal community by giving a clear answer to the question what the argumentative role of the legal principles should be.

When there is a difference of opinion between the higher court and a lower court with respect to the argumentative role of legal principles higher courts, like the Dutch Supreme Court in this case, often operate in a strategic way and leave certain decisions implicit . From the perspective of the rationality of legal argumentation the question arises whether the justification of higher courts can be considered acceptable from the perspective of the rationality of legal decision-making. To this end, it must be established whether courts operate in an acceptable way.

In what follows I shall present an analysis of the strategic maneuvering in the decision of the Dutch Supreme Court in the famous case of the 'Unworthy Spouse'.[4] An analysis of the strategic maneuvering in this case can clarify which discussion

---

[1]Cf. The case of Riggs v. Palmer, 115 N.Y. 506, 22 N.E. 188 (1889) discussed by Dworkin (1986:15–20) as an example of a systematic interpretation of the law of inheritance with the aim of clarifying the underlying legal principles.

[2]See the relevant parts of the text of the decision of the court of appeal and the Supreme Court in 2A and 2B at the end of this contribution.

[3]See also the comments of the annotator E.A.A. Langemeijer with regard to this view on the way the Supreme Court operates in using the legal principles as supporting argumentation for the exception on the basis of reasonableness and fairness. The annotator states that the Court of Appeal already considered the two legal principles as sufficient reasons to deny L. his claim, and is of the opinion that also reasonableness and fairness points in the same direction. In the view of the annotator the Supreme Court takes its 'own way'. He characterizes the way the Supreme Court operates in giving the legal principles a subordinate role as the 'safe way' because it gives more space for considering the circumstances of the specific case. The annotator is of the opinion that it corresponds with the line already taken in other decisions by the Supreme Court.

[4]For a description of the theoretical starting points see the contribution by Harm Kloosterhuis in this volume. For a more extended analysis of this case see Feteris (2011). For other analyses of strategic maneuvering in legal decisions see Feteris (2008, 2009a, b).

strategy is used by the Dutch Supreme Court in the context of an implicit difference of opinion between the lower court and the Supreme Court about the role of legal principles. To explain how the Supreme Court operates, in my analysis I will use the concept of 'strategic maneuvering' as developed by van Eemeren (2010) and van Eemeren and Houtlosser (2006, 2007), which forms part of the pragma-dialectical theory of argumentation described in the contribution by Harm Kloosterhuis in this volume.

The idea of strategic maneuvering is that each attempt to convince is an attempt to reconcile the dialectical reasonableness norm of trying to resolve a difference of opinion in a reasonable way with the rhetorical effectiveness norm of trying to reach a resolution that is most favourable to the arguer in the concrete discussion context with the intended audience. In the analysis of a particular discussion move it is established how the arguer tries to reconcile dialectical and rhetorical goals by making an opportune selection from the topical potential of dialectically relevant moves in a particular discussion stage and by using presentational techniques that are attuned to the intended audience.

In my analysis of the strategic maneuvering of the Dutch Supreme Court in the case of the Unworthy Spouse I will explain how the court tries to reconcile the goal of resolving the difference of opinion in a rational way with the goal of steering the discussion in a particular direction that is desirable from the perspective of the development of law.

## 6.2 The Case of the 'Unworthy Spouse'

In the case of the 'Unworthy Spouse' (HR 1991/593 07-12-1990) L., who has taken care of the 72-year Mrs. van Wylick, marries her. Five weeks after the marriage he kills Mrs. van Wylick, for which he is convicted and imprisoned for 12 years. The question in the civil case is whether, in the circumstances of the specific case in which a spouse is convicted for murdering his wife, it is justified to make an exception to article 1:100 of the Dutch Civil Code on the basis of which a spouse is entitled to half of the community of matrimonial property. The courts answer the question whether, in the circumstances of this specific case, it is allowed to make an exception and if such an exception would be possible, how the exception could be justified.[5] (For the relevant passages of the decisions of the court of appeal and the Supreme Court see 2A and 2B at the end of this contribution).

From a legal and argumentation-theoretical perspective in this case the interesting problem is that the different courts, the lower court and the Supreme Court, adopt the same main standpoint, i.e. that L. is not entitled to his share in the community of matrimonial property, but that they differ with respect to the question how this exception must be justified. The court of appeal is of the opinion that an

[5]For an overview of the relevant legal rules see 1 at the end of this contribution.

exception can be justified on the basis of two general legal principles that can be summarized as 'crime does not pay'. Furthermore in an 'obiter dictum' the court states that the exception can also be justified on the basis of the derogating function of reasonableness and fairness as formulated in the new article 6:2 of the Dutch Civil Code (that was going to be introduced as new law the moment in which the Supreme Court decided about the case). The Supreme Court, however, is of the opinion that the exception must be justified on the basis of reasonableness and fairness in the circumstances of the specific case in light of the two general legal principles. In its presentation of the argumentation, the Supreme Court does not explicitly say that it has a different view in this matter than the court of appeal and why this is the case. In my analysis of the strategic maneuvering I will show that the Supreme Court evades to address this difference of opinion in a strategic way by steering the decision in a way that is, in its view, most desirable from the perspective of the development of the law in the field of matrimonial property.

## 6.3 Dialectical Analysis of the Argumentation of the Supreme Court

To demonstrate how the Supreme Court operates strategically, I will first give a *dialectical analysis* of the contributions of the court of appeal and the Supreme Court. In this way I can clarify which standpoints have been adopted by the courts, which arguments they have put forward and what the structure of the argumentation is. On the basis of the analysis of the argumentation structure it can be explained what the difference is between the way in which the court of appeal has presented the structure of the argumentation and the way in which the structure of the argumentation is (for strategic reasons) interpreted by the Supreme Court.

The dialectical analysis provides a reconstruction of the decisions in terms of the standpoints and arguments that are put forward and the relation between them. In this reconstruction it is necessary to translate the relation between the standpoint and arguments that the courts (often for strategic reasons) leave implicit to clarify the supporting relations in the argumentation structure.[6] Because the aim of this contribution is to clarify in which respects the way in which the Supreme Court interprets the argumentation structure of the justification of the court of appeal differs from the way in which the argumentation structure is intended, I use a uniform notation and formulation of the standpoints and arguments to make the comparison possible (as a supplement at the end of this paper I give the relevant parts of the decisions).

In the dialectical analysis I use the theoretical starting points (described earlier in the contribution by Harm Kloosterhuis in this volume) in combination with the

[6]See for a general discussion of the dialectical reconstruction of argumentative relations in the justification of legal decisions Plug (1990).

methodological principles of the pragma-dialectical theory, being the principles of *externalization, functionalization, socialization* and *dialectification*.[7]

In the dialectical analysis of the argumentation of the court of appeal and the Supreme Court I apply the principle of *externalization* which implies that I depart from verbally expressed standpoints and arguments and the commitments that are created by putting forward certain standpoints and arguments as a court in the context of a legal procedure.[8]

In the analysis I also apply the principle of *functionalization* on the basis of which a legal procedure is considered as a goal-oriented activity which is aimed at realizing the institutional aim of the procedure in cassation. To promote a uniform application of the law the Supreme Court must check whether the lower court, in this case the court of appeal, has applied the law correctly. The argumentative activity is considered as instrumental in realizing this goal, which implies for the analysis that the argumentative elements are viewed as contributions aimed at a critical test of the standpoint and argumentation of the court of appeal that forms the basis of the difference of opinion between the plaintiff in cassation and the court of appeal about the correct application of the law.[9]

In the analysis the application of the principle of *socialization* implies that the discussion is considered as a verbal interaction aimed at achieving certain communicative and interactive goals. As I have explained in the previous contribution, the justification of a legal decision can be considered as an attempt to make the decision acceptable to the parties, other (higher) courts and the legal community.

Finally I apply the principle of *dialectification* which implies that the procedure in cassation is reconstructed as a critical discussion that is conducted to resolve a difference of opinion about the correct application of the law between the plaintiff in cassation and the court of appeal. In this discussion the Supreme Court must critically test whether the argumentation of the court of appeal is in accordance with the legal discussion rules (rules of procedure) and common legal starting points (rules of material law, general legal principles, etc.).

On the basis of this dialectical analysis I give an analysis of the strategic maneuvering in which the rhetorical dimension is also taken into account. In this analysis I reconstruct the *discussion strategy* of the Supreme Court by determining how the contributions of the Supreme Court to the discussion can be analysed as a design of discussion moves aimed at steering the result of a particular discussion stage, and the discussion as a whole, in a particular direction. A discussion strategy consists of a systematic, co-ordinated and simultaneous exploitation of the

---

[7]See for a discussion of these principles van Eemeren and Grootendorst (1991, 1992), van Eemeren 2010.

[8]For a pragmatic analysis of the commitments that are incurred when performing certain speech acts in the context of a legal procedure in terms of the theory of Brandom see Canale and Tuzet (2009).

[9]For an analysis of the speech acts that are performed by the judge in the justification of his decision see Feteris (1989) and Kloosterhuis (2006).

dialectical and rhetorical possibilities in a particular stage of the discussion. In my analysis I show how the discussion strategy of the Supreme Court can be described as a consistent attempt to steer the result of the discussion in a particular direction in accordance with the institutional conventions and constraints of the procedure in cassation.

## 6.4 Dialectical Analysis of the Contributions to the Discussion of the Court of Appeal and the Supreme Court

As I have indicated, the goal of the Dutch procedure in cassation is to check whether the law has been applied correctly by the court of appeal, starting from the cassation grounds that have been presented by the plaintiff. The Supreme Court is not allowed to give a decision about the case in its entirety because it must depart from the facts as established by the court of appeal.[10] These institutional constraints are related to the legal task of the Supreme Court to safeguard legal certainty, to guarantee a uniform application of the law and to contribute to the development of the law.

In our case the Supreme Court must check whether the court of appeal has applied the law correctly when making an exception to article 1:100 of the Dutch Civil Code. From this perspective the dialectical goal of the discussion is to establish whether the court of appeal has justified its decision sufficiently in light of the critique that the plaintiff has brought forward in the cassation grounds. In the analysis of the strategic maneuvering I will show how the Supreme Court tries to reconcile this dialectical goal with the rhetorical goal of evading a result that would be unacceptable from the perspective of the development of the law.

### *6.4.1 Dialectical Analysis of the Contributions of the Court of Appeal*

In dialectical terms the task of the court of appeal is to give a decision in the context of a difference of opinion between the district court and the plaintiff in appeal. The court of appeal must evaluate the argumentation of the district court on the basis of the critique the plaintiff has formulated in his grounds for appeal. The argumentation given by the court of appeal in its justification forms an account of this evaluation. The court of appeal establishes whether the critique of the plaintiff in appeal is justified by checking whether the argumentation of the district court is in accordance with the common legal starting points.

[10]On the basis of article 419, 2 of the Dutch Code of Civil Procedure the Supreme Court must depart from the facts that have been established by lower judges.

1 The claim of the plaintiff, stating that he is entitled to his share in the marital community of property, must be dismissed

↑<br>
1.1<br>
L. should not profit from the marital community of property

↑<br>
1.1.1<br>
*An exception to article 1:100 is justified on the basis of legal principle P1 and P2*

↑<br>
1.1.2<br>
**An exception to article 1:100 is justified on the basis of reasonableness and fairness in the concrete case**

↑<br>
1.1.2.1a -&- 1.1.2.1b<br>
The exceptional circumstances of the concrete case<br>
*Legal principles P1 and P2*

**Scheme 6.1A** Argumentation of the Court of Appeal

The evaluation given by the court of appeal implies that the critique of the plaintiff in appeal is unjustified because the district court has not made the mistakes in the application of the law as were stated by the plaintiff. According to the court of appeal the district court rightly decided that it is allowed to make an exception to article 1:100 of the Dutch Civil Code. The court of appeal defends its decision by pointing out that, other than the plaintiff states, the general legal principle applied by the district court (legal principle 1, LP 1) can be considered as a common legal starting point because it is based on several legal rules.

In Scheme 6.1A I give a dialectical analysis of the argumentation of the court of appeal.[11] In the dialectical analysis the statements are reconstructed in terms of standpoints and arguments. In Scheme 6.1A 1 is the standpoint, 1.1 the main argumentation and 1.1.1 and 1.1.2 two independent lines of justification. In the analysis it is made clear that the justification consists of two justifications that are both presented as independent. The court of appeal chooses to present the two legal principles as one line of independent justification and the reference to reasonableness and fairness (again supported by the principles) as another independent line presented as an 'obiter dictum'. (For a more detailed analysis see 3A at the end of this contribution).

## 6.4.2 *Dialectical Analysis of the Contributions of the Supreme Court*

In terms of the tasks and roles specified in the model of critical discussion the task of the Supreme Court is to give a decision regarding the difference of opinion between the plaintiff and the defendant about the question whether the court of

[11]For the relevant passages of the decision see 2A, and for a more extensive dialectical analysis see 3A at the end of this contribution.

1 The claim of the plaintiff, stating that he is entitled to his share in the marital community of property, must be dismissed

↑
1.1
L. should not profit from the marital community of property

↑
1.1.1
**An exception to article 1:100 is justified on the basis of reasonableness and fairness in the concrete case**

↑
1.1.1.1a -&- 1.1.1.1b
The exceptional *Legal principles P1 and P2*
circumstances
of the concrete case

**Scheme 6.1B** Argumentation of the Supreme Court

appeal has applied the law correctly. In the legal counterpart of the argumentation stage the Supreme Court must evaluate the argumentation of the court of appeal in light of the critique presented by the plaintiff in the cassation grounds. In its decision, in the legal counterpart of the concluding stage, the Supreme Court decides that the decision of the court of appeal can be maintained because the line of argumentation 1.1.2 of the court of appeal (presented in consideration 18 in the original text), in which the court of appeal justifies the exception on the basis of reasonableness and fairness, can be considered as an independent and acceptable justification of the decision. The Supreme Court justifies this decision by stating that an exception is not completely excluded if strict application would be unacceptable according to standards of reasonableness and fairness (legal consideration 3.3). According to the Supreme Court the court of appeal has decided that in the special circumstances of this case and also considered in light of the mentioned general legal principles the claims of L are so unreasonable and unfair that he must be denied the exertion of these rights completely. In its justification the Supreme Court does not answer explicitly the question whether the attack of the plaintiff on the line of argumentation 1.1.1 is successful or not, the only thing the Supreme Court says is that the statements of the plaintiff that the court of appeal has used these principles as a direct legal ground 'misses a factual basis'.

In the dialectical analysis in Scheme 6.1B the statements of the Supreme Court are reconstructed in terms of a standpoint (1) and a complex argumentation consisting of the main argumentation 1.1, the sub-argumentation 1.1.1, and the subsubargumentation 1.1.1.1a and 1.1.1.1b.[12]

In the dialectical analysis of the contributions of the court of appeal and the Supreme Court I have clarified how the justifications can be analysed as parts of what can be considered as the argumentation stage of a legal discussion.

[12]For the relevant passages of the decision see 2B, and for a more extensive dialectical analysis see 3B at the end of this contribution.

I have shown how the justifications can be analysed in terms of the evaluation of the argumentation of a lower court and the justification of this evaluation. With the aid of the dialectical analyses it can be demonstrated that in its evaluation of the argumentation of the court of appeal, the Supreme Court gives an interpretation that departs from the way in which the argumentation was intended by the court of appeal. The Supreme Court 'ignores' the line of argumentation 1.1.1 (printed in italics in Scheme 6.1A) and takes the line of argumentation 1.1.2 (printed in bold in Scheme 6.1A) as the only justification. To clarify how the Supreme Court operates strategically, in the next section I will give an analysis of the discussion strategy of the Supreme Court.

## 6.5 Analysis of the Discussion Strategy of the Supreme Court

To clarify what the discussion strategy of the Supreme Court exactly amounts to for the different stages of a critical discussion I specify how the Supreme Court makes a selection of the dialectical possibilities to steer the result of the discussion in the desired direction.[13]

In the *opening stage* in which the common starting points are established the discussion strategy consists of a design of moves that are aimed at deciding that the starting points the court of appeal has used as points of departure for its decision can be considered as common legal starting points. From a legal point of view the Supreme Court has a certain latitude to maneuver strategically because on the basis of article 25 of the Dutch Code of Civil Procedure it is the task of the judge to supply the legal grounds.[14] In this case the Supreme Court uses the legal space to supply the legal grounds as a possibility to decide that it is allowed to make an exception to article 1:100 of the Dutch Civil Code. At the moment the Supreme Court was asked to decide about the case, in Dutch law there was no rule that specified when someone is unworthy to inherit.[15] To evade a result that would be unacceptable from the perspective of the sense of justice, the Supreme Court wants to create a possibility to make an exception to the right of the spouse because of unworthiness on the basis of certain common starting points. The Supreme Court finds these common starting points in the two general legal principles mentioned by the Court of Appeal that can be considered as underlying certain statutory rules about inheritance and benefaction. In its decision the Supreme Court specifies on

[13]In the procedure in cassation the Supreme Court has no space to maneuver strategically in the legal counterpart of the confrontation stage because the plaintiff in cassation defines the difference of opinion in the cassation grounds.

[14]At the moment of this case it was article 48 of the Dutch Code of Civil Procedure.

[15]In 1999 the Dutch law of inheritance has been changed. The articles from book 3 and 4 that are applicable in this case have been changed. In 1 at the end of this contribution the relevant articles are given.

which grounds, in this special case, it is justified to make an exception, that is, on the basis of application of the requirements of reasonableness and fairness in the exceptional circumstances of this specific case and the application of the two general legal principles. In this way the Supreme Court contradicts in the first place the statement of the plaintiff that the justification cannot be based on the general legal principles by explicitly recognizing the existence of the principles. Secondly the Supreme Court contradicts the statement of the plaintiff that the justification cannot be based on the application of reasonableness and fairness by explicitly recognizing such a possibility, in anticipation of the introduction of article 6:2 of the new Dutch Civil Code.

Apart from giving a decision about the existence of the general legal principles and the possibility to apply the standards of reasonableness and fairness as common starting points, the Supreme Court also gives a decision about the argumentative role of these starting points. The Supreme Court does this in an implicit manner with its statement in consideration 3.3 in which it rejects the statements of the plaintiff. By stating that the argument 1.1.1 of the court of appeal cannot be considered as an independent justification of the decision but that the decision is supported by 1.1.2, the Supreme Court implicitly says that the general legal principles do not form an independent justification of the decision of the court of appeal, although they have been presented as such:

> As appears from the cited formulation, in this context the legal principles play only the role that they have contributed to the decision of the court that the requirements of reasonableness and fairness make the exertion of the right to his share in the community of property inadmissible. As far as the parts A and B read in legal consideration 5.18 that the court has used these principles as a direct legal ground for denying this right, they lack a factual basis.

As has been clarified in the dialectical analysis in Scheme 6.1B, the Supreme Court gives an interpretation of the argumentation of the court of appeal that departs from the way the argumentation was presented. The Supreme Court gives an interpretation of the argumentative role of the legal principles as arguments that are subordinate as a support for application of the standards of reasonableness and fairness, together with other considerations, and not as an independent justification on the main level.

In the 'legal counterpart' of the *argumentation stage* in which the Supreme Court must evaluate the argumentation of the court of appeal, the discussion strategy consists of a design of discussion moves that are aimed at establishing that the attacks of the plaintiff in cassation fail. To this end the Supreme Court uses the common starting points that have been established in the opening stage. The discussion strategy manifests itself in the statements of the Supreme Court in consideration 3.2 in which it decides that the cassation grounds A and B cannot lead to cassation because they lack interest, because they lack a factual basis and because they depart from a wrong conception of the law. Furthermore the strategy manifests itself in the statements of consideration 3.3 in which the Supreme Court states that the critique of the plaintiff in part C regarding the exception on the basis of reasonableness and fairness is wrong.

The evaluation on the basis of these common starting points implies in dialectical terms that in the opinion of the Supreme Court the attacks of the plaintiff in the cassation grounds A and B on the line of argumentation 1.1.1 of the court of appeal fails because the Supreme Court has established in the opening stage that the legal principles exist. The attack in cassation ground C on the line of argumentation 1.1.2 also fails because the Supreme Court has decided in the opening stage that in the exceptional circumstances of this case it is possible to make an exception on the basis of reasonableness and fairness. To be able to decide in the argumentation stage that the critique of the plaintiff cannot lead to cassation on the basis of the reasons mentioned, in the opening stage the Supreme Court has made a particular selection of common starting points that makes it possible to give this decision in the argumentation stage.

Finally, in the legal counterpart of the *concluding stage,* the Supreme Court decides on the basis of the evaluation in the argumentation stage that the decision of the court of appeal can be maintained. The Supreme Court uses the space it has within its dialectical tasks and the legal authority to decide about the correct application of the law and to establish the result of the discussion in an authoritative and final way.

The discussion strategy of the Supreme Court implies that the court does two things at the same time. First the Supreme Court decides in its evaluation that the attacks of the plaintiff in cassation on the argumentation of the court of appeal have failed so that the decision can be maintained. Second the Supreme Court gives an implicit interpretation of the argumentation of the court of appeal that departs from the way in which the argumentation was intended. This interpretation is not necessary to accomplish the dialectical goal of the argumentation stage because the Supreme Court can also reject the appeal in cassation without this interpretation because the decision of the court of appeal is also supported by argument 1.2. The interpretation of the Supreme Court can be considered as an implicit 'obiter dictum' consideration in which the Supreme Court addresses the legal community in its role as court of cassation who wants to give a signal to the legal community about the desired direction of the development of law in cases of matrimonial community of property. By choosing an interpretation in which the exception to article 1:100 of the Dutch Civil Code is justified on the basis of article 6:2 clause 2 of the New Dutch Civil Code that still had to be introduced, the Supreme Court indirectly makes clear that it does not want to consider the two general legal principles as the main argumentation to derogate from article 1:100 in the specific case. According to the annotator, EAAL (E.A.A.L. Langemeijer) the Supreme Court chooses the 'safe way' in the interest of legal certainty in family law by not departing from the law in family matters on the basis of general legal principles.

## 6.6 Conclusion

In this contribution I have explained how the theoretical starting points of the pragma-dialectical theory can be used in the analysis of the strategic maneuvering of the Dutch Supreme Court in a case in which there is a difference of opinion about the argumentative role of certain legal principles. In this case the question was how a judge can justify an exception to existing law if strict application would lead to a result that would be unacceptable from the perspective of the sense of justice. At the moment this case had to be decided, there was no legal rule regarding unworthiness and there was no general rule on the basis of which a judge could make an exception on the basis of reasonableness and fairness to a rule in a particular case. Anticipating the development of future law on these two points, the Supreme Court gives a decision in which it follows a particular discussion strategy.

In the different stages of the discussion the Supreme Court makes certain choices from the dialectical possibilities to steer the discussion in the desired direction. These choices are based on the way in which a certain behaviour that is considered as repugnant to justice can be characterized in a particular way in terms of Dutch civil law with the aim of denying the plaintiff his rights as a spouse in the community of property on the basis of article 1:100 of the Civil Code.

In its discussion strategy the Supreme Court aims at maintaining the decision of the court of appeal while at the same time making a correction so that the decision is in line with the way in which the Supreme Court wants to make an exception to article 1:100. Therefore the Supreme Court develops a discussion strategy in which it first (in the legal counterpart of the opening stage) recognizes the possibility to make an exception on the basis of reasonableness and fairness. Proceeding from this possibility it gives an interpretation of the justification of the decision of the court of appeal in which it corrects the justification, without explicitly saying that the interpretation concerns a different interpretation of the structure of the argumentation. In doing so the Supreme Court uses the space it has within its dialectical tasks as court of cassation to establish the starting points in the opening stage. In this case it uses the possibility to supply the legal grounds by giving an interpretation of the argumentative function of the general legal principles that departs from the way the court of appeal had used the principles. The discussion strategy consists of a specific, systematic and coordinated choice of the dialectical possibilities in the different stages of a critical legal discussion, consisting of particular choices of common starting points and particular choices in the evaluation of the argumentation. These choices are aimed at steering the discussion in a particular direction so that a particular result is reached that would be desirable from the perspective of certainty, from the perspective of justice in the specific case, and the perspective of the development of law with respect to the role of general legal principles and reasonableness and fairness.

## 1. Legal rules applied in the case of the Unworthy Spouse

*Article 1:100 of the Old Dutch Civil Code*

1. The spouses have an equal share in this divided community of property, unless a different division is established by means of a marriage settlement ( . . . ).

*Article 4.3 of the New Dutch Civil Code (introduced after 1990)*

1. Legally unworthy to profit from an inheritance are: He who has been condemned irrevocably because he has killed the deceased, he who has tried to kill the

deceased or he who has prepared to kill the deceased or has participated in preparing to kill the deceased.

*Article 6:248, 2 of the Dutch Civil Code*

An arrangement that is valid between the creditor and the debtor on the basis of the law, a custom or a legal act, does not apply if this is unacceptable from the perspective of the standards of reasonableness and fairness

*Article 3:12 of the Dutch Civil Code*

When establishing what reasonableness and fairness require, generally accepted legal principles, legal convictions that are generally accepted in the Netherlands, and social and personal interests in a particular case, should be taken into account.

## 2A. TEXT OF THE DECISION OF THE COURT OF APPEAL NJ 1989/369, 24-11-1989

( . . . )

5.13 Since the district court has assumed that Mrs. Van Wylick intended with the marriage – that also according to L was a marriage of convenience – a financial benefit for L, the district court has rightly stressed that to the factual situation described in the foregoing the general legal principle is applicable that he, who has deliberately caused the death of someone else, who has favoured him, should not profit from the this favour.

( . . . )

5.16 In this context it is also important to mention that the aforementioned legal principle is closely related to another legal principle, i.e. that one should not profit form the deliberately caused death of someone else, which principle has among others been expressed in article 885 under 1 book 3 CC. ( . . . )

5.17 Application of the mentioned legal principles leads under the aforementioned facts and circumstances to the conclusion that L is not entitled to the benefit that is the consequence of the community of property created by the marriage without a marriage settlement ('huwelijkse voorwaarden') with mrs. van Wylick.

5.18 Also an examination of the claims of L in light of the requirements of reasonableness and fairness according to which he is supposed to behave in the community of property that is created by the marriage, as is stated by Brouwers c.s., leads to the conclusion that L should not profit from the marital community of property. In this case the court applies a strict standard because the appeal to reasonableness and fairness is aimed at preventing the claims of L completely. Also when applying such a strict standard the court is of the opinion that the claims of L must be considered as so unreasonable and unfair, in the aforementioned special circumstances of this case and also considered in light of the mentioned general legal principles, that the exertion of the claimed rights must be denied (to him?) completely.

## 2B. TEXT OF THE DECISION OF THE SUPREME COURT NJ 1991/593 07-12-1990

Supreme Court:

(...)

3. Evaluation of the means of cassation

3.1.1 In cassation the following must be taken as a starting point:

L who is born in 1944, has taken care of the 72-year old van Wylick from January 1983 receiving payment in compensation for the care, initially several days per week and in a later stage on a daily basis. On September 29, 1983 L has married mrs. Van Wylick without making a marriage settlement. The marriage took place in another place than where the future spouses lived and no publicity was given to the marriage.

L owned practically nothing while mrs. Van Wylick brought in a considerable fortune. Both knew that the marriage would cause a considerable shift of property.

Since 1976 L had a relation with another man, which relation has not been broken.

Five weeks after the marriage L has killed van Wylick in a sophisticated way and with a gross breach of the trust that had been put in him. L has been condemned to a long term imprisonment for murder.

3.1.2 Furthermore, on the basis of these circumstances, in particular the short time between the marriage and the murder of mrs. Van Wylick, in the absence of any offer of proof to the contrary, the court has taken as a starting point that the sole reason for L to marry mrs. van Wylick was that he intended to appropriate her property and that already during the wedding, and in any case almost immediately after, L had the intention to kill mrs. van Wylick if she would not die in a natural way.

3.1.3 The court of appeal has, in a similar way as the district court, ruled that the question whether L has a right to half of the property belonging to the community property in the context of the partitioning and division of the community property, as far as this is brought in by mrs. van Wylick, must be answered negatively. This decision is contested by the means of cassation.

3.2 In the legal consideration 5.10 the Court of Appeal has taken as a starting point in answering the aforementioned question that in the light of the 'exceptional circumstances of this case' on the one hand consideration must be given to the general legal principles and on the other hand to the requirements of reasonableness and fairness according to which L is supposed to behave in the community property.

Furthermore the court has stated in legal consideration 5.13–5.17 that in this case two general legal principles apply and that on the basis of these principles L is not entitled to the benefits that originate from the community property. Against these two considerations the parts A and B of the means of cassation are aimed in vain.

As far as these parts are based on the statement that the general legal principles formulated by the court do not exist at all, this statement, that has not been substantiated, must be rejected as incorrect.

As far as these parts A and B are intended as an argument in support of the statement that these legal principles do not apply in a case as the case at hand because, briefly stated, the nature of the acquisition resulting from the community of property impedes that this acquisition can be considered as something that is equal to a 'favour' or an 'advantage' as mentioned in these principles, they cannot lead to cassation because of a lack of interest. For the decision of the court is supported by the independent judgement formulated in consideration 5.18 that is, as will be explained below, contested in vain.

3.3 In legal consideration 5.18 the court has ruled that in the exceptional circumstances of this case 'and also considered in light of the mentioned general legal principles' the claims of L are so unreasonable and unfair that he must be denied the exertion of these rights completely. ***As appears from the cited formulation, in this context the legal principles play only the role that they have contributed to the decision of the court that the requirements of reasonableness and fairness make the exertion of the right to his share in the matrimonial community of property inadmissible. As far as the parts A and B read in legal consideration 5.18 that the court has used these principles as a direct legal ground for denying this right, they lack a factual basis.*** As far as they express the complaint that those principles cannot contribute to the decision of the court, they depart from a wrong conception of the law.

Part C attacks legal consideration 5.18 with the statement that the judge is not allowed to make an exception to 1:100, 1 of the Civil Code on the basis of reasonableness and fairness. This statement is wrong in its generality. For an exception is not completely excluded. The court has correctly stated that such an exception can only be made in very special circumstances, where the court speaks of' a very strict standard' . In the circumstances that the court has taken as a starting point, the court has correctly decided that the unimpaired application of the equal division of the community of property based on the rule of article 1:100 clause 1 of the Civil Code between spouses in a dissolved matrimonial community, would, in the wording of article 6:2 clause 2 of the new Civil Code, be unacceptable according to standards of reasonableness and fairness.

On this ground the court has concluded that in the division of this community L is not entitled to the share in the community of property that has been brought in by van Wylick.

(...)

3.5 Since, as has been stated above, none of the parts succeed ('treffen doel'), the appeal in cassation must be dismissed.

4. Decision

The Supreme Court:

dismisses the appeal;

### 3A. Pragma-dialectical analysis of the decision of the Court of appeal

1. The claim of L, stating that he is entitled to his share in the marital community of property, must be dismissed

    1.1. L. should not profit from the marital community of property (5.17, 5.18)

        1.1.1. *In the special circumstances of the concrete case an exception to the legal division on the basis of article 1:100 of the Dutch Civil Code is justified on the basis of the following two legal principles:*

1.1.1.1a. He, who deliberately causes the death of someone else, who has benefited favoured him, should not profit from this favour (5.13) (*legal principle P1*)

1.1.1.1a.1. Article 3:959 of the Dutch Civil Code and article 4:1725 sub 2e of the Dutch Civil Code (5.14)

1.1.1.1b. One should not profit from the deliberately caused death of someone else (*legal principle P2*)

1.1.1.1b.1. Article 3:885 sub 1e of the Dutch Civil Code

1.1.2. **In the concrete case an exception to the legal division of the marital community of property on the basis of article 1:100 of the Dutch Civil Code is justified on the basis of reasonableness and fairness as specified in article 6:2 section 2 of the New Dutch Civil Code**

1.1.2.1a. The exceptional circumstances of the concrete case
1.1.2.1b. He, who deliberately causes the death of someone else, who has favoured him, should not profit from this favour (5.13) (*legal principle P1*)

1.1.2.1b.1. Article 3:959 of the Dutch Civil Code and section 4:1725 sub 2e of the Dutch Civil Code (5.14)

1.1.2.1c. One should not profit from the deliberately caused death of someone else (*legal principle P2*)

1.1.2.1c.1. Article 3:885 sub 1e of the Dutch Civil Code

**3B. Pragma-dialectical analysis of the decision of the Supreme Court**

1. The claim of L, stating that he is entitled to his share the marital community of property, must be dismissed

1.1.1. **In the concrete case an exception to the legal division of the marital community of property on the basis of article 1:100 of the Dutch Civil Code is justified on the basis of reasonableness and fairness as specified in clause 6:2 section 2 of the New Dutch Civil Code**

1.1.1.1a. The exceptional circumstances of the concrete case
1.1.1.1b. *In the concrete case an exception to the legal division on the basis of article 1:100 of the Dutch Civil Code is justified on the basis of the following two legal principles:*

1.1.1.1b.1a. He, who deliberately causes the death of someone else, who has favoured him, should not profit from this favour (5.13) (*legal principle P1*)

1.1.1.1b.1a.1. Article 3:959 of the Dutch Civil Code and article 4:1725 sub 2e of the Dutch Civil Code (5.14)

1.1.1.1b.1b. One should not profit from the deliberately caused death of someone else (*legal principle P2*)

1.1.1.1b.1b.1. Article 3:885 sub 1e of the Dutch Civil Code

## References


Canale, D., and G. Tuzet. 2009. Inferring the ratio: Commitments and constraints. In *Argumentation and the application of legal rules*, ed. E.T. Feteris, H. Kloosterhuis, and H.J. Plug, 7–14. Amsterdam: Sic Sat.

Dworkin, R. 1986. *Law's empire*. London: Fontana.

Feteris, E.T. 1989. *Discussieregels in het recht. Een pragma-dialectische analyse van het burgerlijk proces en het strafproces. (Discussion rules in law. A pragma-dialectical analysis of the dutch civil process and criminal process)*. Dissertation Amsterdam. Dordrecht: Foris.

Feteris, E.T. 2008. Strategic maneuvering with the intention of the legislator in the justification of judicial decisions. *Argumentation* 22: 335–353.

Feteris, E.T. 2009a. Strategic manoeuvring in the justification of judicial decisions. In *Examining argumentation in context. Fifteen studies on strategic manoeuvering*, ed. F.H. van Eemeren, 93–114. Amsterdam: John Benjamins.

Feteris, E.T. 2009b. Strategic manoeuvring with linguistic arguments in the justification of legal decisions. In *Proceedings of the Second Conference Rhetoric in Society*, Leiden University, 22–23 Jan 2009. (cd-rom).

Feteris, E.T. 2011. Strategic maneuvering in the case of the "Unworthy Spouse". In *Exploring argumentative contexts*, ed. F.H. van Eemeren, B.J. Garssen, 149–164. Amsterdam: John Benjamins.

Kloosterhuis, H. 2006. *Reconstructing interpretative argumentation in legal decisions. A pragma-dialectical approach*. Amsterdam: Sic Sat.

Plug, H.J. 1990. *In onderlinge samenhang bezien. De pragma-dialectische reconstructie van complexe argumentatie in rechterlijke uitspraken*. Dissertation Amsterdam. Amsterdam: Thela Thesis.

van Eemeren, F.H. 2010. *Strategic manoeuvering in argumentative discourse. Extending the pragma-dialectical theory of argumentation*. Amsterdam: John Benjamins.

van Eemeren, F.H., and R. Grootendorst. 1991. The study of argumentation from a speech act perspective. In *Pragmatics at issue. Selected papers of the International Pragmatics Conference*, ed. J. Verschueren, Antwerp, August 17–22, 1987. Volume I (pp. 141–170). Amsterdam: John Benjamins.

van Eemeren, F.H., and R. Grootendorst. 1992. *Argumentation, communication, and fallacies*. Mahwah: Erlbaum.

van Eemeren, F.H., and P. Houtlosser. 2006. Strategic maneuvering: A synthetic recapitulation. *Argumentation* 20: 377–380.

van Eemeren, F.H., and P. Houtlosser. 2007. Seizing the occasion: Parameters for analysing ways of strategic manoeuvring. In *Proceedings of the sixth conference of the International Society for the Study of Argumentation*, ed. F.H. van Eemeren, J.A. Blair, Ch.A. Willard, and B. Garssen, 375–381. Amsterdam: SicSat.

# Chapter 7
# Legal Argumentation and the Normativity of Legal Norms*

**Carlos Bernal**

## 7.1 Introduction

Legal argumentation has differing relations with the concept of normativity. On the one hand, normativity plays an important role in legal argumentation. This is because legal norms are elements of the arguments which go together to make up legal discourse. On the other hand, legal argumentation also plays a relevant role in grounding the normativity of legal norms. The normativity of legal norms is not only based on authority, but also on correctness, and correctness is achieved, at least in part, by compliance to rules governing legal argumentation.

The aim of this paper is to analyse the most significant relationships between normativity and legal argumentation. To achieve this aim, the paper will consider four aspects: the normativity of the different kinds of legal norms, the rules of legal argumentation, the role played by the rules of legal argumentation in grounding the normativity of legal norms, and the role played by legal norms in legal argumentation. The main claim that I would like to endorse here is that compliance with rules governing correct legal argumentation provides a foundation for the normativity of the primary and secondary norms of law. This paper aims to explain how this foundation is provided.

*The author thanks Eveline Feteris, Stanley Paulson, and an anonymous reviewer of Cogency for valuable feedback. This paper has been originally published in English in Cogency Vol. 3, No. 2, 2011.

C. Bernal (✉)
Macquarie Law School, Sydney, Australia
e-mail: carlos.bernal-pulido@mq.edu.au

C. Dahlman and E. Feteris (eds.), *Legal Argumentation Theory: Cross-Disciplinary Perspectives*, Law and Philosophy Library 102, DOI 10.1007/978-94-007-4670-1_7,

## 7.2 The Normativity of Different Types of Legal Norms

Various concepts of normativity have been stated throughout the history of philosophy and general jurisprudence. This is not hardly surprising if it is remembered that the concept of normativity designates the "evaluative or prescriptive" property of a statement (Hare, *The Language of Morals,* 1972:1). Statements which boast this property and which contrast with factual statements are relevant to law, ethics and religious orders, and also to theories concerning themselves with these orders. There are strong debates between the many different accounts of normativity endorsed in these fields.[1]

With reference to law, the concept of normativity is the subject of interesting discussions concerning, among other things, how to understand the normativity of law and whether the law bears a special kind of normativity that is different from the normativity of moral norms.[2] For the present purposes, the relevant question is what the normativity of legal norms consists of. It should be pointed out that law is made up of various types of legal norms, and that the normativity of each one of these types of norms boasts certain individual properties. Two typologies of norms need to be considered for the present analysis. There is a connection between these two typologies, which gives rise to four types of normativity. Every one of these four types of normativity has a particular relationship with the rules governing legal argumentation. The first typology is the well-known differentiation between rules and principles; the second one is the Kelsenian distinction between primary and secondary norms.

The differentiation between rules and principles gives rise to two types of normativity: the normativity of rules, and the normativity of principles. The normativity of rules is an all-or-nothing affair. Rules apply in their entirety or they do not apply at all for resolving a specific case. If the de facto assumption envisaged in the rule has been proven, the judge should apply it in full. If, on the other hand, the de facto assumption envisaged in the rule is not verified, or despite the fact that it has been proven, an exception stipulated in it occurs as well, the judge should rule out the idea of applying it (Dworkin 2000:14). The normativity of principles, meanwhile, is a *prima facie* normativity (Ross 1930:19; Hare, *Moral Thinking,* 1981:27; Searle 1978:84). As Alexy maintains, principles are "requirements to be optimized" with *prima facie* validity, which order their content to be realised to the greatest extent possible, as far as legal and factual possibilities are concerned. The range of legal possibilities is determined by the opposing principles. While rules are definitive commands which apply by means of subsumption, principles are *prima facie* requirements which are applied by means of balancing (Alexy, *A Theory of Constitutional Rights,* 2002:47).

[1]On these debates in ethics, see Korsgaard (1996:1 f).

[2]On the normativity of law, see: Bertea (2009:1 f).

The difference between primary and secondary legal norms also gives rise to two types of normativity. This is a distinction stated by Hans Kelsen. According to Kelsen, a primary norm gives the judge the power to impose the legal consequence, once the de facto assumption has been proven. A secondary norm, on the other hand, states the action that should be taken in order to prevent the legal consequence.[3] It is arguable in Kelsen's doctrine whether the secondary norm is addressed to the subject or whether it is a mere reflection of the primary norm (Bernal, Las normas de competencia, 2004:107). It is nevertheless true that these two types of norms are endowed with a different type of normativity. The normativity of primary norms is one that can be called weak (Paulson, Zwei radikale Objektivierungsprogramme, 2005:191 f.). Kelsen referred to this meaning of normativity when he wondered what the specific normativity of law (Gesetzlichkeit des Rechts) consisted of. According to Kelsen, "imputation is recognised in the Pure Theory of Law as the particular lawfulness, the autonomy, of the law" (Kelsen 1996:23). This normativity consists in the power of the judge to impute the legal consequence. There is a strong normativity concept alongside this weak one. The strong concept could characterise the normativity of secondary norms better.[4] Joseph Raz alludes to this concept when he says that "aspects of the world are normative in as much as they or their existence constitute reasons for persons, that is, grounds which make certain beliefs, moods, emotions, intentions or actions appropriate or inappropriate" (Raz 1999:67). Applying this concept to law would justify the legal obligation of the subject (Paulson, Zwei radikale Objektivierungsprogramme 2005:191 f.). The secondary norms are addressed to the subjects of law and they provide them with reasons for actions according to the law.

It has to be recognised that the classification into primary and secondary normativity has so far been carried out more with respect to rules. Kelsen's developments referred to norms which had a hypothetical, conditional structure and the properties of rules. It should nevertheless be pointed out that principles – and their normativity – can also be characterised as primary and secondary. Secondary principles have the structure COx, in which the 'C' stands for a command, and 'O' for optimization. These principles command the addressees of the principle

[3]I refer here to the classification into primary and secondary norms according to Kelsen, and not to the differentiation between primary and secondary rules, as stated by Hart. According to Kelsen: "Thus, the norm that establishes sanction-avoiding behaviour – behaviour the legal system aims to bring about – is a legal norm only on the presupposition that it is saying something (in abbreviated form for the sake of convenience) that the reconstructed legal norm alone states fully and correctly: given as condition, behaviour opposite to that which the norm establishes as sanction-avoiding, then a coercive act is to be forthcoming as consequence. This reconstructed legal norm is the legal norm in its primary form. The norm establishing sanction-avoiding behaviour can only be regarded, then, as a secondary legal norm" (Kelsen 1996:30).

[4]Despite his tendency to consider that the weak thesis of normativity applies to all law, even Kelsen himself appears to defend the strong thesis on occasions, when he states that legal norms are mandates drawn up in a categorical, imperative form, and that they are addressed to the legal subject via a secondary norm. See: Paulson, An Empowerment Theory, 1998:60 f.

to optimise the object of the principle (for example, Article 20 in the Spanish constitution – which guarantees the right to privacy – establishes a principle which orders, amongst other things, an employer to optimise a worker's privacy when using e-mail at his place of work).[5] This optimisation requirement could be called the strong normativity of principles. It is addressed to every public or private subject of the principle, since principles – especially when they are constitutional rights – are binding on all public and private powers.

Alongside this dimension, principles also have a weak normativity. This normativity is addressed to the judge, and becomes effective at the moment the principle is applied. This normativity is explicit in the norm governing the power to carry out a balancing exercise, or to be more precise, to apply the principle of proportionality and thus determine the maximum measure possible where the principle should be realised, taking into consideration the legal and factual reasons against it. In the example, Article 18 in the Spanish constitution gives the judge the power to balance the principle of protecting privacy against other relevant principles in a specific case, for instance protecting freedom of enterprise on the part of the employer.

The combination of these four types of normativity can be shown in a table.

| | Strong Normativity | Weak Normativity |
|---|---|---|
| Rules | Command to do or not do x | Power to impose the penalty |
| Principles | Requirement to optimise x | Power to balance |

## 7.3 A Concept of Legal Argumentation

Secondly, the concept of legal argumentation needs to be specified. Legal argumentation can be defined as an interlocution or dialogue exercise between everyone involved in legal practice. As Feteris says, "someone who presents a legal thesis is expected to put forth arguments to support it" (Feteris 1999:1). Whether or not a thesis ought to be accepted and adopted as the solution for a practical question will

[5]The Article 20 of the Spanish Constitution states that: "(1) The following rights are recognised and protected: (a) the right to freely express and disseminate thoughts, ideas and opinions trough words, in writing or by any other means of communication; (b) the right to literary, artistic, scientific and technical production and creation; (c) the right to academic freedom; (d) the right to freely communicate or receive accurate information by any means of dissemination whatsoever. The law shall regulate the right to invoke personal conscience and professional secrecy in the exercise of these freedoms. (2) The exercise of these rights may not be restricted by any form of prior censorship. (3) The law shall regulate the organisation and parliamentary control of the social communications media under the control of the State or any public agency and shall guarantee access to such media to the main social and political groups, respecting the pluralism of society and of the various languages of Spain. (4) These freedoms are limited by respect for the rights recognised in this Title, by the legal provisions implementing it, and especially by the right to honour, to privacy, to personal reputation and to the protection of youth and childhood. (5) The confiscation of publications and recordings and other information media may only be carried out by means of a court order."

depend on the extent to which these arguments are right. Legal argumentation is thus a practical activity, one which attempts to answer the practical question *par excellence* in concrete cases: what ought to be done? Legal argumentation sets out to ground a right answer to this question. However, because of the many conceptions of the good existing in every society, and because of the existence of moral disagreements, no attempt can be made to achieve a right answer by deriving it from a single system of values that is coherent in itself, rather by following certain rules of procedure which make legal argumentation rational. It is very true that adhering to these rules of procedure offers no guarantee that a single right answer will be arrived at in each case. However, if these rules of procedure are broken, it is indeed a serious sign of a lack of correctness in the answer to a case or the justification of it.

This explains why the main activity of legal argumentation theorists has been to create legal argumentation models which make the rules explicit for developing a rational legal argumentation (Atienza, *Las razones del derecho* 1991:1 f.). No single catalogue of rationality rules for legal argumentation exists in legal theory. This is one thing that has led to the most intricate of doctrinal controversies (Tugendhat 1980:1 f.; Neumann 1986:94 f.). All in all, the best known rules, and the ones most widely accepted by doctrine, are those relating to (1) clarity and conceptual consistency, (2) normative consistency, (3) saturation, (4) adhering to deductive logic, (5) adhering to argumentation burdens, (6) honesty, (7) argumentation consistency, and (8) coherence. According to these rules, the more a legal argumentation is developed through arguments (1) which boast conceptual (Alexy, Grundgesetz und Diskurstheorie 1996:344) and linguistic clarity and consistency (Alexy, *A Theory of Legal Argumentation*, 1989:185; Aarnio 1987:254), (2) which can also justify the same interpretative results when they are applied to the same assumptions (Peczenik 1983:189), (3) which are complete – in other words, which contain all the premises belonging to them (Alexy, *A Theory of Legal Argumentation,* 1989:236), (4) which adhere to deductive logic (Atienza, Para una razonable definición de razonable, 1987:193), (5) which adhere to argumentation burdens, (6) which correspond to the real thoughts of those who put them forward, (7) which have no internal contradictions (MacCormick 1984:43 f.), and (8) which are supported by general rules or principles, the more rational it will be (Alexy and Peczenik 1990:115 f.; Baum Lavenbook 1984:355; and Alexy, Juristische Begründung, System und Kohärenz 1990:97 f.).

## 7.4 Legal Argumentation in Normativity

These legal argumentation rules play a leading role when it comes to grounding the normativity of primary rules (4.1) and primary principles (4.2) at the time of their application.

### 7.4.1 *Legal Argumentation and Primary Rules*

Firstly, the exercising of the judicial powers established in primary rules should not depend on the will or discretion of the judge, but rather should be the result of a correct legal argumentation. These powers are exercised by means of subsumption, the simplest structure of which is as follows:

| | |
|---|---|
| Major Premise: | (1) (x) (Tx → PRx) |
| Minor Premise: | (2) Ta |
| Conclusion: | (3) PRa (1) (2)[6] |

This structure expresses the step from the primary rule (1) to the individual norm (3), and is made up of the following elements: (1) the primary rule, consisting of a de facto assumption (Tx), the imputation link (→) which symbolises the power (P) the judge has been given to impute the legal consequence (Rx) if the de facto assumption (T) has been proven, and also the aforementioned legal consequence; (2) the minor premise (Ta), in other words, the subsumptive judgement according to which, fact (a), the individual example of facts in general (x), meets the conditions established by the de facto assumption (Tx) of rule (1); and the individual rule of competence (PRa), according to which, the judge is given the power to attribute legal consequence (R) to fact (a).

Legal argumentation rules perform a double function in this structure. Firstly, the very subsumption structure establishes an argumentation process which respects the rules of deductive logic. Secondly, the rules of rationality in legal argumentation should be applied in order to determine the major and minor premises of the subsumption. Identifying the primary rule which takes the place of the major premise is thus the result of a process whereby provisions are interpreted in the sources of law. Adhering to the rules of clarity, consistency and coherence is not only a limit and an orientation criterion merely for finding the normative meaning of the provisions which are relevant to the case; it is also useful for resolving contradictions or inconsistencies between various primary rules which are valid at one and the same time. Coherence rules are essential for resolving normative contradictions or inconsistencies. Clarity, consistency, coherence and saturation rules should moreover act as guide when evidence is being examined which leads to establishing whether fact (a) has been proven, and, in particular, to the formulation of the subsumptive statement (Ta). Viewed rationally, reducing the possible lack of determination in the primary rule is not something that should be left to the discretion of the judge, but rather should be the product of a reasoning compliant with the rules of legal argumentation.

It is clear from the institutional viewpoint that determining the major and minor premises of the subsumption depends on the judge exercising his authority. However, this exercising of authority will only be considered correct from a critical perspective if the judge also adheres to the rules of legal argumentation.

---

[6]See, on this formula as a logical formula for the internal justification of jurisdictional decisions in general: Alexy, Die logische Analyse juristischer Entscheidungen 1995:20 f.

### 7.4.2 Legal Argumentation and Primary Principles

Legal argumentation rules should likewise serve as guide for applying primary principles through balancing, or more extensively, through the principle of proportionality. The primary normativity of principles gives the judge the power to apply the principle of proportionality. This principle is a linked group of three sub-principles: suitability, necessity and proportionality in the strict sense of the word. Each of these sub-principles expresses a requirement which every interference in a principle should meet, if it is to be legally legitimate. These requirements can be summarised in the following terms (Bernal, *El principio de proporcionalidad,* 2007:797; Alexy, *A Theory of Constitutional Rights,* 2002:66 f).

According to the suitability sub-principle, every interference with a legal principle should be adequate and suitable for contributing to the realisation of another legal principle.

According to the necessity sub-principle, every interference measure with a principle should be the most benign, with respect to the principle which is being interfered with, of all measures which are at least equally suitable for helping to achieve the proposed goal.

Finally, the principle of proportionality in the strict sense of the word establishes that the importance of the goals sought by any interference with a principle should bear a corresponding relation to the meaning of the principle which is being interfered with.

As with subsumption, legal argumentation rules determine the very structure of the principle of proportionality. If this principle is observed closely, it will be seen to have a precise argumentation structure, consisting of various burdens of argumentation that are free of contradiction, which makes it clear what factual and normative variables are relevant for applying the principles at stake. Factual variables are expressed in the sub-principles of suitability and necessity, and also in the balancing exercise, when this determines the extent of factual interference between the principles which are relevant to the case. Normative variables, meanwhile, appear when the weight of the principles is being determined in the balancing exercise.

Using saturated, consistent and coherent chains of arguments will allow each variable to be given a correct answer. These chains will possibly lead in some cases to a single correct answer for each variable. In other cases, however, the only correct answer will be that there is no correct answer. In these cases, even from the point of view of correctness, the judge will have an irreducible margin of discretion.

## 7.5 Normativity in Legal Argumentation

Finally, it is necessary to take into account the effect of normativity on legal argumentation. The strong normativity of secondary rules and principles has a bearing on subsumption and on balancing. In a legal system, this normativity not only means that secondary rules and principles constitute reasons for actions to their addressees which pre-empt other types of reasons, it also implies that together with the power to subsume and to balance, primary rules likewise impose a duty on the judge to impute the legal consequence, assuming that the de facto assumption has been proven, while primary principles impose a duty on him to resolve the case in the manner established in the principle which prevails in the balancing exercise. This duty expresses the special weight that normativity places on rules and principles, in comparison with other types of general, practical arguments which interfere with both the subsumption and the balancing exercise.

As far as subsumption is concerned, this duty which expresses the normativity of rules means that their argumentation structure varies, in the manner stated below.

| | |
|---|---|
| Major premise: | (1) (x) (Tx → ORx) |
| Minor Premise: | (2) Ta |
| Conclusion: | (3) ORa (1), (2) |

In the major premise, the judiciary has the power to impute the legal consequence (→ Rx) and also is commanded to impute it (→ ORx). This command means that when the judge exercises this power, she should pre-empt other types of reasons which result in a consequence other than (Rx) being arrived at. The primary rule is thus a reason which rules out other types of general practical arguments.

Something similar happens with balancing. The principles which come together in the structure of balancing bear also the normativity of reasons for action This is nevertheless not a definitive normativity, as is the case with rules, but rather just a *prima facie* normativity. Firstly, this normativity prevents the judge from disregarding a principle in a balancing exercise in a case which has at least a semantic property that enables it to be connected with this principle. Thus, if a specific case has a semantic property which links it to principle *P1* and a semantic property which links it to principle *P2*, and the legal solutions deriving from *P1* and *P2* are incompatible with each other, the judge must necessarily establish whether *P1* should take precedence over *P2* in case (C), or vice versa: that is, if *P1*P*P2* or *P2*P*P1*. In addition, and secondly, the *prima facie* normativity of the principle which has taken precedence in the balancing exercise forces the judge to resolve the case in the manner established by that principle. Thus, for example, if *P1* should have precedence, the judge should extract an ascribed norm from the balancing exercise which has the structure of a rule: (x) (Tx → ORx). In this structure, *Tx* is the de facto assumption consisting of the properties that are relevant in the specific case, and *ORx* expresses the command to impute the consequences established under principle *P1*.[7]

[7]This is called by Alexy "Law of Competing Principles". According to this rule: "The circumstances under which one principle takes precedence over another constitute the conditions of a rule which has the same legal consequences as the principle taking precedence". See Alexy, *A Theory of Constitutional Rights*, 2002:54; Alexy, Logische Analyse der juristischen Entscheidungen 46.

## 7.6 Conclusions

The preceding analysis leads to the following conclusions:

The combination of typologies of legal norms that was taken into account here, namely, the distinction between rules and principles, on the one hand, and primary and secondary norms (endowed with a weak and a strong normativity, respectively), on the other, gives rise to four types of normativity of legal norms. Primary rules have a weak normativity. They empower the judge to impose the legal consequence foreseen in the rule if the de facto assumption of it has been proven. Secondary rules have a strong normativity. They command legal subjects to perform or not to perform a type of action. Primary principles have a weak normativity. They empower the judge to balance principles in collision. Finally, secondary principles have a strong normativity. They require their addressees to optimise their object (a right or a common good).

The rules governing legal argumentation concerning clarity and conceptual consistency, normative consistency, saturation, adhering to deductive logic, adhering to argumentation burdens, honesty, argumentation consistency, and coherence play a leading role when it comes to grounding the normativity of primary rules and primary principles at the time of their application. First, the exercising of the judicial powers established in primary rules should not depend on the will or discretion of the judge, but rather should be the result of a correct legal argumentation. These powers are exercised by means of subsumption. While the very subsumption structure establishes an argumentation process which respects the rules of deductive logic, the rules of rationality in legal argumentation should be applied in order to determine the premises at stake in the subsumption. Second, the rules of legal argumentation should likewise serve as guide for applying primary principles through balancing, or more extensively, through the principle of proportionality. As with subsumption, legal argumentation rules determine the very structure of the principle of proportionality. In addition, using saturated, consistent and coherent chains of premises will allow avoiding some incorrect results in the application of this principle.

Finally, the strong normativity of legal norms displays also an effect upon legal argumentation. The strong normativity of secondary rules and principles has a bearing on subsumption and on balancing. In a legal system, this normativity not only means that secondary rules and principles constitute reasons for actions to their addressees which pre-empt other types of reasons, it also implies that together with the power to subsume and to balance, primary rules likewise impose a duty on the judge to impute the legal consequence, assuming that the de facto assumption has been proven, while primary principles impose a duty on him to resolve the case in the manner established in the principle which prevails in the balancing exercise. This duty expresses the special weight that normativity places on rules and principles, in comparison with other types of general, practical arguments which interfere with both the subsumption and the balancing exercise.

## References

Aarnio, Aulis. 1987. *The rational as reasonable: A treatise on legal justification*. Dordrecht: Reidel.

Alexy, Robert. 1989. *A theory of legal argumentation. The theory of rational discourse as theory of legal justification*. Oxford: Oxford University Press.

Alexy, Robert. 1990. Juristische Begründung, System und Kohärenz. In *Rechtsdogmatik und Praktische Vernunft. Symposion zum 80. Geburstag von F. Wieacker*, ed. O. Behrends, M. Diesselhorst, and R. Dreier, 97–120. Göttingen: Vondenhoeck & Ruprecht.

Alexy, Robert. 1995. Die logische Analyse juristischer Entscheidungen. In *Recht, Vernunft, Diskurs. Studien zur Rechtsphilosophie*. Frankfurt: Suhrkamp.

Alexy, Robert. 1996. Grundgesetz und Diskurstheorie. In *Legitimation des Grundgesetzes aus Sicht von Rechtsphilosophie und Gesellschafstheorie*, ed. Brugger Winfried, 344–360. Baden – Baden: Nomos.

Alexy, Robert. 2002. *A theory of constitutional rights*. Oxford: Oxford University Press.

Alexy, Robert, and Alexander Peczenik. 1990. The concept of coherence and its significance for discoursive rationality. *Ratio Juris* 1: 115–147.

Atienza, Manuel. 1987. Para una razonable definición de razonable. *Doxa* 4: 189–202.

Atienza, Manuel. 1991. *Las razones del derecho. Teorías de la argumentación jurídica*. Madrid: Centro de Estudios Constitucionales.

Baum Levenbook, Barbara. 1984. The role of coherence in legal reasoning. *Law and Philosophy* 3: 355–374.

Bernal, Carlos. 2004. Las normas de competencia en la Teoría Pura del Derecho de Kelsen. In *Hans Kelsen 1881–1973*, ed. Luis Villar Borda, 117–137. Bogotá: Universidad Externado de Colombia.

Bernal, Carlos. 2007. *El principio de proporcionalidad y los derechos fundamentales*. Madrid: Centro de Estudios Políticos y Constitucionales.

Bertea, Stefano. 2009. *The normative claim of law*. Oxford/Portland (Oregon): Hart.

Dworkin, Ronald. 2000. *Taking rights seriously*. London: Duckworth.

Feteris, Eveline. 1999. *Fundamentals of legal argumentation. A survey of theories on the justification of judicial decisions*. Dordrecht/Boston/London: Kluwer.

Hare, Richard. 1972. *The language of morals*. Oxford: Clarendon.

Hare, Richard. 1981. *Moral thinking. Its levels, method and point*. Oxford: Clarendon.

Kelsen, Hans. 1996. *Introduction to the problems of legal theory* (trans: Paulson, Bonnie Litschewski and Paulson, Stanley L.). Oxford: Clarendon Press.

Korsgaard, Christine M. 1996. *The sources of normativity*. Cambridge: Cambridge University Press.

MacCormick, Neil. 1984. Coherence in legal justification. In *Theorie der Normen. Festgabe für Ota Weinberger zum 65. Geburstag*, ed. W. Krawietz, H. Schlesky, G. Winkler, and A. Schuamm, 43–63. Berlin: Duncker & Humblot.

Neumann, Ulfrid. 1986. *Juristische Argumentationslehre*. Darmstadt: Wissenschaftliche Buchgesellschaft.

Paulson, Stanley. 1998. An empowerment theory of legal norms. *Ratio Juris* 1: 58–72.

Paulson, Stanley. 2005. Zwei radikale Objektivierungsprogramme in der Rechtslehre Hans Kelsens. In *Hans Kelsen, Staatsrechtslehrer und Rechtstheoretiker des 20. Jahrhunderts*, ed. Paulson Stanely and Stolleis Michael, 191–220. Tuebingen: Mohr Siebeck.

Peczenik, Aleksander. 1983. *Grundlagen der juristischen Argumentation*. Vienna/New York: Springer.

Raz, Joseph. 1999. *Engaging reason. On the theory of value and action*. Oxford: Oxford University Press.

Ross, William David. 1930. *The right and the good*. Oxford: Clarendon.

Searle, John. 1978. Prima facie obligations. In *Practical reasoning*, ed. Joseph Raz, 84–90. Oxford: Oxford University Press.

Tugendhat, Ernst. 1980. Zur Entwicklung von moralischen Begründungsstrukturen im modernen Recht. *ARSP Beiheft* 14: 1–20.

# Chapter 8
# Weighing and Balancing in the Light of Deliberation and Expression

**Bruce Anderson**

## 8.1 Introduction

Legal theorists such as Marko Novak and Robert Alexy appeal to a process of "weighing and balancing" to resolve legal conflicts, examples of which include conflicts of principles, conflicts between constitutional rights and legislation, differences in the interpretations of a rule, and competing constitutional rights. For these writers the problem is that there is in these situations no clear rule by which to settle the conflict. By 'clear rule' they mean a major premise for a deductive justification. In this context, the challenge for these writers is how to rationally incorporate elements such as intuition, discretion, and judgments of value – which they believe are irrational and subjective – and how to legally justify decisions reached by a process of weighing and balancing.

By contrast, I have argued that the actual judicial decision making process – comprised of asking questions, achieving insights, and making judgments of value – is conscious, deliberate, intelligent, and rational. Further, in my view the legal decision-making process is not a distinct discovery process independent of the process of justification. Evaluating proposed outcomes is a normal part of any legal decision-making process.

To be more specific, I have explained the decision-making process as the operation of 13 mental activities. They are sensible presentations/memories, What-questions, direct insights, interpretations/definitions/explanations, Is-questions, reflective insights, judgments of fact, What-can-be-done-questions, practical insights, courses of action/options/alternatives/plans, What-should-be-done-questions, practical reflective insights, judgments of value, and decisions. In this light the decision-making process comprised of the mental operations named immediately above is

B. Anderson (✉)
Saint Mary's University, Halifax, NS, Canada
e-mail: Bruce.Anderson@SMU.CA

C. Dahlman and E. Feteris (eds.), *Legal Argumentation Theory: Cross-Disciplinary Perspectives*, Law and Philosophy Library 102, DOI 10.1007/978-94-007-4670-1_8,

the real ground of legal reasoning, not a subsequent process of legal justification. Further, it follows that a written or oral expression of a judicial decision is something quite different from either the decision-making process itself or its justification (Anderson 1996: 131–170).

In recent discussions weighing and balancing are portrayed as a process of justification. But such analyses assume that the process itself must be rationally controlled where 'rational' means a clear set of logical rules. The purpose of this paper is to explore how an understanding of aspects of the actual decision-making process might enrich our understanding of the process of weighing and balancing. Further, this approach has the potential to critique accounts of legal rationality dominated by deductive logic. I begin with a general discussion of deliberation. Next I focus on practical reflective insights and judgments of value which I consider to be the key mental elements relevant to any talk about weighing and balancing. Then I discuss aspects of the work of Marko Novak (2010) and Robert Alexy (2003a, b) in light of that perspective. I end with a discussion of the differences between deliberation and written expression and make some connections to Eveline Feteris' (2008) work.

## 8.2 Deliberation

### *8.2.1 The Process of Deliberation*

Recently, when I had to decide whether or not to recommend increasing a faculty member's teaching load searching for a rule was not the first thing that came to mind. On the contrary, my concern was to figure out, as best I could, what exactly the situation was and then to figure out what was the best thing to do in the situation as I understood it. I was puzzled and deliberated about what I should do. I did read and considered the relevant articles of the Collective Agreement but these rules were not the key elements of my deliberations and subsequent decision. Rather, I noticed that I posed all sorts of questions about my colleague's research interests, what he had published, connections between teaching and research, and the aim of a university. I also asked my colleagues for their views. I was awake at night thinking about these issues. I had insights and made value judgments about the responsibilities of faculty, about the research of other faculty members, and about this particular colleague's teaching and research. Finally, I reached a decision and sent a memo to the Dean recommending increasing the teaching load. But what is deliberation? What was happening when I was deliberating? It is obvious that something precedes memos and written judicial decisions. But what is it? What act or activities occur? What, precisely, is deliberation?

Deliberation is an activity that is future-oriented in that it is aimed at deciding what you should do. It involves coming up with plans and selecting an option. It involves anticipating possibilities, evaluating those possibilities in concrete specific situations, and then doing something. Because judges are provided with alternatives by lawyers the major concern of judges is to evaluate alternatives and to choose between competing options. Judges deliberating are concerned with doing something practical, changing the current situation in some way, for instance either permitting advertisements for tobacco products or forbidding them. In fact, the situation envisaged by a judge deliberating does not yet exist. So far, no decision has been reached.

When it is obvious that someone has deliberated well in a concrete and specific situation we might ask "How did they do that?" How did they come up with that? It is this concern with "how something was done" that I want to explore. Hence I will provide a partial answer to the question *What is deliberation*? by tackling the questions: *What do you do when you are deliberating*? *How do you reach a decision*?

When we face a situation that calls for some sort of action, there are two things that we have to do. One, we have to discover and judge what the situation is. And two, we have to discover what is worthwhile, suitable, or the best thing to do in that situation. Before deciding whether a plaintiff wins or loses, or the amount of damages to award, a judge has to understand, what in fact happened. Analyzing the process of judging what, in fact, happened in a particular case would be an interesting thing to do. However, my focus in this paper is the subsequent practical process, that is judging what should be done.

How does a judge figure out what to do? The concern is with what can be done in this situation. Alternatives are proposed by opposing lawyers. But these options have to be tested. Which option is the most suitable? The options are evaluated by asking questions about their suitability. The judge *grasps* that one alternative is more suitable than the other and a *judgment of value* is made that one alternative is better than the other. This ends deliberation. What is interesting about deliberation is that a judgment of value cannot but be embodied by a judge. Lawyers differentiate between good and bad judges. Sloppy or bad deliberation leads to judgments of value and decisions that are unsuitable or corrupt. On the other hand, we admire good deliberation when it leads to judgments of value that suit a particular concrete situation. There is no escaping the attentiveness, intelligence, and values of a judge when they deliberate. That is why we want experienced and wise judges to deal with nuanced and complex situations, not legal technicians. A *decision* to act on the value judgment that one option is better than another follows a judgment of value: the judge drafts an Order.

So far I have merely mentioned the mental operations involved in the decision making process. But such a brief glimpse at the nature of deliberation in legal decision making, will, perhaps, indicate its complexity. However, it is worth noting that my discussion of deliberation represents a shift from a common sense discussion of weighing and balancing to an effort to appreciate particular mental activities comprising deliberation and how these activities are related. The discussion provides at least some evidence that deliberation, not rules, is the centrepiece of judicial decision-making. But let's examine deliberation in more detail.

### 8.2.2 *Questions, Practical Reflective Insights, and Judgments of Value*

When a judge listens to lawyers' competing arguments about how a case should be decided questions are provoked. Does the legislation violate the constitutional right to freedom of expression? Is the violation justified? Does a particular interpretation of the rule conflict with its purpose? And so on.

Two overarching questions – Is this alternative feasible? and Is this alternative more suitable than the other? – capture the attitude of a judge engaged in evaluating options. Questions are posed about the options and their implications are worked out. Answering these questions calls for a full evaluation of the implications of the proposed alternatives and the discovery of which one is the most appropriate solution in the circumstances as they are understood by the judge. In fact, we jump to value judgments when we settle which is the best solution in a situation. The normal process of deliberation is one of posing questions, seeking and finding answers, jumping to conclusions, and working out their implications.

The key activity in this deliberation process is practical reflective insight. Practical reflective insights are concerned with evaluating the suitability of proposed courses of action. They grasp the relevant issues and their implications concerning plans and options. The relevant issues and implications that are discovered might include reasons that support the plan, the exact steps required to implement the plan, the consequences of the plan, the alternatives it excludes, whether the steps are feasible. Practical reflective insight grasps the links among the relevant aspects of a particular situation, plans or options, and the reasons for and against the plans or options and discovers whether a plan is possible or sufficiently suitable for the circumstances. They do not occur out of the blue. They draw on sensible presentations, imaginations, memories, direct insights, interpretations, reflective insights, judgments of fact, practical insights, plans and options. It does not alter any of the contents of these mental activities. Rather, it creates a unity or order among them so that they are grasped in a new way, as relevant in action.

The emergence of practical reflective insight depends on personal factors such as the judge's familiarity with the actual situation, how serious they consider the situation, and their openness to further questions. Practical reflective insight does not depend on a set of rules. The criteria for whether a practical reflective insight is correct is whether the judge is convinced that a particular option or plan is the most suitable for the situation. The practical reflective insight will be correct if, in fact, all the relevant questions have been asked and satisfactorily answered. Further, the correctness of practical reflective insights depends on the judge achieving adequate direct insights, reflective insights, and practical insights.

Practical reflective insights are subsequently formulated as judgments of value such as "The legislation should be struck down" or "The rule should not be interpreted strictly." In other words, the evaluation of alternatives ends with a judgment of value. However, a decision by the judge brings deliberation to an end.

Decision confers actuality on a course of action. For instance, the judge signs their written judgment and it is published, reads the written legal decision to the litigants in court, or mails it to them.

The move from judgment of value to decision is complicated in the sense that a judge might know what should be done but fails to do it. Or the evaluation and judgment of value might be rash and then a bad decision follows. There is no avoiding the fact that a judge's education, experience, personal biases, intelligence, reasonableness, and degree of openness for instance are an important part of deliberation. But none of these mental activities seem to be essentially arbitrary, irrational, or unconscious. On the contrary, deliberation is essentially intelligent, deliberate, and conscious.

Perhaps the most surprising aspect of this portrait of deliberation is the discovery that a creative mental operation, namely practical reflective insight plays an essential role in evaluating and testing proposed plans, options, or alternative courses of action. In fact, practical reflective insights test alternative courses of action. Further, practical reflective insights are essentially open and creative acts. They are not achieved by following rules of logic. Rather, they grasp relations among facts, options and judgments of value that were previously unknown. Also, practical reflective insights are ultimately justified when there are no further relevant questions that need to be answered, not because they could be subsumed under general legal principles or rules or because they were coherent and consistent with other valid legal rules and principles in the legal system. Finally, this analysis suggests that legal reasoning is fundamentally an open and creative activity, rather than a process that is essentially closed and rule-bound.

The structure of deliberation as asking questions, achieving practical reflective insights, and making judgments of value can give precision to the notion of weighing and balancing. In this context weighing and balancing need to be understood as the process of deliberation. 'Weighing' would be conceived as the process of asking questions about competing outcomes, rights, principles, or rules and making value judgments. The key element in 'balancing' would be an overarching practical reflective insight, an insight that in a single moment discovers the relations among the current situation, the proposed alternatives, the pros and cons of each alternative, and the sufficiency of the suitability of each alternative in the case. To be clear, what I mean by weighing and balancing is the performance and achievement of practical reflective insights and judgments of value.[1]

This discussion of deliberation can be used to call into question aspects of recent accounts of weighing and balancing such as those by Marko Novak and Robert Alexy. Marko Novak claims that due to the subjective and irrational character of intuition and judgments of value in the balancing process an independent rational proportionality test and a strict *stare decisis* of balancing are required in order

[1]There is a second type of weighing and balancing oriented to agreeing or disagreeing with, affirming or denying, assenting or dissenting to, a proposition. Weighing and balancing in this context involve Is-questions, reflective insights and judgments of fact.

to "rationalize intuitions" and "persuade us that balancing was predominantly rational..." (Novak 2010: 105). He writes that "[i]n the case of balancing in order for a decision to be well reasoned (i.e. justified) the whole process of decision making, including (ir)rational elements, must go through a rationality test of justification" (Novak 2010: 105). By contrast, my view is that the process of asking questions about possible courses of action, achieving practical reflective insights, making judgments of value, and deciding is rational in the sense of being intelligent, conscious, and deliberate. I also claimed that practical reflective insight itself is the central element in an evaluative process, and that the achievement of a practical reflective insight is a creative act. This act is rational if your definition of rationality is not overly narrow and restricted to logic. Finally, a distinct justificatory process over and above deliberation is not necessary. Practical reflective insights and judgments of value are the key elements in testing options.

Let's consider Robert Alexy's analysis of weighing and balancing. For Alexy, balancing is the key ingredient in proportional judgments. He writes that constitutional rights can be violated only if they can be justified and they are justified only if they are proportional. Proportional judgments, he continues, presuppose balancing (Alexy 2003b: 436). He understands balancing in terms of a rule he calls the Law of Balancing. The Law of Balancing stipulates that "The greater the degree of non-satisfaction of, or detriment to, one principle, the greater the importance of satisfying the other" (Alexy 2003a: 136). He breaks down this Law into a three stage process. Step one is judging the intensity of the interference with the right as either light, moderate, or serious. Step two is judging the importance of satisfying the competing principle as either light, moderate, or serious. And step three is comparing the intensity of the interference with the right and the importance of satisfying the competing principle in order to judge whether or not the interference is justified. For instance, limited restrictions placed on tobacco advertising judged to be a moderate interference with the right to free expression would be compared to the high importance placed on protecting health by limiting tobacco advertising. However, the procedure is not a deductive procedure. Reasons are supposed to be given for these judgments, and these judgments presuppose standards not found in the Law of Balancing. Alexy finds commensurability between the judgments made in steps one and two by appealing to the fact that the same scale (light, moderate, serious) is used to measure the interference with one right and the importance of the competing right, and by stipulating that comparisons must be made in terms of what is correct in light of the constitution.

His next move in his analysis is to express the formal structure of balancing as a Weight Formula which he says functions as a set of premises from which a legal result can be inferred. He believes that "the weight formula allows one to grasp the interplay between the six elements which are relevant in order to determine the concrete weight of a principle when two principles collide" (Alexy 2003b: 448). The concrete Weight Formula is:

$$\mathrm{Wij} = \frac{\mathrm{Ii\ Wi\ Ri}}{\mathrm{Ij\ Wj\ Rj}}$$

In this formula i and j are the conflicting rights or principles. Ii/Ij is the relative degree of interference with the conflicting rights or principles. Wi/Wj is the relative abstract weight of the conflicting rights or principles. Ri/Rj is the relative degree of reliability of empirical assumptions grounding the conflicting rights or principles. According to Alexy this "weight formula represents a scheme which works according to the rules of arithmetic... [However] the real premises of the weight formula are not numbers, but judgments about degrees of interference, the importance of abstract weights, and degrees of reliability... The weight formula, then, connects judgments indirectly or analogously by interpreting the judgments through numbers..." (Alexy 2003b: 448). Alexy however does plug numbers into the weight formula. He uses the following scale: 1 = light, 2 = moderate, and 3 = serious. In this fashion Alexy offers a rational reconstruction of balancing, is able to calculate whether or not a decision is justified, and shows that balancing is rational.

Although Alexy notes that judgments are important elements in weighing and balancing, and that judgments presuppose standards not found in the law of balancing his view lacks the precision offered by the discussion of practical reflective insight. He is not able to account for the creativity and openness of practical reflective insights and judgments of value. Rather, his weight formula, by fixing the procedure and the criteria for choosing one side over another, is more likely to suppress relevant questions, practical reflective insights, and judgments of value that do not fit the structure. Using arithmetic to help explain balancing obscures and over-simplifies what is, in fact, a very complex and nuanced process that is fundamentally creative and open.

My critique above is consistent with work on balancing done by psychologists Amos Tversky, Shmuel Sattath, and Paul Slovic. Their view is that choice is contingent insofar as it depends on how a particular problem is framed and the procedure selected to resolve the conflict. They stress that in decision making "preferences are not simply read off some master list; they are constructed" (Tversky et al. 2004: 846). For them the crux of the problem of choosing among two or more alternatives is the difficulty of comparing options and trading off one competing factor against another. One procedure is to choose the option with what is considered to be the superior or most important attribute among numerous competing factors. This procedure would be appropriate when qualitative factors are relevant. You can imagine the situation where a judge is deliberating and has listed the pros and cons in favour of one party and the other. In the list there might be far more pros in favour of one side, but the other side wins because one factor in their favour was judged to be more important than all the other factors considered.

Another type of procedure would be appropriate when a quantitative assessment is required. When the factors being assessed are expressed in the same measurable units such as money, percent, or test scores it is possible to compare the factors associated with each alternative using the same scale. Their general point is that different types of choices call for different procedures and that these two different procedures are likely to result in different choices. In light of this work Alexy's

Weight Formula would be seen as too rigid and his mathematics of balancing would be seen as inappropriate because he uses a quantitative decision procedure when a qualitative procedure is called for.

More broadly, Amos Tversky and Daniel Kahneman take it for granted that decision making is rational, but they don't mean it in the narrow sense of rationality dominated by logic and "conceived as a normative model of an idealized decision maker" (Tversky and Kahneman 2004: 593). In fact, they argue for a description of the behavior of real people and conclude that the two accounts – normative and descriptive – cannot be reconciled because the actual behavior of people deviates so much from the expectations of normative models of decision making. My concern is that the weight formula has the same problem insofar as it deviates from explanations of deliberation and choice.

## 8.3 Expression Is Not Jusification

Marko Novak and Robert Alexy's analyses of weighing and balancing provoke questions about the relation between mental activities and expression and justification. It is worth stressing that the focus of my portrait of weighing and balancing has been on our mental operations, not on expression. But we are faced with a problem when we want to investigate the decision-making process of a judge. It is impossible for you or me to experience what another individual such as a judge saw and heard, the questions they asked, the insights they achieved, the judgments they made, the decisions they reached. We are not able to climb into someone's mind. Hence when investigating the decision-making process of another person we must initially focus on expression. We can recognize by spoken and written words the mental activities that the other person experienced and, by our own efforts, reproduce these mental activities in order to answer the same questions or solve the same problem the judge posed. Here expression is the raw material for analysis. The link between expression and the 13 mental elements is that particular types of expression correspond to, and depend on, particular mental activities. For instance, writing that "The rule should not be interpreted literally" depends on questions about What-should-be-done, practical reflective insights, and judgments of value. Further, we can attend to the decision-making procedure that we follow in order to answer the same question or solve the same problem as another person in order to understand, assess, and evaluate the decision-making process of the other person.

It is important to notice, and to distinguish between, the inner coherent perspective demanded of judges, which they occasionally reach, and the expression of that inner perspective in written words. There is a type of expression corresponding to options, judgments of value, and decisions. But judgments of value are distinct from their expression. The ground of whether one course of action is better than another resides in a practical reflective insight grasping the full implications of the alternatives. In this context written judicial opinions are elements in a problem-solving process which correspond to, and depend on, the mental activities that preceded them. Expression is a subsequent activity. It follows that the ground of the distinctiveness of legal reasoning does not lie in expression. Expression, then, should not be treated as the primary and dominating feature of legal reasoning. My point is that an analysis of deliberation provides a fuller context for studying weighing and balancing in the sense that justification and expression should be understood as distinct activities. Whether a legal decision is justified or not can now be seen as depending on a judge performing at his or her best – being attentive to human affairs, being intelligent, that is grasping unnoticed or unrealized possibilities, being reasonable, that is correctly judging what is true and false, being responsible in the sense of grasping the full implications of courses of action and choosing the best one. The problem with recent discussions of weighing and balancing, by Novak and Alexy for instance, is that they do not sufficiently distinguish between deliberation and expression, give priority to expression over the decision-making process, thereby neglecting the guts of legal reasoning, namely questions, practical reflective insights, and judgments of value.

In fact, when we talk about the spirit and the letter of the law we are noticing some sort of a difference between deliberation and expression. Eveline Feteris' discussion of whether a rule should be interpreted literally or in light of its purpose implicitly marks a distinction between deliberation and expression (Feteris 2008). The distinction is also evident when we ask whether the decisions of the nineteenth century judges are less justified than twenty-first century judges. The practice of presenting two or more majority opinions in some Supreme Court of Canada judgments also highlights a difference between deliberation and expression. Conflicting majority and minority opinions in a particular decision point to the fact that deliberation is a key part of legal decision-making. For instance, see *Alberta (Information and Privacy Commissioner) v. Alberta Teachers' Association* [2011] SCC 61 and *R v. Barros* [2011] SCC 51.

We can distinguish, in expression, between two extreme forms. There is the form that is patterned in accord with the discovery process. This patterning is illustrated by judges' talk of weighing and balancing. The aim of this type of expression is to provoke readers' questions, insights, judgments, and decisions. The other extreme is axiomatic expression and we can think of Neil MacCormick's portrait of first-order justification, Robert Alexy's portrait of subsumption, and Eveline Feteris' rational reconstruction of judicial decisions. However, these two types of presentation are not independent. The presentation via discovery tends to be inadequate insofar as identification and formulation have not been adequately pursued. Identification involves precision regarding the relevant data. Formulation involves working out the implications of insights and judgments and their relation to other insights and judgments in an effort to reach sufficient understanding, reasonable judgments, and adequate expression.

However, axiomatic presentation tends to be inadequate insofar as it ignores the educational level of readers. The primary purpose of this type of expression is to set forth clearly and exactly the terms, relations, and implications that proceed from understanding and to provide the materials for judgments and decisions. Such expression may reveal inattention, misunderstanding, unreasonable judgments, and irrational courses of action. The normal inadequacy of expression is summed up in the cautionary proverb "Don't jump to conclusions!" but the reality of deliberation, in fact, is that there is no other way to arrive at a judgment of value. In fact, we do not balance conflicting rights, principles, or interpretations. Rather, we choose one alternative or the other.

The more general issue provoked by an examination of deliberation is that many legal theorists discuss the problem of justification and expression without an adequate conception of the distinctions I have made here. In light of the distinction between mental activities and expression, the accepted ideal of legal justification *would seem* to be the ideal of adequate expression acceptable to the legal profession. But in the context of my portrait of deliberation what they should have in mind is the cluster of questions, insights, judgments that give rise to this adequate expression.

Not noticing the basic distinction between the performance of mental activities and expression gives rise to problems about expression and hides problems relating to the adequacy of courses of action and judgments of value themselves. Stressing the form of the expression that would be adequate and hence legally justified may lead a reader to dispense with relevant questions about the implications and suitability of the outcome of a case. Also, the focus on expression and the neglect of deliberation is unlikely to help judges achieve sufficiently suitable insights, judgments, decisions or to help readers towards understanding and evaluating judicial decisions.

To state it bluntly, options, practical reflective insights, and judgments of value are inner events. Their external expression is always fundamentally inadequate. A written decision cannot capture the educated attentiveness of an experienced judge, the ease with which a judge understands familiar situations, the way a judge homes in on the relevant aspects of unfamiliar situations, the feeling a judge has when someone is lying that is followed by just the right questions that expose the lies, and the unbiased and thorough evaluation of conflicting proposals by a judge reaching for a suitable outcome. Further, no matter what we say or write there will always be presuppositions. Expression, then, is never complete expression. Complete expression would require us to express everything we know. But we know that questions, practical reflective insights and judgments of value depend on previous practical reflective insights and judgments of value. And that those questions, practical reflective insights, and judgements of value depend on questions, practical reflective insights, and judgments of value and so on, and so on.

The adequacy of written expression corresponds to what a writer intends to communicate to a reader. A writer can communicate feelings, noise, thoughts, judgments, and decisions. The crucial point is that a writer's thoughts, judgments, decisions themselves are not passed on, transferred, or directly given to a reader. The reader must discover and achieve their own thoughts, judgments, decisions. The writer's words, may express judgments of value and decisions, but the words themselves are the raw materials, data for a reader's insights, judgments, decisions. In other words, the way a judicial decision is written does not mean it is justified. Justification, in this fuller context, is understood as the discovery of sufficient reasons for a course of action, and this process of discovery is part of the actual decision-making process. Testing or justifying practical reflective insights or judgments of value does not involve a further process that occurs over and above the actual decision-making process.

In this context legal theorists' efforts to define adequate expression in the legal context and to equate expression with justification miss the key point that emerges from analyzing deliberation, namely that the suitability of a legal decision rests primarily on the adequacy of mental events, not on the adequacy of the expression. What we would call justification is related to the mental activities comprising deliberation. To repeat myself, expressions themselves do not justify legal decisions. Moreover, the form of expression, whether rhetorical or axiomatic, simply invites or facilitates readers' insights and judgments. Expression, then, represents the *possibility* of a reader understanding and evaluating a legal decision.

For Eveline Feteris expression is not the same as justification. Her claim that the aim of a teleological-evaluative rational reconstruction is to make a judge's choices explicit is consistent with my perspective, and her strategy to reveal these choices is quite sensible. Revealing the underlying values and rules in a judicial decision is definitely a good idea. But her desire that a balancing rule should be drawn from one case makes sense only insofar as it is possible to find subsequent cases where "If *all* these circumstances occur and *all* these value judgments are made, then the outcome should be the same." Because practical reasoning depends on particular situations, calling for the creation of a prescriptive universal rule based on one case seems to be reaching beyond the limits of practical reasoning. But there is certainly nothing wrong with rules of thumb.

## References


Alexy, R. 2003a. Constitutional rights, balancing, and rationality. *Ratio Juris* 16(2): 131–140.

Alexy, R. 2003b. On balancing and subsumption. A structural comparison. *Ratio Juris* 16(4): 443–449.

Anderson, B. 1996. *Discovery in legal decision-making*, Law and philosophy library, vol. 21, 131–170. London: Kluwer Academic Publishers.

Barden, G. 1990. *After principles*. London: University of Notre Dame Press.

Feteris, E. 2008. The rational reconstruction of weighing and balancing on the basis of teleological-evaluative considerations in the justification of judicial decisions. *Ratio Juris* 21(4): 481–495.

Lonergan, B. 1992. *Insight: A study of human understanding*. Toronto: University of Toronto Press.

McShane, P. 1975. *Wealth of self, wealth of nations*. New York: Exposition Press.

Novak, M. 2010. Three models of balancing (in constitutional review). *Ratio Juris* 23(1): 101–112.

Tversky, A., and D. Kahneman. 2004. Rational choice and the framing of decisions. In *Preference, belief, and similarity: Selected writings of Amos Tversky*, ed. E. Shafir, 593–619. Cambridge: MIT Press.

Tversky, A., S. Sattath, and P. Slovic. 2004. Contingent weighing in judgment and choice. In *Preference, belief, and similarity: Selected writings of Amos Tversky*, ed. E. Shafir, 845–874. Cambridge: MIT Press.

# Chapter 9
# Construction or Reconstruction? On the Function of Argumentation in the Law

**Jaap Hage**

## 9.1 Introduction

Derek is a thief. In an electronics shop, he took away a mobile phone without paying and with the intention to keep it. For this reason, Derek is punishable, because there is a rule that makes thieves punishable.

Derek's punishability apparently comes into being, even if nobody were to pay any attention to it. This is from the legal point of view an easy case, and the rule that makes Derek punishable seems, so to speak, to 'apply itself'. The interpretation and application of the rule apparently were not only uncontroversial, but also 'automatic'. The legal outcome was seemingly already there, without any need for argumentation. If an argument is produced, its apparent function is merely to *reconstruct* the application, and possibly also the interpretation, of the rule that attaches its legal consequences to the case of Derek.

Not all cases are so easy. Take for instance the following case about hate speech. In 2010 the Dutch politician Geert Wilders was prosecuted for hate speech against Muslims. The issues at stake were both legal-technical and fundamental. The legal-technical issue was whether hate speech against the Islam counts as hate speech against Muslims. The fundamental issue was whether some members of society and in particular politicians should be allowed to express their opinion about other members of this society, or their religion, even if they do so in a manner that may be considered as insulting and may very well evoke hatred. Neither one of these issues has an easy answer and the case might very well be considered to be a hard one. Several arguments were adduced, pleading in different directions and the court of first instance discharged Geert Wilders (Rechtbank Amsterdam 13-1-2011).

J. Hage (✉)
Department of Foundations and Methods of Law, University of Maastricht, Maastricht, Netherlands
e-mail: jaap.hage@maastrichtuniversity.nl

C. Dahlman and E. Feteris (eds.), *Legal Argumentation Theory: Cross-Disciplinary Perspectives*, Law and Philosophy Library 102, DOI 10.1007/978-94-007-4670-1_9,

What matters for the present purposes is that in this case it is less likely that the legal outcome was already there, only to be discovered by means of an argument that reconstructs the operation of legal rules. In such a hard case, it seems that the outcome may go anywhere, and depends strongly on the arguments that are actually adduced in the legal debate. It appears that the legal consequences of the case are *constructed* by means of the arguments, and not merely reconstructed. The legal consequences of a case would then be what the best (possible[1]) legal argument says they are.

Apparently the distinction between easy cases and hard cases signifies a distinction between two kinds of law. In easy cases the law would consist of self-applying rules that 'automatically' generate legal consequences for cases. Legal arguments then merely have the function to reconstruct legal consequences which are already there. In hard cases, the law cannot operate in this independent fashion. It is necessary to produce arguments to determine the legal consequences of a case. This determination is not merely epistemic, aimed at obtaining knowledge of independently existing legal consequences. It is constructive: the legal consequences are created by means of the argumentation.

If the distinction between easy and hard cases is really so important, it has also implications for the role of legal argumentation. In easy cases, the role of argumentation would epistemic, aimed at discovering the legal facts. In hard cases, the role of argumentation would be constitutive. Argumentation determines the legal consequences of cases and standards for legal argumentation would therefore have a role that is on the same footing as substantive legal rules and principles.

Going by the examples, the view that there are two different roles for legal argumentation seems attractive. When we encounter an 'easy' case, it seems obvious that the legal consequences are already there, only to be recognized by the observer. An argument is not really necessary, but may be useful to give an explicit justification of an obvious conclusion. When we encounter a 'hard' case, the proper legal consequences are – by definition – hard to see, and we need arguments to determine which legal consequences should be attached to the case. Notice the change in terminology: the consequences are not there yet, but have still to be attached to the case. Moreover, it seems that we, humans, are the ones attaching the legal consequences to the case, not the independently operating law.

Attractive as this twofold division between easy and hard cases and the different roles for legal reasoning may seem at an intuitive level, it becomes problematic on second thought. Is there really a sharp difference between easy and hard cases, with different roles for legal reasoning, legal reasoners and the law? And if there is, how can 'the law' know that it must attach legal consequences to a case independently. Can 'the law' recognize easy cases? Do easy cases wear the label 'easy' on their sleeves? The use of this metaphor already illustrates that there is something seriously wrong with this way of looking at easy and hard cases. The adoption of legal constructivism for both easy and hard cases restores the desired uniformity in

[1]The relevancy of this insertion of 'possible' will become clear in Sect. 9.4.

legal reasoning, but at a cost. How can we explain on a uniform constructivist model the difference in experience when we have to deal with easy and with hard cases? This leads us to the central question of this paper.

The central question with which this paper deals is *whether the constructivist view of legal argumentation is correct, and if so, whether it is only correct for hard cases or that it also holds for easy cases*. In the next section this question will be elaborated and to that purpose some useful distinctions will be introduced.

## 9.2 Legal Constructivism

Amongst others through the influence of Dworkin, who proposed a theory of law according to which legal judgments are the result of constructive interpretation (Dworkin 1986b, chapters 2 and 7), constructivist theories of the law have become quite popular (e.g. for the Netherlands Smith 2009 and Soeteman 2010).

In Dworkin's constructivist theory of law, two aspects of constructivism can be distinguished. First, Dworkin offers an account of how to arrive at legal judgments. This is through constructing a theory of law which must on the one hand fit with existing legal materials such as case law and legislation and which must on the other hand be substantively right (Dworkin 1986b, chapter 7). Second, Dworkin considers the judgments thus arrived at as law, *for the reason that they are part of such a constructed theory*. Legal reasoning is in the view of Dworkin not a way to arrive at legal judgments which were true for some other reason such as correspondence with some kind of legal reality. It is precisely the other way round: legal judgments are true because they are the outcome of a correct construction. Dworkin (1986b, 225) states it as follows:

> According to law as integrity, propositions of law are true if they figure in or follow from the principles of justice, fairness, and procedural due process that provide the best constructive interpretation of the community's legal practice.

### 9.2.1 *Types of Procedure*

If the legal consequences of cases are connected to legal arguments, it is important to distinguish between two different ways in which this connection may be viewed. Here, the Rawlsian distinction between perfect, imperfect and pure procedures is relevant (Rawls 1972, 86). In all three cases there is a procedure which leads to a particular outcome. The question is how the correctness of the outcome relates to the nature of the procedure. In the case of perfect and imperfect procedures, the correctness of the possible outcome is given independently.

A perfect procedure is such that it is guaranteed to lead to this correct outcome. An example of such a perfect procedure is to divide a cake in equal pieces by using a well-functioning balance on which pieces of an equal weight are measured out.

Whether the pieces are equal does not depend on weighing them, but weighing with a perfect balance, if properly conducted, is guaranteed to lead to equal pieces.

This guarantee of a correct outcome is lacking in the case of imperfect procedures. A criminal trial, set up to determine whether a suspect is guilty, is an example of such an imperfect procedure. Whether the suspect is guilty is a fact that does not depend on the procedure. The criminal procedure is defined – we may hope – in such a way that the chance of a correct outcome is optimized, but there is no guarantee that the verdict of the judge or jury will be true to the facts.

In case of a pure procedure, the correctness of the result depends on the proper execution of the procedure. More in particular, the correctness is not defined independent of the procedure. A good example is a lottery. Which ticket wins the prize is determined by the drawing. There is no independent standard for the rightness of the outcome (e.g. the poorest ticket holder should win the prize). As long as the drawing of the winning ticket was performed in accordance with the rules of the lottery, any outcome is correct, and it is correct *because* it is the outcome of the correctly performed drawing.

The distinction between on the one hand perfect and imperfect procedures, and on the other hand pure procedures, has implications for whether a procedure has really to be executed or whether a 'simulation' is equally good. A nice example of such a simulation is provided by Rawls' contract theory. Rawls' two principles of justice would derive their status, not from their content, but from the fact that they *would be* chosen under the ideal circumstances represented by means of the original position and the veil of ignorance. It is not necessary that the principles are actually chosen. If we look at Rawls' argument in *A Theory of Justice*, we see that it is based on a simulation of a decision making procedure. Rawls argues that people in the original position *would* choose the principles he proposes, and that would sufficiently justify those principles. That this simulation suffices, shows that Rawls considers his principles to reflect justice independently of their being chosen. The hypothetical contract merely aims to show that it would be rational to choose the two principles of justice. It is a case of a perfect procedure. Contrast this with a real contract, which is binding, not because its content is rational, but because the contract parties really agreed to it. Real contracts represent pure procedures, while hypothetical contracts provide perfect or imperfect procedures.

As we will see, it is important in connection with legal constructivism whether the role of legal argumentation is to arrive at conclusions that are independently correct (or incorrect), or that argumentation, if properly performed, determines what the legal consequences of a case are.

### 9.2.2 Degrees of Objectivity

For a proper understanding of the different versions of constructivism it is also useful to consider a related issue, namely the objectivity of law. In this connection, Leiter (2002) has distinguished between four versions of objectivity or the lack thereof, which are here slightly adapted to the purposes of this paper:

- *Subjectivism* assumes that whether a legal consequence obtains depends on the view of the cognizer (the person who holds a belief about the legal consequence).
- *Minimal objectivism* assumes that whether a legal consequence obtains depends on views held within the group of cognizers (e.g. the officials of a particular legal system).
- *Modest objectivism* assumes that whether a legal consequence obtains depends on the views which would under appropriate or ideal circumstances (e.g. full rationality and maximal knowledge of the facts) be held by the group of cognizers.
- *Strong objectivism* holds that whether a legal consequence obtains does not depend on anyone's views.

Strong objectivism is generally adopted with regard to hard 'physical' facts, such as the fact that the North Sea borders on the Belgian shore, or that Mount Everest is the highest mountain. If we reason to arrive at such facts, the reasoning is purely reconstructive, because the facts in no way depend on it.

Modest objectivism is an attractive view with regard to the outcome of mathematical puzzles, such as: What is the first derivative of the formula '$x^2 + 2x - 3$'?[2] Most people (with the exception of so-called 'Platonists') do not believe that the derivative of this formula exists somewhere 'outside' just like physical objects. Neither do they believe that the proper outcome depends on the beliefs of a single persons or a group of persons. It does depend on what they would believe if they were purely rational.

Minimal objectivism seems an attractive view with regard to the existence of social phenomena, such as the leaders of informal groups, and the existence of customary law or other social rules in the sense of Hart (1994, 55–57).

Pure subjectivism, finally, seems the most appropriate view with regard to phenomena which are considered to be just a matter of taste, such as whether cauliflower is more tasteful than spinach, or whether 'Layla' by Derek & the Dominoes is a better piece of music than Bach's 'Erbarme Dich'.

Constructivism seems to be particularly relevant for those facts to which the modestly objectivist approach is applicable. The appropriate or ideal circumstances under which judgments about these facts can be given are then specified in terms of standards for good argumentation. These standards determine what are good arguments, and maybe[3] also what is the best possible argument and what one should believe if one were purely rational and omniscient.

### 9.2.3 What Is at Stake?

Given the distinctions made in the previous subsections, it is possible to formulate the central issues of this paper more precisely.

[2]'$2x + 2$' is the correct answer.

[3]But see Sect. 4.2.

The first issue is whether legal argumentation is aimed at reconstructing legal consequences which are already 'there', or whether it aims at constructing the legal consequences. This is essentially the distinction between imperfect procedures ('perfect' procedures would be unrealistic) and pure procedures. In case the procedure were to be imperfect, the independently existing legal consequences would probably exist in a mixture of the minimally and modestly objective fashion.

The second issue arises if legal argumentation is constructive, aimed at creating legal consequences rather than merely reconstructing them. In that case it must be established exactly which argumentation creates the legal consequences. In this connection two questions arise:

1. Which arguments are sufficiently 'legal' to lead potentially to legal consequences?
2. If there are sufficiently legal arguments which lead to incompatible conclusion, which of them determines the legal consequences of a case?

Both questions ask for standards to distinguish between arguments. The one asks for a standard to distinguish between legal arguments (which are relevant for legal consequences) and non-legal ones (which are not relevant). The second requires a standard to determine which of two or more conflicting legal arguments determines the legal consequences. What is the 'best' legal argument?

If there is to be any objectivity in this approach to legal reasoning, it must be of the modest kind, because what the legal consequences of a case are depends on the application of standards, and therefore on some idealized reasoning procedure.

## 9.3 Reconstruction

In the example about Derek the thief, it seems that the argument is merely a reconstruction of the legal consequences that came about independently, and of the rule application that brought these consequences about. This view of the relation between legal arguments and legal consequences sits together well with the so-called institutional theory of law.[4]

### *9.3.1 The Institutional Theory of Law*

The institutional theory of law assumes that the law is a part of social reality, that is characterized by it that legal entities and facts are the result of the application

[4] There are many expositions of the institutional theory of law (e.g. MacCormick and Weinberger 1986, Lagerspetz 1995, La Torre 1999, Ruiter 1993, 2001, and MacCormick 2007), and the following cannot be more than a very brief summary of the main ideas behind them.

of rules. We are all familiar with the physical world. It consists of a large number of 'things'. These things have characteristics and stand in relations to each other. That things have these characteristics and stand in these relations to each other, are *facts*. The facts in the physical world obtain to a large extent independent of human beings. This is the domain of Leiter's objectivism. The social world, or social reality, does not only depend on what is physically the case, but also – and to a large extent – on what people believe and accept about the social world. A legal example would be that some rules (those of customary law) exist as legal rules because sufficiently many people that participate in a legal system accept these rules as legal rules and believe that others do the same. This is the domain of Leiter's minimal objectivism.

In modern societies, however, most legal rules derive their existence and status as *legal* rules from being made in accordance with rules that specify how to make legal rules. They exemplify a second way in which facts in social reality can obtain, namely through the operation of rules which exist in social reality, including legal rules. The part of social reality that is the result of the application of rules may be called the *institutionalized part of social reality*. Typical phenomena within the institutionalized part of social reality are money, promises, the law and everything created through the law, such as officials, legally defined organizations, contracts, last wills, permits, and most legal rules.[5]

According to the institutional theory of law, large parts – if not all – of the law exist in the institutional mode, that is as the result of the application of rules. Although it is seldom formulated explicitly, the rules which create institutional reality are taken to apply 'automatically'. Given the rule which makes thieves punishable and the fact that Derek is a thief, Derek is punishable. This is a fact in the institutionalized part of social reality, because the rule attaches this status to Derek as he is a thief. This happens, even if nobody knows that Derek is a thief. In that case, Derek will be punishable without anybody knowing it.

Notice that the facts in institutional reality have an objectivity that is in part minimally and in part modestly objective in Leiter's sense. They are minimally objective to the extent that the rules which make the institutional facts possible must in the end be based on collective acceptance. They are modestly objective because the operation of these rules, if reflected in the human mind, is a matter of logical thinking. It would be misleading however, to think that according to the institutional theory of law legal consequences depend on logical thinking on the basis of rules. The rules are assumed to operate independently, and the arguments merely mimic the operation of the rules.[6]

'Correct' arguments lead to conclusions that are true independently, as the result of self-applying rules. If there are standards for legal reasoning, these standards might in theory be validated by checking whether their application – that is if the

[5]Extensive discussions about the mode of existence of social reality can be found in, amongst others, Searle 1995 and Tuomela 2002.

[6]Rules are taken here to include legal principles, rights and whatever other entities which may lead to legal consequences.

reasoning was correct – leads to true conclusions. In theory, because there is no way to check whether the conclusions of legal arguments are true other than by producing another legal argument. Notice, however, that on the institutional theory of law this impossibility of an independent check does not imply that the argument determines the legal consequences. The problem is 'merely' epistemic: there is no other test for the truth of propositions about legal consequences than a legal argument.[7] In theory, a legal argument may therefore lead to a false conclusion about the legal consequences. Legal reasoning is on this view an imperfect procedure.

### 9.3.2 *Intermezzo: Dworkin's 'One Right Answer' – Thesis*

In his early work, Dworkin (1978, chapter 13 and 331–335; 1986a, chapter 5) famously defended the thesis that (almost) every case has one right answer, even if legal experts do not agree about what it might be.

The most likely explanation of this view is that the legal rules, principles, and rights in a sense apply themselves to cases and generate legal consequences, and this makes these rules etc. into reasons why the cases have the legal consequences they have. Moreover, the self-application of the rules etc. can be reconstructed mentally and that leads to arguments about what the legal consequences may be. The best possible argument exactly reconstructs the operation of the rules etc. and therefore leads to the correct conclusion. If a case is hard, it is not simple to discover what the correct argument is and therefore also not what the right answer is. But since the rules etc. apply themselves, the argument is not necessary for their operation and therefore not for the legal consequences either. Obviously, this interpretation sits well together with the institutional theory of law and with ontological constructivism.

### 9.3.3 *Preliminary Conclusion*

Because there does not exist a test to determine whether a conclusion about legal consequences is true, other than another legal argument, there exists always uncertainty about the conclusions of legal arguments. In this sense, all cases are hard cases, because one can never be certain that one knows the truth about the legal consequences of the case. The 'best' that can be obtained is a theory about the legal consequences that is widely shared. But even that is no guarantee for the legal truth. In theory it is always possible that the best argument until now will be

[7]It should be realized that this not exceptional in epistemology. There is, in the end, no other test for the correctness of observational beliefs than the performance of a new observation, with as result another observational belief.

improved upon. Whether that is the case can, however, only be 'determined' on the basis of more argumentation. Even if it were the case that legal rules apply 'automatically', there is no way to establish this, and neither is there a way to discover the results. Therefore the idea that law is self-applying and that legal argumentation is merely reconstruction is at best an assumption that can neither be verified nor falsified.

## 9.4 Ontological Constructivism

As we could see in the previous section, the institutional theory of law leads to a number of unattractive consequences such as legal consequences about which we can never be certain and legal rules which operate without anybody noticing it. These consequences should make us reluctant to accept the institutional theory of law, even for easy cases. So it may be worthwhile to have a closer look at legal constructivism, and see if and under which circumstances that might work. We will do so in two steps. First we will consider the theory that the law is what the best possible legal argument says it is. This view will, for reasons to be discussed later, be called *ontological (legal) constructivism*. It will turn out that the plausibility of ontological constructivism presupposes that the law forms a closed domain. That the law forms a closed domain is not above dispute. Therefore we will consider in the next section *procedural (legal) constructivism*, the view that the law is what the best actual argument says it is.

If the law is what the best possible legal arguments says it is, we must be able to identify all possible legal arguments, and we must have a standard to compare these arguments in order to determine what is the best one. These demands are not easy to satisfy, but to give an impression of what is at stake we will have a brief look at a field in which both demands are satisfied. That field is the constructivist version of mathematics and logic.

### *9.4.1 Constructivism in Mathematics and Logic*

Mathematical 'Platonists' assume that the mathematical facts somehow exist objectively, only to be discovered by human reason.[8] Constructivists, on the contrary, assume that mathematical objects, such as the smallest prime number above 10.000.000, only exist if they can be constructed. Moreover, mathematical facts only obtain to the extent that they can be proven from a set of axioms that does not include the law of the excluded middle. In this connection it is important that the proof is given by applying the inference rules of the logical system to the axioms

[8]See http://plato.stanford.edu/entries/platonism-mathematics/ (last consulted on October 28, 2011).

of the system and to the theorems that were already derived from the axioms. In particular it is *not allowed* to prove a theorem by means of a *reductio ad absurdum*.[9]

According to logical constructivism, a sentence is a logical truth if and only if it can be, or has been, proven from the axioms of the system. The difference between these two possibilities will turn out to be crucially important. A proof in the form of derivation of a theorem from axioms is a kind of argument, and a theorem is only a theorem if, *and because*, it is the conclusion of such an argument. Under logical constructivism, logical truths derive their status as such from the fact that they are the conclusions of valid arguments with premises which are axioms. The function of arguments under logical constructivism is not merely to show that a sentence is a theorem of the logical system; they *make* sentences into theorems. Together the axioms and the inference rules determine what are the theorems (logical truths) of the system.[10] There is no independent standard, apart from the axioms and inference rules, which determines what are logical truths. Notice that this standard deals with two issues at the same time. In the first place it separates correct[11] mathematical and logical arguments from incorrect ones. And in the second place it selects the best arguments, because any correct answer leads to a true conclusion. So there cannot be competition between stronger and weaker arguments. All correct arguments are equally strong, and if their conclusions conflict, the logical system is inconsistent.

However, there is no guarantee that we can check whether a sentence is a logical truth if we do not have the argument yet. Maybe a correct argument with this sentence as conclusion *can* be constructed, but as long as this has not been done, we cannot be sure. The question therefore arises what we need for a logical truth under constructivism. Does it suffice that the axioms and the inference rules of the system make it possible to construct a sound argument, or should we require that the sound argument has actually been produced?

The literature on constructivist (intuitionist) logic is not very clear about this issue (Van Dalen 2001, 224–227), but there is no need for us to make a choice. We can distinguish between *ontological constructivism*, according to which a sentence is a logical truth if it is possible to construct a proof of it, and *procedural constructivism*, according to which there must be an actual proof for every logical truth.[12]

---

[9]Such a proof consists in showing that if a sentence were true, an inconsistency follows. Since an inconsistency cannot be true, the sentence cannot be true and *therefore its negation must be true*. An example of such a derivation is that the sentence ‘A and not-A’ is inconsistent and can therefore not be true. Therefore its negation, either not A or not-not-A (the same as A) must be true. In this way the logical truth of the disjunction A or not-A can be proven, without even knowing whether A or not-A is true.

[10]That axioms and inference rules have similar roles can also be seen from the fact that one and the same logic can be characterised both by means of axioms and inference rules and by only inference rules (a larger number of them, then).

[11]The informal term ‘correct’ is here meant to express the same as ‘sound’ in more precise logical work.

[12]The reason why the first version is called *ontological* constructivism is that it relies on the range of *possible* arguments. The reason why the second version is called *procedural* constructivism is that it relies on the arguments that were actually produced.

### 9.4.2 The Law as a Closed Domain

In the introductory section legal constructivism was introduced as the view that the legal consequences of a case are what the best (possible) legal argument says they are. We are now in a position to recognize that 'the best legal argument' would refer to the procedural version of legal constructivism, while 'the best possible legal argument' would refer to the ontological version. Following up on the discussion of constructivism in mathematics and logic, we will now first consider the possibility that the law is what the best possible legal argument says it is. If the law on a particular issue is what the best possible argument about this issue says it is, there must be a best possible argument.

The phrase 'best possible argument' has two presuppositions. One presupposition is that arguments can be compared in order to determine what the best one is; it will be discussed in Sect. 9.5.2. The other presupposition is that it is possible to identify the 'possible arguments'. Is this a reasonable presupposition if we are not dealing with logic, but with the law?

Only if the law is a closed system in the sense that the number of rules, rights and principles etc. that can be used in legal arguments is finite,[13] and if the number of facts that characterize a case is finite too,[14] the number of possible legal arguments can be finite. Although both the assumptions that the law is a closed system and that the number of case facts is finite are dubitable, it is instructive to see why the combination of these two assumptions leads to the possibility to identify the set of possible arguments.

To show that there is a finite and identifiable set of possible arguments, a few additional assumptions will be made. These assumptions are there for expository purposes only and dropping them would not lead to a different conclusion, but merely to a more complicated demonstration.[15] The additional assumptions in question are that the law consists of rules only and that all arguments are of the 'detachment' or 'modus ponens' – type, that is of the form 'if A then B; A, therefore B'.

If these two assumptions are made, any argument that answers a legal question can be seen as having a tree-structure. This will be illustrated by means of a very

[13]It is assumed here that legal arguments are arguments in which legal rules, principles, rights etc. are employed. Some support for this assumption can be found in, for instance, Alexy 1978, 283/4. What is needed for the finiteness of the number of legal arguments is that this test is exclusive, and that there are no other legal arguments. That is not what Alexy had in mind.

[14]This assumption also covers 'rules' by means of which case facts can be derived from other case facts, such as the 'rule' that if X takes away something that belongs to Y, and if X and Y are not the same person, then X takes away something that does not belong to him or her. In other words: so-called 'world knowledge' is taken to be included in the set of case facts, and is therefore also temporarily assumed to be finite.

[15]The demonstration would for instance have to take defeasible argumentation into account. That would be more complicated, but also in that case a finite set of premises leads to a finite and identifiable set of arguments. See Hage 2005, chapter 8.

simple example. The issue at stake is whether Derek was punishable after he took away the mobile phone from the electronics shop. Any argument concerning this issue would have as its conclusion either that Derek was punishable or that he was not.[16] Such an argument would have two premises: (the validity of) a legal rule with this conclusion and a conjunction of (descriptions of) case facts. Both these premises must either be included in the finite set of rules, respectively the finite set of case facts, or must be derivable from them. Any argument by means of which the premises can be derived must have the same structure, and therefore have premises that are either in the finite set of premises or are derivable from this set. In the end, any argument with the conclusion that Derek is punishable, or that he is not, will have a tree structure with as a root this conclusion and with branches ending in premises that can be found in the finite set of premises. On the assumption that all arguments have the form of a detachment, the set of arguments that meet these two conditions is finite, and this finite set contains all the possible arguments. This means that if there is a standard for comparing these arguments, it is possible to identify the best *possible* argument. And then legal constructivism in its ontological version would be a viable option.

However, the assumption that the law is a closed domain is rather controversial. It seems that it can only be defended on some variant of legal positivism according to which the law must exist as a matter of social fact. And even then the additional assumption must be made that there is only one correct interpretation of social reality, because if more interpretations are possible, the arguments concerning these interpretation can draw from an in principle unlimited set of premises, therewith opening the domain of arguments that seemed to be closed by the assumption that the law exists as a matter of social fact. In fact, there are many reasons why the law would not be a closed domain, including that:

- there may be exceptions to rules which cannot be listed on beforehand;
- sometimes legal rules conflict without there being a clear standard for prioritizing the one above the other;
- the law sometimes contains 'gaps', where a gap is to be understood as a kind of case to which the law seems not to connect any legal consequences although it should have a legal consequence[17];
- the terms used in legal rules have a fuzzy scope of application (actually a special case of a gap, because the law does not answer the question when a term is applicable);
- legal rules are sometimes 'open-ended' in the sense that they implicitly refer to evaluative standards (also a special case of a gap);
- the law contains standards (e.g. legal principles) which cannot be identified by means of their pedigree (Dworkin 1978, chapter 2).

[16]In theory a third possibility might exist, namely that the law does not answer the question at issue. However, in case of punishability it is plausible to assume that a criminal suspect is not punishable if it cannot be shown that he is.

[17]This is only a reason why the law would be 'open' on the assumption that there is law where there is a gap, but that this law cannot be identified easily on the basis of, for instance, pedigree.

It seems therefore useful to see what the implications are for the viability of legal constructivism if the assumption is dropped that the law is a closed domain. If we assume that the law is 'open', it is unclear how there could be a best possible legal argument. Even if one disregards the question whether there is a standard by means of which arguments can be compared, there is the impossibility to determine which legal arguments are possible. Possibility can only exist in the presence of constraints which draw the borderline between what is possible and what is impossible. If the law is an open domain, in theory any argument might be presented as a legal argument. Therefore one cannot identify which arguments are possible, let alone which of the possible arguments is the best one. As a consequence, *ontological legal constructivism as the view that the law on an issue is what the best possible legal argument says it is, is not a viable view.*

## 9.5 Procedural Constructivism

It seems that it is either one of two. Either the law is closed in the sense that there exists a finite number of valid legal rules, principles etc. Then it is possible to identify the possible legal arguments. Or the law is an open domain in the sense that the set of valid legal rules, principles etc. is not finite. Then it is not possible to identify the possible legal arguments. However, there is an intermediate position between these two assumptions and their conclusions. This intermediate position can be found by abandoning a static, a-temporal perspective on the law, which assumes that the possible legal arguments can be generated 'automatically'. Then it is possible to allow that the law is open in the sense that there is no finite, given set of true legal premises, and still to work with a finite set of arguments. The crucial step in this connection is not to work with all possible legal arguments, but with all *actual* legal arguments. This means that we take the step from ontological constructivism to procedural constructivism.

### *9.5.1 The Erlanger Approach*

The inspiration for taking this step can be found in the ideas of the so-called Erlanger Schule, and in particular the work of Schwemmer and Lorenzen (1973). In this work, justificatory arguments – and this would apply to legal arguments as well as to other justificatory arguments – are not interpreted in a timeless way as structured sets of propositions, but as actual contributions to a discussion. Any such argument must have premises. Instead of assuming that these premises must be traced back to a given set of premises which are above criticism, Schwemmer and Lorenzen proposed the idea that these premises would just be assumed to be true or justified, unless they were disputed. Notice that this assumption only holds for the premises of arguments that were somehow really produced; not to all possible arguments, however possibility might be defined in this connection. Moreover, the disputation of premises must be real argument steps too, and not merely possible disputations.

Such an approach to arguments presupposes that there are rules that specify which arguments can be adduced, and how and under which circumstances arguments may be disputed. For instance, it may be forbidden to dispute the truth of premises which were also used in earlier arguments by the person disputing them.[18] These rules only specify which argument 'moves' are *possible*, however. The defining characteristic of the 'Erlanger approach' is that the real argument moves have to be made in *actual* argumentation. That the argumentation must be 'actual' does not necessarily mean that the arguments must be formulated explicitly and communicated to another person or auditory than the person who made the argument. It is possible that arguments are merely mental, merely were thought of by a person who is wondering which conclusion to draw. The crucial point, however, is that the number and nature of the arguments is determined by events that actually took place, and not by a pre-given set of premises and rules that specify which arguments can be formulated on the basis of these premises. It will not do that an argument can be generated by, for instance, a computer program; it must somehow actually be produced.

The demand that arguments are somehow actually produced makes that for any legal question there will be a finite set of actual arguments that plead for or against a particular answer to that question. As a consequence, the 'Erlanger approach' resembles the assumption that the law forms a closed domain as far as the issue is concerned whether it is possible to identify all the arguments. It resembles the assumption that the law is open, however, by allowing the introduction in the argumentative process of any premise. On beforehand, there is no fixed and finite set of possible legal premises, but at any moment in time there is a fixed, limited set of valid arguments that were actually adduced. This set may be empty.

The 'Erlanger approach' does not solve the problem posed by the assumption that the law is an open system, the problem that there is no set of possible legal arguments and that it is therefore impossible to identify the best *possible* legal argument. The reason is that the 'Erlanger approach' does not lead to a set of possible legal arguments but merely to a finite set of *actual* legal arguments. Does this mean that the 'Erlanger approach' cannot defend legal constructivism against the criticism that the open nature of law allows an infinite set of possible legal arguments and in that way makes legal constructivism an impossible enterprise? Yes and no. The criticism that the open nature of law allows an infinite set of possible legal arguments still stands and if one assumes that the law is an open domain, legal constructivism in its ontological form cannot be maintained. However, the 'Erlanger approach' suggests how legal constructivism can be amended in such a way that it is compatible with the open nature of law. On this amended version legal constructivism would be the position that the law on an issue is what the best actual legal argument on this issue says it is. This is a variant of procedural legal constructivism.

[18]Such rules, which govern legal 'dialogues', are discussed in Lodder 1999.

### 9.5.2 Comparing Arguments

The amended, procedural, version of legal constructivism has an additional advantage, namely that it allows the comparison of arguments, even where the premises seem to be incommensurable. As was noted above, legal constructivism in its ontological form makes two assumptions. One is that there is a finite set of possible legal arguments; the other that there is a criterion at the hand of which it can be established which of those arguments is the best one. By amending legal constructivism as proposed, the first assumption has been turned into the more likely one that there is a finite set of *actual* legal arguments. This leaves the second assumption open for discussion: how is it possible to select the best argument, given a finite set of arguments?

Rather than discussing this in abstract, I will give an example that illustrates how the comparison of arguments can be handled.[19] The example is the hate speech case about Geert Wilders, mentioned in the introduction. The issue is whether Geert Wilders should be punishable for his insulting utterances about the Islam. To simplify the issues at stake, I will assume that there are two reasons. One reason, pleading for punishability, is that the utterances insult Muslims through their religion and that they evoked hatred between groups within the Dutch population. The other reason, pleading against punishability is that Geert Wilders expressed his opinion, and that the freedom of expression is a fundamental right which deserves even extra protection in the case of politicians. So we have two arguments, one pleading for, and the other pleading against punishability. How can we decide which is the stronger?[20]

It has been argued that in such cases there is no common scale on which the two values (on the one hand no conflicts between population groups and on the other hand freedom of expression) can be balanced (Chang 1997, 1). In a dialogical setting, in which parties can adduce arguments against each other's positions, there may be a way out however. It is for instance possible that the party arguing against punishability adduces the argument that freedom of expression is, in this particular case, more important than the avoidance of hate speech. If this argument is not attacked by the other side, it stands and a balance has been struck between the two values. If the other side does not immediately accept this additional premise, a dialogue about this premise may be started and it is not excluded on beforehand that this dialogue will end with a conclusion about the relative weight of the two values in this particular case. If that happens, the dialogue about the punishability of Wilders comes to an argued end. If that does not happen, the case remains undecided, and there is no 'best' argument.

---

[19]An abstract discussion can be found in my paper *Dialectical Models in Artificial Intelligence and Law* (Hage 2005, chapter 8) and in the literature mentioned there.

[20]For the sake of easy exposition, I assume that these two arguments are the only relevant ones.

The point of having the dialogue is that even where a common scale is originally lacking, the parties in the dialogue *may* come to an agreement about a criterion to determine which value prevails under the given circumstances. In other words, even where a common scale seemed to be lacking, it may come to be recognized. That is the advantage of real dialogues over the automatic generation of arguments on the basis of a fixed set of premises. In the course of a dialogue, the standard for determining what the best actual argument is can be introduced on the fly. If such a standard is already available, or can be introduced, for all the arguments that deal with the issue at stake, it is at least in theory possible to determine what the best actual argument is. If such a standard cannot be found, there is no best argument and there are – on a constructivist approach – no legal consequences.

Notice, by the way, that in this example the comparison of arguments has been reduced to a (potential) discussion about one of the premises of the argument, namely about the premise that the one reason outweighs the other reason. This means that the 'Erlanger approach' is not only suitable to solve problems about the premises of arguments, but also to deal with the comparison of arguments. The 'trick' is to move the comparison of arguments from the meta-level (a relation between arguments) to the object level (a proposition about the relative weight of reasons). This is not the place to go into details,[21] but it seems in general possible to treat the information that is necessary for the comparison of arguments as premises for arguments. As a consequence the problem of comparing arguments is 'reduced' to the problem of reaching agreement about the premises for justificatory arguments.

### 9.5.3 *Reification of the Law*

A procedural approach to justification and to the determination of legal consequences has a major advantage. It is that the limitation to actually adduced arguments avoids the problem of potentially infinitely many arguments that is the consequence of the open nature of the law. There is a corresponding drawback however, and that has to do with the fact that there is no guarantee that all plausible arguments for or against a position will actually be adduced. Let us return to the easy case about Derek the thief, who stole a cellular phone from an electronics shop. It seems obvious that he is punishable. Suppose, however, that Derek is only an eight year old boy who was pushed by his father to steal the thing. If this fact were adduced in a legal procedure it would probably change the conclusion from the punishability of Derek to his non-punishability. But what if it is not adduced? Would that mean that Derek is still punishable, or merely that his punishability is wrongly assumed to have been proven? Another, rather theoretical, possibility is that nobody thinks of it that Derek is punishable, not even Derek himself. Would that mean that Derek is not punishable, or merely that his punishability has not been shown and is unknown?

[21]More details can be found in Hage 1997, and in chapter 3 of Hage 2005.

Somehow the view that legal consequences are automatically attached to cases and that legal argument is merely a reconstruction of these independently existing legal consequences remains attractive. In hard cases, like the hate speech one, it has lost its attraction however. There are two ways to deal with this seeming inconsistency. The one is to assume that the law works differently in easy cases and in hard cases: it attaches legal consequences automatically to easy cases, and in hard cases it waits for the arguments that are actually adduced. The other one is to explain why the law seems to deal differently with easy and with hard cases, although this is not really the case. The first way to deal with the inconsistency is not attractive, if only because it requires that we can distinguish between easy cases and hard cases. Moreover, this distinction should be made on another ground than that the law operates differently in easy cases than in hard cases, because otherwise the argument would be circular. A convincing way to distinguish between easy cases and hard ones has not been offered yet,[22] and therefore the second way to deal with the inconsistency is the more attractive one.

How can we explain that the legal consequences of a case depend on the actual arguments adduced about them, while it seems that the law attaches the legal consequences automatically in easy cases? Tentatively I want to mention the inclination in modern legal thinking to reify the law. In Roman law, legal reasoning was less aimed at establishing legal positions such as owing an object, or being punishable, but more at the possibility to get things legally done. The question was less whether particular behavior was punishable than whether an action aimed at punishment would succeed. This action-oriented style of thinking is still more prominent in the common law tradition than in the civil law tradition, but also in the common law tradition there is a tendency towards reification of the law and of legal consequences.

A consequence of this style of thinking is that the question 'Should Derek be punished?', which is future-oriented, is easily transformed into 'Is Derek punishable?' which is past-oriented. Moreover, where the former question is easily interpreted in terms of decision making, which must be done by individual persons or bodies of persons, the latter question is more naturally interpreted as dealing with a matter of fact which must be the same for everybody. And if it is to be a matter of fact whether Derek is punishable, this fact must have been brought about and then the rule which made Derek punishable must have applied 'automatically'.

This reifying style of thinking may be useful to create a body of law which is intersubjective and can function as a social order that creates the same expectancies about future behavior in most of its participants. It is less useful, and possibly even confusing, when it comes to thinking about the nature of law and the operation of legal rules. It creates the appearance that rules operate 'automatically' and that legal arguments merely reconstruct legal consequences which were already there.

[22]In an earlier paper (Hage et al. 1994) I have tried to define the distinction in procedural terms, and as will be clear from this paper, I still believe this to be the right approach. The details of that earlier paper appear unsatisfactory me now.

This appearance is deceptive. Even in easy cases, legal rules are used by human reasoners to attach legal consequences to cases.[23] It is in actual legal arguments that the law is created, and it is only because of a reifying way to look at the law that the impression is created that the legal consequences were already there.

## 9.6 Conclusion

The central question of this paper is whether and to what extent legal constructivism, the view that the legal consequences of case are created, constructed in legal argumentation is correct. Its alternative is legal reconstructivism, the view that legal argumentation merely reconstructs the operation of legal rules etc. and aims at discovering facts which were already there. An important representative of this reconstructive view is the institutional theory of law.

The problem with reconstructivism is that it seems only attractive in easy cases, where everybody with the appropriate knowledge of the law can easily 'see' the legal consequences which the legal rules allegedly attached to the case. In hard cases, reconstructivism seems far-fetched, even to the extent that a judge of superhuman powers, Hercules, is needed to discover the law (Dworkin 1978, chapter 4). On the assumption that the operation of legal rules is not fundamentally different in hard cases than in easy cases, a unified account of the operation of legal rules is asked for. This account should either adopt constructivism and explain why legal rules *appear* to operate automatically in easy cases, or adopt reconstructivism and explain why it only *seems* that they cannot operate automatically in hard cases. The former alternative is the more attractive one, because the latter can neither be verified nor falsified. Moreover, I have argued that the seemingly automatic operation of legal rules in easy cases may be explained from the tendency to reify the law and in particular the generation of legal consequences.

In the case of constructivism, we can distinguish between ontological constructivism, which identifies the legal consequences of a case with what the best possible legal argument says they are, and procedural constructivism, which identifies the legal consequences of a case with what the best actual legal argument says they are. Ontological constructivism makes only sense if it is possible to identify the possible legal arguments. Such an identification is only possible if the domain of law is closed. There are, however, many reasons to assume that the domain of law is not closed, and the conclusion is therefore that ontological legal constructivism does not make sense.

---

[23]This also explains the defeasibility of legal reasoning, a phenomenon that cannot well be accounted for on a reifying view of the law. See Hage (1997, 113f), where the application of a rule is treated as a kind of action to give a good account of defeasible reasoning in the law, and Hage (2005, 69f) where the reifying perspective is adopted and the defeasibility of legal reasoning is down-played.

By elimination of its two alternatives we therefore arrive at procedural legal constructivism, the view according to which the law is what the best actual argument says it is. At first sight, this view may seem implausible, because there is no guarantee that the best legal argument until now leads to a correct conclusion. This appearance is deceptive, however, because it is the consequence of the (implicit) assumption that the legal consequences are already there. But, as we have seen, we have no evidence at all for that view, and its attractiveness is better explained from the inclination to reify the law than from the existence of legal consequences which cannot be perceived nor proven or disproven. Legal consequences are not independent entities, but are essentially conclusions of law-applying arguments. It is in these arguments that the consequences are created, and the final result is what the best argument, the best actually produced argument, says it is.

**Acknowledgment** The author thanks Anne Ruth Mackor for useful discussions on the topic of this paper and her comments on a draft version.

## References

Alexy, R. 1978. *Theorie der juristischen Argumentation*. Frankfurt a/M: Suhrkamp.
Chang, R. (ed.). 1997. *Incommensurability, incomparability, and practical reason*. Cambridge: Harvard University Press.
Dworkin, R. 1978. *Taking rights seriously*. London: Duckworth.
Dworkin, R. 1986a. *A matter of principle*. Oxford: Clarendon.
Dworkin, R. 1986b. *Law's empire*. London: Fontana.
Hage, J.C. 1997. *Reasoning with rules*. Dordrecht: Kluwer.
Hage, J.C. 2005. *Studies in legal logic*. Dordrecht: Springer.
Hage, J.C., R.E. Leenes, and A.R. Lodder. 1994. Hard cases; a procedural approach. *Artificial Intelligence and Law* 2: 113–167.
Hart, H.L.A. 1994. *The concept of law*, 2nd ed. Oxford: Oxford University Press.
La Torre, M. 1999. *Norme, Instituzioni, Valore: per una teoria instituzionalistica del diritto*. Rome: Laterza.
Lagerspetz, E. 1995. *The opposite mirrors*. Dordrecht: Kluwer.
Leiter, B. 2002. Law and objectivity. In *The Oxford handbook of jurisprudence and the philosophy of law*, ed. Jules Coleman and Scott Shapiro, 969–989. Oxford: Oxford University Press.
Lodder, A.R. 1999. *Dialaw. On legal justification and dialogical models of argumentation*. Dordrecht: Kluwer.
MacCormick, N. 2007. *Institutions of law*. Oxford: Oxford University Press.
MacCormick, N., and O. Weinberger. 1986. *An institutional theory of law*. Dordrecht: Reidel.
Rawls, J. 1972. *A theory of justice*. Oxford: Oxford University Press.
Ruiter, D.W.P. 1993. *Institutional legal facts*. Dordrecht: Kluwer.
Ruiter, D.W.P. 2001. *Legal institutions*. Dordrecht: Kluwer.
Schwemmer, O., and P. Lorenzen. 1973. *Konstruktive Logik, Ethik und Wissenschaftstheorie*. Manheim: Bibliographisches Institut.
Smith, C.E. 2009. Het normatieve karakter van de rechtswetenschap: recht als oordeel. *Rechtsfilosofie en rechtstheorie* 38: 202–225.
Soeteman, A. 2010. *Rechtsgeleerde waarheid*. Amsterdam: Afscheidsrede Vrije Universiteit Amsterdam.
Van Dalen, D. 2001. Intuitionistic Logic. In *The Blackwell Guide to Philosophical Logic*, ed. L. Goble, 224–257. Oxford: Blackwell.

# Chapter 10
# The Argument from Psychological Typology for a Mild Separation Between the Context of Discovery and the Context of Justification

**Marko Novak**

## 10.1 Introduction

In accordance with legal argumentation theory the entire process of adjudication is divided into the process of discovery and the process of justification of a legal decision. The first phase of deciding, which concerns the process of establishing the upper premise as well as the lower premise of logical syllogism, and entails the discovery of all relevant information concerning both premises so that a logical conclusion is reached, is part of an internal process of a judge, which is usually not disclosed to the public. Such a process of discovery is often the subject of research into the psychology of decision-making. It is the phase of decision-making that importantly includes irrational elements as well as rational elements.

The majority of legal theorists, especially those interested in legal argumentation, have claimed that only the context of justification, in which a judicial decision is justified in the reasoning of the decision by arguments or reasons, can be rationally reconstructed. Such scholars rigidly separate the context of justification from the context of discovery since they believe the latter includes (intuitive) hunches, which are non-rational and non-logical. For that reason, they have preferred to leave this subject to psychologists to study the entire process of reaching decisions. However, according to Bruce Anderson, here they have unfortunately been quite unsuccessful (Anderson 2010). It seems that the legal theorists' disinterest in the context of discovery and decision-making comes from the traditional notion that there is no place in law for irrationality and intuition, and that if we must admit that it actually exists it should be minimised as much as possible in the process of decision-making which is left to psychologists, while more law-oriented lawyers should deal with the process of justification as the core of rationality in decision-making.

M. Novak (✉)
European Faculty of Law, Nova Gorica, Slovenia
e-mail: marko.novak@evro-pf.si

C. Dahlman and E. Feteris (eds.), *Legal Argumentation Theory: Cross-Disciplinary Perspectives*, Law and Philosophy Library 102, DOI 10.1007/978-94-007-4670-1_10,

In this article I also do not agree with a rigid separation of the two contextes of legal decision-making and support a more moderate separation between the two. I realise that in this perspective the outcome of my position is similar to that of Bruce Anderson; however, I use different arguments to support that.

Thus, in the first chapter I describe the traditional role rationality has played in the context of legal decision-making and law in general. However, this traditional picture of law as being predominantly a rational activity has been seriously attacked by the postmodernist movement that has also tried to deconstruct it, to which I refer in the second chapter. In this context I present the role of the Critical Legal Studies' perspective and that of its ancestors, the American Legal Realists.

In the third chapter I briefly outline the post-postmodern status concerning the role of rationality in law. I particularly refer to the contemporary relevance of legal argumentation theory which regarding the legal decision-making process has mainly emphasised the phase of the justification of legal decisions. However, in the fourth chapter I raise the issue of the importance of the process of discovery which stems from the fact that our decision-making process does not only include a rational part, but also an irrational part, most notably intuition.

It is intuition in particular that connects both parts, and from that it entails that both processes of decision-making could to some extent be connected. In order to emphasise the role of (irrational) intuition I then use an argument from psychological typology to prove that every decision-making process is partly irrational and that it is impossible to exclude it from decision-making. Finally, instead of claiming the rigid separation of the abovementioned two phases of decision-making, it is more important to recognise their connection and interrelation. However, it is also important to put the discovery phase and the justification phase in the right perspective and still argue their mild separation if we prefer rational legal decisions.

## 10.2 The Traditional Predominance of Rationality in Law and Judicial Decision-Making

Law has traditionally been considered as a typical rational activity.[1] "Rational" usually pertains to the human faculty of reason,[2] which in philosophy is contrasted with experience. Being non-rational, such experience can thus exist in the form of religious revelation, sensory experience, emotion etc. (Mautner 2000: 479). Moreover, there has traditionally been a distinction between two types of rationality,

[1]The discussion concerning the rationality and irrationality of law is not new among contemporary legal scholars. For a discussion about that in Slovenia, see Cerar (2001).

[2]The etymology of this English word is as follows: "ME [Medieval English] *resound,* fr. OF [Medieval Old French] *raison,* fr. L [Latin] ration-, *ratio* reason, computation, fr. *reri* to calculate, think; prob. akin to Goth *rathjo* account, explanation"(Merriam-Webster's Collegiate Dictionary, 1993: 974).

namely practical and theoretical (also practical and theoretical reason).[3] This distinction is recognised even in modern philosophy. Practical reason is considered to deal with normative questions, such as what one ought to do and what it would be best to do. These questions are interested in the matter of value and action. In contradistinction with that, theoretical reason deals with reflection, with matters of fact and their explanation. It is concerned with belief and, as such, is more typical of natural and social sciences (Wallace 2000). Surprisingly, it is not that far from what in scholastic philosophy has been understood as the division between *ratio* and *intellectus,* the former being the ability of a discursive way of thinking, with the latter being the ability of direct intelligence (Maritain 1951: 111). To some extent, this would correspond to the division in the English language between reason and intellect (or intelligence).[4]

Furthermore, in a historical perspective, rationality in law has had at least two different meanings that have been reflected in various theories of law. First, those who have supported a metaphysical-rational empistemological approach to law, either in its older version (such as Lao-Tze, Confucius, Aristotle, Cicero and Aquinas) or in its modern version (e.g. Geny, Dabin, Cohen, Fuller, Finnis) (Prakash Sinha 1993: V-XII), have found true law in rational principles that have been accessible to persons through their ability to grasp and understand certain internal idea(l)s (such as God, nature, morality etc.). As mentioned, such a manner of the operation of the human mind that is directed to the overall connectedness of knowledge and the possibility of ideas has traditionally been considered as "intellect" (lat. *intellectus*). Below we will see that such rationality was mostly influenced by intuition, as a cognitive function, and might thus be called intuitive rationality.

The second understanding of "rational" refers to *ratio* or to the capacity of abstracting, differentiating, analysing, making concepts, of applying means to ends (the so-called instrumental (Horkheimer 1974) or empirical rationality). Such approaches to legal theory have traditionally been labelled as empiricist-positivist empistemological approaches to the understanding of the concept of law (especially positivist theories of law) (Prakash Sinha 1993: V-XII). Such views mostly appeared at the beginning of modernity and have to some degree been extended to the present.

According to the modern understanding of the concept of law, the rationality that is typical of law today is predominantly considered to be of a practical character (i.e. practical reason). In practical contexts, rationality is the adaptation of means to ends (MacCormick (2008; 2005: 470)). From its social aspect, by its aspiring

---

[3]Gr. *practices* pertaining to action, in contrast with theoretical (gr. *theōria* viewing; speculation; contemplation) which relates to thought (Mautner 2000: 440, 563).

[4]The etymology of these two words, i.e. intellect and intelligence, is as follows: "ME, fr. MF [Middle French] or L; MF, fr. L *intellectus,* fr. *intellegere* to understand"; and "ME, MF, fr. L *intelligentia,* fr. *intelligent-, intelligens* intelligent" (Merriam-Webster's Collegiate Dictionary, 1993: 608).

to (practical) rationality law serves important social goals, such as providing social order, stability and predictability, as well as serving as an important means for the resolution of major social disputes.

I accept the general framework of the already mentioned traditional distinction between *ratio* and *intellect* but understand it in a different way. I view it according to the philosophic psychology concerning the understanding of cognitive functions or the psychological type theory that was developed by C. G. Jung in his Psychological Types (Jung 1921), and was subsequently empirically tested, and to some extent even extended, by K. Myers and I. Myers Briggs (Briggs Myers and Myers 1980). Myers and Briggs invented a special indicator to measure the predominance of certain cognitive functions in tested people. That indicator was then patented as the MBTI (Myers-Briggs Type Indicator) (Briggs Myers and Myers 1980: XIX).

According to Jung, the four cognitive functions, i.e. thinking, feeling, sensation and intuition, are divided into two larger groups of which one is rational and the other irrational. In this manner, thinking and feeling are rational functions whereas sensation and intuition are irrational functions. With irrational functions we perceive objects, people, events and ideas, while with rational functions we evaluate what we have perceived. In every person, Jung argued, there is one superior function, one auxiliary function, and one inferior function (Jung 1921). Jung's theoretical inventions were empirically tested by Myers and Briggs and their contemporary followers (Daicoff 2004). According to such research, it has been proven that in the case of lawyers, the superior cognitive function is to a great extent thinking, as a rational function. According to these results, the percentage of lawyers with their superior thinking function is around 75, in contrast with 25% of those with their superior feeling function. (Daicoff 2004: 32–36). The auxiliary functions that to some extent direct and determine thinking are both sensation and intuition. According to all MBTI tests that I have managed to examine, the ratio between the predominance of intuition and sensation as an auxiliary function among lawyers is somewhat 50/50. According to the results of the surveyed MBTI tests, it depends, however, on which kind of legal professions were tested. In general, intuition was found to as prevail in the general group of lawyers and law students, while sensation prevailed in the event of judges (Daicoff 2004: 64–65).

From these findings and in line with the abovementioned trends in the history of legal thought, I seems that there have been two general types of thinking (and rationality) in law. The first is the mentioned empirical rationality in which thinking (evaluation) obtains relevant data or information (perception) mostly from sensation, by experiencing the facts of a case and the relevant legal standards by the senses, evaluating such by thinking, and making a final decision. In the continuation, I will argue that today such empirical rationality is most typically applied in clearer cases. Further, there is a certain use of intuition but in such cases it is not determinate for the result of the decision-making process (the so-called instrumental intuition). Secondly, there is also the mentioned intuitive rationality which is applied more in unclear cases through, e.g., moral legal principles. Such intuition could also include political or economic solutions to a problem at issue. In this framework, the so-called creative intuition is determinate for the result of the decision-making.

Here thinking obtains relevant legal information from intuition because sensation cannot help much as the text of the legal norm has gaps, is vague, ambiguous – in short, unclear.

Finally, everything mentioned above in connection with the predominance of rationality in law in general naturally also applies to judicial decision-making and the judiciary in general, as one of the most prominent legal professions. It is the judicial profession that I mostly focus on in the rest of this article, where I discuss in particular the extent to which judges embrace both rational and irrational aspects of the decision-making process, and that their ideal relation is the one in which the irrational is in the service of the rational.

## 10.3 A Postmodern Attack on the Essential Connection Between Law and Rationality

### *10.3.1 The Critical Legal Studies Movement*

A central goal of postmodernism was to deconstruct the "meta-narratives of modernity" (Lyotard 1984). One such meta-narrative of modernity, especially of the Enlightenment, was certainly the authority of rationality and reason (Mautner 2000: 359). In comparison with the pre-modern world, through the scientific revolution modernity had empiricised reason by instrumentalizing it (Horkheimer 1974) to become *ratio,* in relation to which reason's pre-modern intellectual (intelligent) dimensions were subsequently left to metaphysics.

In contemporary legal theory, one of the most known attacks on rationality in law came from the Critical Legal Studies (CLS) movement in the United States in the 1970s and early 1980s. To an important extent their deconstructionist approach to legal doctrine, exposing the "indeterminacy of the text and delegitimizing liberal legalism's claim about the existence of a knowable, objective, and value-neutral (and rational) law (Prakash Sinha 1993: 310)," certainly represented a postmodernist position in legal theory (Minda 1995: 126).

In contradistinction with liberalism, which claimed that rationality distinguished legal discourse from other kinds of social force and that in law there is a rational foundation for doctrine and development, CLS rejected such a position as a myth claiming that passion (Unger 1986) or will are not excluded from law. Moreover, CLS proponents argued that law was nothing but an expression of politics, or "an instrument of political propaganda that legitimates the class structure by masking exploitation with apparent fairness" (Prakash Sinha 1993: 312–13).

This position of CLS concerning the critique of rationality in law was not surprising given that CLS adherents claimed to be descendants of the American Legal Realists (ALR). The ALR argued that law and legal reasoning often contain indeterminacy, subjectivism, non-formalism and irrationality, or that "legal reasoning can rarely require, in an objective sense, a particular result" (Prakash Sinha

1993: 306). Moreover, CLS proponents also found support for their ideas in the deconstructivist movement regarding the interpretation of texts, claiming that texts have no objective meaning and that the founding of meaning in a text is the result of an act of interpretation by the reader and not of an inherent objective meaning of the text. In such a manner, the interpretation of a text or a social action is allegedly the function of power, not proof. This allegedly contributed to the indeterminacy of the text and the non-existence of a knowable, objective and value-neutral law (Prakash Sinha 1993: 310).

If CLS took from the ALR the idea that law is necessarily subjective, informal and irrational, they did not however accept from them the notion that the irrational in law is not necessarily something bad, negative and arbitrary (Anderson 1996). This is even more so if we understand the psychological typology of general decision-making, which also applies to the way in which judges decide cases, which I will be outlining below. For that reason I will briefly refer to their ancestors, the ALR. Given that many ALR were former judges at different American courts, their pre-postmodern reflection on how judges in concrete cases actually proceed and adjudicate can be very useful.

### *10.3.2 The American Legal Realists (ALR)*

One of the protagonists of the intellectual movement of the American Legal Realists was Jerome Frank. Frank, who at some point in his career was a judge, looked at the concept of law from a psychoanalytical perspective. In his work Frank addressed certain psychological specialties of an individual that might affect the (excessive) emotionality of his or her judgments (e.g. impatience, irrational irritation when faced with unpleasant thoughts that refer to wishes, hatred, the sense of power, loyalty to certain groups) (Frank 1930: 206).

According to Frank, law is uncertain, indefinite and subject to unpredictable changes. However, such uncertainty about law is not an unfortunate fact but an important social value since otherwise society would be too tightly restricted and unable to adjust to the reality of incessant social, economic and political changes (Frank 1930: 207–08).

Furthermore, Frank asserted that in terms of psychology the process of adjudication rarely begins at the upper syllogistic premise, on the basis of which the judge only deduces or makes an inference. Quite the contrary, Frank opined that judges generally make their judgments in the opposite direction, i.e. stemming from speculative conclusions made in advance. Judgments are thus based on judges' internal premonitions. He called such premonitions or stimuli hunch producers, which as political, economic and moral prejudices tell the judges to reach certain decisions that are formally based on rules and principles. According to Frank, there are also other hunches and premonitions that depend on the characteristics of an individual judge who is to make certain conclusions or decisions. Therefore, in Frank's opinion, a judge's personal traits, his or her psychological dispositions, prejudices, sympathies and antipathies (in relation to, e.g., witnesses or parties to proceedings) decide on what is to be the right decision in a particular case. From this perspective, the judge does not differ from other "mortals" (Frank 1930: 207–08).

According to Frank, following such use of intuition, the judge *a posteriori* begins to apply rational arguments in order to check (or supervise) whether it is possible by such to justify the conclusion that was *a priori* made by virtue of his or her intuition. This entails that the conclusion made in advance, or *a priori,* essentially determines the arguments used in the reasoning. In Frank's opinion, if this is not possible, then the judge will have to choose another conclusion except he or she is "arbitrary or insane" (Frank 1930: 203).

Following Frank if we wish to know something more about hunches that contribute to lawmaking we should know the judge's personality. Thus, law changes in accordance with the personality of a judge that decides on a certain case. However, such a distinction between judges cannot be disclosed in connection with the writing of their judgments particularly due to their ability to use different tricks in order to disguise disharmony between them. In such a manner, true irrational inclinations are hidden behind the veil of a rational structure of reasoning. However, from time to time we learn something about judges' personal preferences only through their interviews, biographies, literary works about them, as well as from brilliant and bad reasoning of their decisions. Although rules and principles are foundations of law they are only instigations for the activity of judges. Accordingly, Frank was certain that the main factor in the operation of law is a judge's personality (Frank 1930: 206).

Frank's ideal was a fully grown-up lawyer (judge) who does not need external authority but possesses constructive doubt that enables him or her to create law in accordance with a developing civilization. At the same time, such a judge is (to be) aware of his or her prejudices, take(s) them into consideration, and deal(s) with such rationally in order to achieve a decision that would be as just (and objective) as possible (Frank 1930: 212).

Following Frank, judges necessarily have discretion when they apply abstract rules to concrete facts, i.e. they necessarily create law by making value judgments, since legal creativity is the essence of the life of law. According to Frank, the ideal judge would not abuse power but take care of the enforcement of justice by applying their knowledge of law and being aware of their potential prejudices and weaknesses (i.e. his or her human nature) (Frank 1930: 210).

In general the ALR have criticised legal formalists or legal positivists who claim that law or law application is (fully) determined by mere legal provisions, in the framework of which (according to the most extreme position, that of German mechanical jurisprudence) judges are to be completely neutral (even mechanical) "technicians" who merely apply abstract legal norms to concrete facts. The main tasks of the ALR were certainly to destroy the myth pointing to such full (even scientific) autonomy of law and the narrowly perceived empiricist's perception of the application of law.

I am very much aware of the ALR's valuable contributions to disclosing the idea that law and a lawyer's psychological predisposition are interconnected, and that law is merely a result of the projection of lawyers' activities when creating or applying the law. I agree with their perspective that law can be indeterminate as it depends on, e.g., judges as human beings, and also on how the law is interpreted and applied in a particular case. This certainly proves the fact that a judge is necessarily subjective when adjudicating cases, but this subjectivity, such as judge's hunches (intuitive ideas), are not necessarily something bad if they are taken in the overall context of the profession of a judge as a responsible actor. As already mentioned, it seems that CLS proponents did not take from the ALR the position that irrationality in law can also be positive, not necessarily negative.

I take into consideration everything that the ALR said regarding the subjective inclination of judges when deciding cases, and proceed with some additional (more objective) requirements that come up in this connection. As we will see in the section on typology and judicial decision-making, the issue of psychological typology and law addresses both irrational and rational elements in adjudication, and tries to put them in the right perspective so that the emphasis is on the value of thinking as the ultimate rational cognitive function.

## 10.4 The Post-postmodern Return of Rationality in Law: Legal Argumentation Theory and the Justification of Judicial Decisions

The fact is that the postmodernist movement in law unmasked such as being merely objective, formal, and rational in the direction of also proving its subjectivity, informality and irrationality. However, if it was very much successful at criticising the traditional picture of rationality in law, it was unsuccessful in replacing it with some constructive alternative contents.

Thus, what remains for a post-postmodernist approach in law concerning the role of rationality in it, which entails that the irrational cannot finally supersede the rational in law if we would like to retain quality legal decision-making, is the fact that "hence in the context of law we must count with the irrational rationally" (Kaufmann 1992: 25). It seems that a post-postmodernist approach in legal theory has brought reaffirmation of rationality in law. A major contribution to that, especially in the field of public discourse, was Habermas' work (Habermas 1987). Habermas is one of the most prominent critics of philosophical postmodernism. Against postmodernism he tried to defend argumentative reason in inter-subjective communication against postmodern experimental strategies. In his view, postmodernism is nothing but an illicit aestheticization of knowledge and public discourse. Against this, he sought to rehabilitate modern reason as a system of procedural rules for achieving consensus and agreement among communicating subjects. Insofar as postmodernism introduced aesthetic playfulness and subversion into science and politics, he resisted it in the name of a modernity moving toward completion rather than self-transformation (Aylesworth 2005). Habermas very much influenced some of the pioneers of contemporary legal argumentation, most notably Robert Alexy (Alexy 1989).

Thus, one example of the "comeback" of rationality in law has been the (re)emergence of the theory of legal argumentation, as an integral approach that claims that a legal decision is neither just the result of a determinate text (the traditional – modern position), nor only the result of the will of an interpreter (the postmodernist position), but is the decision that must be reasonable (Pavčnik and Wolcher 2000). In this sense, it seems that the theory of legal argumentation tries to reconcile the tension between the traditional and the postmodern approaches when the role of rationality in law is concerned.

In legal argumentation theory a perspective on adjudication has been established according to which such is divided into two phases: (1) the process of discovery of the premises and deciding thereupon, and (2) the process of justification of the legal decision. Legal argumentation theorists who separate the context of discovery from the context of justification include, e.g., Reichenbach, Alexy, Carter, Hart, MacCormick and Summers (Feteris 1999: 10). The first phase of legal deciding concerns the reaching of a conclusion that appears in the operative provisions of the decision, and is carried out on the bases of a legal norm and a factual situation. Such a process of establishing the upper premise as well as the lower premise of logical syllogism, and of the thereby connected discovery of all the relevant data on both the premises so that a logical conclusion is reached, is part of an internal process of the judge, which is usually not disclosed to the public. The mentioned process of discovery is often the subject of research into the psychology of decision-making (Feteris, 10). It is the phase of decision-making that importantly includes irrational elements (i.e. perception in the form of sensation and intuition) as well as rational elements (such as evaluation in the form of thinking). Certainly, the mentioned irrational elements, most often intuition, do not appear in the reasoning of a decision in which the judge tries to justify his or her decision by using only rational means.

The majority of legal theorists, especially those interested in legal argumentation, have claimed that only the context of justification, in which a judicial decision is justified in the reasoning of the decision by arguments or reasons, can be rationally reconstructed. Such scholars rigidly separate the context of justification from the context of discovery since in their opinion the latter includes (intuitive) hunches, which are non-rational and non-logical. For that reason, they have preferred to leave the phase of discovery to psychologists to study the entire process of reaching decisions. However, according to Anderson, in that those were unfortunately quite unsuccessful (Anderson 2010). It seems that the legal theorists' disinterest in the context of discovery and decision-making comes from the traditional notion that there is no place in law for irrationality and intuition, and that, if we must admit that such actually exists in law, it should be minimised as much as possible in the process of decision-making, which is left to being studied by psychologists while more law-oriented lawyers should deal with the process of justification as the core of rationality in decision-making. Here it seems that legal theorists neglect the emphasis made by the American Legal Realists pointing out that hunches and intuition can play a positive and even an important role in the law, not necessarily a damaging one.

I also do not agree with a rigid separation of the two contextes but support a more moderate separation between them. I realise that in this perspective the outcome of my position is similar to Bruce Anderson. He opposes the rigid distinction between the context of discovery and the context of justification by claiming that "his analysis of the context of discovery supports the claim that whether or not a legal decision is justified depends on whether the judge performed at his or her informed best – that the judge paid attention of the relevant data, intelligently grasped links among the data, made reasonable judgments grounded on sufficient evidence, made responsible value judgments, and reached a decision consistent with his or her value judgment about what is the most suitable solution to the legal problem" (Anderson, ibid.).

However, my arguments for supporting the mild version of the separation between the contexts of discovery and justification of legal decisions are different to Anderson's in that they are mainly embedded in psychological typology. Thus, in the continuation I will try to emphasize the importance of the context of discovery and decision-making, thereby focusing on judicial decision-making, by understanding the "operation" of psychological typology in this context. I argue that the context of discovery, in addition to rational elements, also includes important irrational elements of human (judges') mind, and that such irrational elements do not only play a coincidental or even damaging role in judicial decision-making but can even be very crucial for good (even just or ethical) decision-making. Nevertheless, I insist that judicial decisions should not only be based on irrational elements since in such an event no supervision over judges' activity, such as examining their reasoning, would be possible. Therefore, the context of discovery (decision-making) must be connected with the context of justification (reasoning of the decision) by way of providing a translation of irrational elements into rational ones, i.e. in the manner of providing reasons for the decision in the reasoning which serves as a kind of rational experiment for the one who has taken the decision.

## 10.5 Concerning the Process of Discovery and the Role of Irrationality in Judicial Decision-Making

### *10.5.1 Understanding Judicial Decision-Making Through Psychological Typology*

Although categorising people according to certain psychological types has an ancient origin, the most famous modern approach to psychological typology comes from Carl G. Jung (Jung 1921). According to Jung, the human psyche is divided into two different basic attitudes: (a) extraversion; and (b) introversion. These two attitudes determine where a person obtains energy. While the extravert obtains it from the outside by dealing with external objects, activities, excitements, people and things, the introvert obtains it from the inside by reflecting about ideas, thoughts, interests, ideas and imagination. In addition to the two attitudes, what is typical of the human psyche are four basic cognitive functions: (i) thinking and feeling as rational functions, which are responsible for our evaluation; and (iii) sensation and intuition, which as irrational cognitive functions are the basis of our perception or the manner of taking in data. Our thinking analyses information in a detached, objective fashion. It operates from factual principles, deduces and forms conclusions systematically. It is our logical nature. Feeling forms conclusions in an attached and somewhat global manner, based on likes or dislikes, the impact on others, and human and aesthetic values. It is our subjective nature. Sensing notices the sights, sounds, smells and all the sensory details of the present. It categorises, organises, records and stores the specifics from the here and now. It is reality-based, dealing with "what is". It also provides the specific details of memory and recollections from past events. Intuition seeks to understand, interpret and form overall patterns of all the information that is collected and records these patterns and relationships. It speculates on possibilities, including looking into and forecasting the future. It is imaginative and conceptual (Reinhold 2010).

In every person, one of these functions is superior or dominant, and one inferior. There is also an auxiliary function and a tertiary function, which have some influence on the dominant cognitive function. In accordance with that, Jung developed eight different types. His thought was further developed by the Americans Katharine Briggs and Isabel Briggs-Myers who added to Jungian four cognitive functions another pair of opposites, judging and perceiving, which as two additional cognitive functions define the way how we relate to the external world or determine the type of our lifestyle (Briggs Myers and Myers 1980).

Why is the above-mentioned short description of psychological typology relevant to this article? It is important to demonstrate that every person is (ir)rational due to his or her basic cognitive functions. This certainly applies to the lawyer and their decision-making, as well as to the judge's deciding. However, the fact that in the lawyer's personality the rational part (i.e. thinking and judging as ideal psychological type preferences) prevails or should prevail certainly importantly contributes to the role that law has had throughout history in society, in which it has ensured at least a certain degree of the rationalisation of ever dynamic social relations. From that it follows that the lawyer's cognitive functions are both rational and irrational but the rational elements should predominate. This applies even more to the judge who, in my opinion, is the central figure in the legal profession.

Likewise, the process of discovery, as the initial part of the legal decision-making process according to legal argumentation theory, not only includes rational, i.e. evaluative, elements but also irrational elements since the judge's rationality (i.e. thinking as the predominant cognitive function in legal decision-making) needs certain data or material to begin its evaluation, which receives it through the operation of irrational sensation (i.e. the perception of facts and existing laws) and intuition (i.e. the recognition of the "right" legal norm that is based on certain facts, and the so-called "sense" of justice).[5]

As already indicated, intuition has an important role in legal (or judicial) decision-making. First, it appears in the form of instrumental intuition, by virtue of helping the judge find or recognise the most appropriate legal standard (be it a legal rule or principle) in the legal system to be applied to certain facts of the case. In such an event, this instrumental intuition ("instrumental" hunch) is subject to the so-called internal justification of a decision, as the necessary rational experiment that is necessary for justifying the decision in clear cases. By "internal justification" I understand what MacCormick determined as the first-level or "deductive" justification in which the decision is defended by means of a legal rule and the facts of the case (MacCormick 1978).[6]

Secondly, in the context of their decision-making judges often resort to so-called creative intuition, which is more creative than instrumental intuition as to some extent it exceeds the internal legal system in the event of gaps in the law, ambiguities, vagueness of legal text, implied meanings in it, which are all typical of unclear cases. In such an event, assisted with creative intuition that communicates the necessary information to the judge, he or she must necessarily step from the area of the internal legal system into the realm of the so-called external area of the legal system, whose outer boundaries are the requirements of justice, ethics, morality, legitimacy, (legal) certainty, predictability etc. In this case the decision is justified externally. Here I refer to what MacCormick understood by his second-order justification in which the arguments that are required are to defend the decision by demonstrating that the ruling is in accordance with the prevailing legal order (including in particular legal principles, and arguments from coherence and consistency) (MacCormick, ibid.).[7]

This entails that such a process often includes intuition – especially if the case at issue is unclear (or hard), which means that the combination consisting of sensation, thinking and instrumental intuition is not sufficient to provide the decision-maker with the necessary material for making a conclusion.

However, the phase of justifying a decision is restricted to the thinking and empirical processes of providing rational reasons for the decision, by way of persuading the legal (and general) audience that the decision-maker has decided reasonably. In such a case, the decision that was reached internally is reviewable externally. Thus, the elements of thinking as rational standards (arguments as reasons; as well as the elements of sensation making the experience of such reasons

[5]I suggest that even in English we cease using the syntax "sense of justice" or "feeling of justice" but begin using the expression "intuition of justice," which is the only right expression according to the understanding of psychological typology by Jung, Briggs and Myers.

[6]*Cf.* Alexy's position that internal justification is concerned with whether the decision follows logically from the premises adduced as justifying it (Alexy 1989).

[7]*Cf.* Alexy's perception of external justification by which he understands the defending of the acceptability of the premises by interpretative methods and arguments (Alexy 1989).

possible) play an important role as codes that are decisive for the external mediating and communicating function of law to be ensured. This phase of decision-making as the phase of reasoning is crucially conditioned by the use of rational codes. This is necessarily so as, unlike reason and rationality, intuition as an irrational cognitive function is incapable of being a mediator, common denominator, or common ground on which people can rely when social disputes are to be resolved.

Accordingly, it seems more than probable that the phases of discovery and justification are to some extent connected, as when one decides in a certain manner they simultaneously intuitively anticipate the justification of their selection of a decision. Nevertheless, it may occur when beginning to write down the reasons for a decision that a judge changes their mind, alter their decision, or selects other reasons than those that they anticipated in the initial reaching of the decision. Therefore, it would be very hard to defend the thesis that the process of discovery and the process of justifying a decision can be rigidly separated. This does not say, however, that certain intuitions, senses, perceptions or hunches concerning a legal decision must not be rationally justified or submitted to a rational "test".

Even though, as Frank alleged, in the process of decision-making the judge's personal (psychological) characteristics play an important role, the decision of the same judge must be reasoned or rationally justified. If this is not possible, they must reach another decision that can be justified (rationally).

If the process of justification is more formal and rational, which is reflected in the use of relatively autonomous legal canons (of positive law or legal texts), to demonstrate that the judge has not acted arbitrarily, the process of discovery is more informal and material. In such, as already above-stated, intuition may play a greater role. As briefly mentioned above, the process of reasoning a judicial decision as the process of justifying such pertains to the type of thinking that is mainly supported by the senses in: (a) perceiving the facts of the case; (b) the norms of the legal text; and (c) expressing the reasons for the decision in the reasoning. Such thinking mainly operates on the basis of codes of positive law, or it tries to be close to that or match that as much as possible. This is the world of more or less formal mechanisms of operative-analytical rationalism and legal logic, which enables a decision to pass the empirical and rationality test, in the context of which the judge tries to remain within the relative autonomy of the legal world. If the decision cannot pass such an empirical rational test, than it cannot be a legal decision.

### *10.5.2 More on the Role of Intuition in Judicial Decision-Making, or Why Does the Mild Separation Thesis Matter?*

In order to achieve greater rationality of deciding, the process of deciding itself should be more rationally illuminated. In such a manner it would be easier to understand which psychological factors come into play in deciding. Thus, by also being aware of their irrational part, a judge would adjudicate more reasonably, impartially and objectively. According to Frank, it is in particular the judge who is exposed to emotional dynamism in the court since only an honest judge who is also aware of their competencies, but also of his or her prejudices and deficiencies, can be the best guarantee of justice (Frank 1930: 138). Namely, according to the ALR, the processes of reaching a decision and justifying it includes the following steps: (a) learning the facts of the case and reflection on a just solution; (b) a hunch or intuition about the solution; (c) examining the possibility of such hunches and intuitions in the framework of an existing law (rules, principles and precedents); (d) reaching a decision; and (e) providing the necessary reasons for the decision (Frank 1930: 138). Thus, as already indicated we can see that both phases (discovery and justification) are mutually related to a significant extent.

A Slovenian legal theorist, Boris Furlan, who lived at the time of the American Legal Realists, has similarly emphasized in his treaties on a theory of legal inferring that, in the process of legal decision-making, a practicing lawyer initially derives from his or her internal (legal) sense. Namely, similarly to Frank Furlan argued that, in contradistinction with the predominantly accepted logical syllogism, a practicing lawyer in his or her logical inferring does not stem from the upper premise of the legal norm but actually from the lower premise of the actual case (state of facts). In this way, he or she uses intuitive recognition in order to find a common denominator between the state of facts and the legal norm which is to be applied. Such an act of intuition leads him or her to the upper premise which is then applied in the form of logical syllogism. However, according to Furlan, the judge must rationally justify or reason their intuition in the framework of logical syllogism, since, as we perceive our world in modern times, *ratio* is the most reliable communicator in our external world, which ensures predictability and necessary frameworks for accepted social norms. If the mentioned recognition is an act of intuition, the syllogism is an act of reason. So that our intuition becomes accessible to other people we must translate it into the form of reasons and rationality. Through logical syllogism alone we cannot find appropriate legal norms that would lead to a solution of the case, but only prove the correctness of that which we found by means of intuition. However, deductive syllogism is the only means of rational proving. Finally, legal syllogism has an undisputed role as providing supervision over our intuitive findings so that they are translated into rational codes (Furlan 2002).

From that we can see that the context of discovery in which, beside (rational) evaluation, (irrational) intuition also plays an important role, cannot be rigidly separated from the context of justification as the latter is often only the necessary result and translation of the former. In the process of deciding itself, when a dilemma occurs because we have addressed a hard or unclear case (with several possible solutions which can all be plausible or when "we ran out of the rules"), we usually pay attention to intuition to provide our thinking with an additional guide for resolving the case. Such intuition could lead to a legal rule, (unwritten) principle, (legal) value, policy, some other standard, helping us to find the legal solution in a thinking "obstacle". However, as above mentioned, such decision that is supported by intuition still has to undergo the (empirical) rationality test, which entails that it is to be rationally and empirically justified in the legal reasoning of the decision.

Undoubtedly the role of (not strictly legal) psychological factors in the work of legislators or those who decide on the application of law (especially judges) is usually proportionate to the openness of legal standards that are the criteria for reaching the decision, as well as to the possibility of broadness of interpretation since such "opened-texture" legal provisions can be reasoned in several ways, all of which can be rationally defensible.

Why does then the thesis of a moderate separation between the context of discovery and the context of justification of legal decisions matter?

Intuition which is mostly used in the discovery context (as perception) is important, even indispensible, for getting proper reasons that are applied in the justification context. After all, legal language is a set of symbols which are to an important extent accessible to us by virtue of intuition. In a legal context this occurs, e.g., when a judge initially, before he or she decides on a case and writes the reasoning, finds an analogy between the text of a relevant legal norm and the language of the facts of the case, or between the material facts of a precedent and the essential facts of a case considered. The CLS and ALR's contribution to a debate in legal theory was important as they dimistified the traditional one-sided notion that legal decision-making is entirely rational. Especially the ALR's claim that the judge by the a posteriori application of rational arguments often tries to justify the conclusion that was a priori made by virtue of his or her intuition, seems to support the thesis that in reality the context of discovery and the context of justification cannot be rigidly separated. Thus, the irrational part in the discovery context should not be neglected as totally unimportant since this would idealize too much the justification context. Thus, the interest in the discovery context rather than just in the justification context makes the entire adjudication process to appear more real.

However, a mild version of separation between the two contexts is necessary since it is reasons that decide which intuitions are proper for a reasoning, and which are not. For example, in the reasoning of a decision a judge should use so-called social (or objective) reasons, not their personal subjective reasons which could only be a rationalisation of their subjective preferences. Finally, the mild separation thesis demands that the discovery context be more rationally illuminated. By being aware of the irrationality (positive and negative) that is present in the discovery context we may reach more reasonable, objective and impartial judicial decisions.

## 10.6 Conclusion

In the process of legal decision-making, more narrowly in its process of discovery, it seems that the mentioned two kinds of intuition take place.

First, in deciding clear[8] cases so-called "instrumental intuition" seems to play an important role. In such an event, the judge stems from the given facts of a case (i.e. from the lower syllogistic premise) and uses their intuition (so-called "legal intuition") in order to find an appropriate legal norm under which the facts of the case will subsequently be subsummed. If the case is truly clear (e.g. when the facts of the case are well known and the legal norm substantially understandable and determinate, and quite easily found) the judge's intuition is instrumental since it operates as a means, an instrument or "short-cut" to find the relevant legal norm within the relatively explicit legal rules of the (internal) legal system. Such a clear case would, e.g., be when a thief is caught *in flagranti,* when stealing a coat from a supermarket given that his or her criminal intention was clearly established. Within such a decision-making process the judge's initial intuition (also "hunch"), which is irrational *per se,* is rationally evaluated in their mind before it is expressed as a decision, and subsequently also rationally justified in the form of reasons that are provided in the reasoning of the decision.

Second, in the event of an unclear case, the entire process is carried out at the beginning as was mentioned above: (1) the empirical perception (through the judge's senses) of the facts of the case; (2) rational evaluation in the manner of thinking what to do; (3) an intuition (or hunch) as to which legal norm is a possible solution; (3) a rational evaluation as to whether such a legal solution is indeed possible given the facts of the case; (4) the internal decision made; and (5) the decision expressed and reasons for such provided in the reasoning.

If there is no clear upper premise of the legal norm the role of the judge and their intuition must necessarily be more creative. His or her intuition creatively extends beyond the explicit boundary of the legal text into the area of the implicit text[9] of the unclear legal provision, which still must remain within the legal system for otherwise it cannot be a legal decision. An example of such creative intuition is the implict text of the American Constitution that was discovered in the case of *Griswold v. Connecticut* (381 U.S. 479 (1965)), concerning the right to privacy. It is well known that in this case the US Supreme Court found the previously not explicitly existing right to privacy in the US Constitution in the implicit text of the Constitution by virtue of discovering "penumbras" and "emanations" of certain other explicitly mentioned rights (i.e. several amendments to the US Const.). The problem is then how to justify, rationally, such judicial creativity. It seems that the internal criteria of justification cannot be applied so we have to make use of the external criteria of justification, the role of which is to help us establish a necessary connection between the solution and the legal system. Such creative intuition as a form of judges' irrationality is positive as long as it discovers hidden parts, develop undeveloped parts, or upholds or supports parts of the existing legal system. Such creative intuition must still remain within the legal system.

---

[8]Here I refer to MacCormick's determination of a clear case instead of an easy case as he argued that in a complex society there are no easy cases (MacCormick 2005).

[9]Concerning the meaning of implicit text see Barak 2005: 104–106.

Finally, it follows from the argument from psychological typology presented above that the context of discovery and the context of justification of legal decisions cannot be rigidly separated since every person's decision-making necessarily includes irrational elements which importantly influence his or her rational evaluation. Nevertheless, in order for such irrationality of the judge *(via* intuition as part of perception) to pass the test of the legal system, and therefore be considered as positive, it must be in the service of the internal and external criteria of the justification of judicial decisions, and thereby in the service of the rationality of law. This occurs when an intuition is translated into a legal reason which determines the conditions under which the intuition can be considered as legal intuition. If it departs from being in the service thereof it may be considered as legally invalid irrationality.

## References


Alexy, R. 1989. *A theory of legal argumentation*. Oxford: Clarendon.

Anderson, B. 1996. *Discovery in legal decision-making*. Dordrecht: Kluwer Academic Publishers.

Anderson, B. 2010. Context of discovery, context of decision and context of justification in the law. IVR encyclopaedia of jurisprudence. http://ivr-enc.info/index.php?title=Main_Page. Accessed 26 Mar 2010.

Aylesworth, G. 2005. Postmodernism. Stanford encyclopedia of philosophy. http://plato.stanford.edu/. Accessed 5 Feb 2010.

Barak, A. 2005. *Purposive interpretation in law*. Princeton/Oxford: Princeton University Press.

Briggs Myers, I., and P.B. Myers. 1980. *Gifts differing*. Mountain View: Davis-Black Publishing.

Cerar, M. 2001. *(I)racionalnost modernega prava [The (Ir)rationality of modern law]*. Ljubljana: Bonex založba.

Daicoff, S.S. 2004. *Lawyer, know thyself*. Washington, DC.: American Psychological Association.

Feteris, E. 1999. *Fundamentals of legal argumentation*. Dordrecht: Kluwer Academic Publishers.

Frank, J. 1930. *Law and the modern mind*. New York: Brentano's, Inc.

Furlan, B. 2002. *Problem realnosti prava [The problem of law's reality]*. Ljubljana: Pravna fakulteta in Cankarjeva založba.

Habermas, J. 1987. *The philosophical discourse of modernity*. Cambridge: Cambridge University Press.

Horkheimer, M. 1974. *Eclipse of reason*. New York: Continuum International Publishing Company Ltd.

Jung, C.G. 1921. *Psychologische typen*. Duesseldorf: Patmost Verlag GmbH & Walter Verlag.

Kaufmann, A. 1992. *Rechtsphilosophie in der Nach-Neuzeit*. Heidelberg: Decker und Müller Verlag.

Lyotard, J.-F. 1984. *The postmodern condition: A report on knowledge*. Minneapolis: University of Minnesota Press.

MacCormick, N. 1978. *Legal reasoning and legal theory*. Oxford: Clarendon.

MacCormick, N. 2005. *Rhetoric and the rule of law*. Oxford: Oxford University Press.

MacCormick, N. 2008. *Practical reason in law and morality*. Oxford: Oxford University Press.

Maritain, J. 1951. *Man and the state*. Chicago: The University of Chicago Press.

Mautner, T. (ed.). 2000. *The penguin dictionary of philosophy*. London/New York/Victoria/Toronto/New Delhi/Auckland/Johannesburg: Penguin.

*Merriam-Webster's Collegiate Dictionary* (10th Ed.). 1993. Springfield/Massachusetts: Merriam-Webster, Inc.

Minda, G. 1995. *Postmodern legal movements*. New York: The New York University Press.
Pavčnik, M., and L.E. Wolcher. 2000. A dialogue on legal theory between a European Legal Philosopher and his American friend. *Texas International Journal* 35: 335–386.
Prakash Sinha, S. 1993. *Jurisprudence, legal philosophy*. St. Paul: West.
Reinhold, R. 2010. Personality pathways. Exploring personality types & its applications. http://www.personalitypathways.com/type_inventory.html. Accessed 5 Jan 2010.
Unger, R.M. 1986. *Passion*. New York: Free Press.
Wallace, R.J. 2000. Practical reason. Stanford encyclopedia of philosophy. http://plato.stanford.edu/practical-reason. Accessed 14 Jan 2010.

# Chapter 11
# Constitutive Rules and Coherence in Legal Argumentation: The Case of Extensive and Restrictive Interpretation*

**Antonino Rotolo and Corrado Roversi**

## 11.1 Introduction

### *11.1.1 Motivation and Aim*

The literature in jurisprudence and legal theory has rarely explored the link between argumentation theory and the institutional theory of legal concepts. A remarkable exception that devoted some (non-systematic) effort to this link is, for instance, the work by MacCormick (2005). This paper aims at offering a fresh contribution to this research issue by developing a theory of the extensive and restrictive interpretation of legal provisions. We show that these interpretive techniques correspond to complex revision operations over theories of constitutive rules. Indeed, restrictive and extensive interpretations are typical examples of how courts deal with the open texture of legal language and with penumbral cases by further developing the content of legal rules: courts act in such a way as to expand or restrict the core of determinate meaning of rules taking into account their purposes (Hart 1994, Chap. 7). Herbert Hart suggested that, in those cases, judges act as surrogate legislatures by filling legal gaps. Indeed, this view is confirmed in this paper and made analytically clear: legal concepts can be holistically and inferentially characterized by arbitrarily large and connected theories of constitutive rules, and so, when we expand or restrict the scope of legal concepts we are doing nothing but changing (revising or contracting) those theories. This analysis also sheds light on

*This paper is the result of a joint effort, with Corrado Roversi writing Sects 11.1.2, 11.2, and 11.3, and Antonino Rotolo Sects 11.1.1 and 11.4–11.7.

A. Rotolo (✉) • C. Roversi
CIRSFID, University of Bologna, Bologna, Italy
e-mail: antonino.rotolo@unibo.it; corrado.roversi@unibo.it

C. Dahlman and E. Feteris (eds.), *Legal Argumentation Theory: Cross-Disciplinary Perspectives*, Law and Philosophy Library 102, DOI 10.1007/978-94-007-4670-1_11,

the relation between the legal and the ordinary understandings (if any) of a given concept: in the case they both take place, we should compare and aggregate two corresponding theories, the one corresponding to the ordinary reading and the one corresponding to the legal reading.

The advantages of this approach are thus that it allows us to make these interpretive arguments more transparent and to provide criteria for choosing the best interpretive option on account of requirements such as those of minimal change, inclusiveness and connectedness of legal knowledge.

In a nutshell, our basic intuitions are the following:

- Extensive and restrictive interpretations require to expand and contract the theories of constitutive rules characterizing those concepts that are involved in the interpretive process;
- In the case any relevant concept has both an ordinary and a legal understanding, we should preliminarily compare and merge the corresponding theories;
- The merging and revision processes of theories may lead to multiple results;
- Then the problem is to choose the best option, which requires to develop an argumentation system where different interpretive arguments support different theories for the same concept.

The outline of the paper is as follows. In the remainder of this section, we briefly introduce the reader to the concept of constitutive rule. Section 11.2 explains how we should view constitutive rules in the law in order to make an analytic use of them for reconstructing the interpretation of legal concepts. Section 11.3 further clarifies this view by illustrating what types of conditions constitutive rules can express, how this can lead to a version of concept holism and why constitutive rules are defeasible. Section 11.4 systematically defines all building blocks we use in the remainder. Section 11.5 describes in detail the process of expansion and contraction of legal concepts driven by the goals of norms: these ideas are first informally presented and then made more precise and rigorous. Section 11.6 refines the model of the previous section by discussing how to compare and merge the ordinary and legal understandings of concepts and how to develop arguments for selecting the best theories to support the expansion or contraction of a theory of constitutive rules. A section with some conclusions and a discussion of related work end the paper.

### *11.1.2 Constitutive Rules: Preliminaries*

Since the work of John Searle—and before him with the work of Czesław Znamierowski and John Rawls—the concept of constitutive rule has been playing an important role in the effort of contemporary social philosophy to explain the ontology of institutional facts. Authors who have dealt with this concept have typically maintained that institutional facts are "made possible" and "constituted" by, or "logically presuppose," a given set of rules, which for this same reason are said to be constitutive of those facts. The classic example is that of chess: facts of a chess match such as those denoted by the sentence "the bishop took the queen in two moves" simply could not obtain if some rules—the rules of chess, which dictate what bishops and queen are, what they can do, and also what "taking a piece" is—were not already in place. The conclusion is that (in Searle's own words):

> Regulative rules regulate activities whose existence is independent of the rules; constitutive rules constitute (and also regulate) forms of activity whose existence is *logically dependent* on the rules. (Searle 1964, p. 55, italics added)

So formulated, this statement seems clear. However, when one goes deeper in trying to assess what this "constitutive power" of rules amounts to, problems start to arise. How can rules create facts and activities? What kind of ontology of rules must be presupposed to support this ontology of institutional facts? Searle, and with him many other authors who have dealt with ontological questions in relation to institutions, have been maintaining in recent years what we could call a "rule-realist" approach to constitutive rules. According to this approach, these rules exist and have constitutive power because they are the content of collective intentional states of acceptance, and it is such collective intentionality that "props up" institutions and institutional facts. However, interpretations diverge on how this collective intentionality should be analyzed, namely, whether for example it should be conceived as a set of individual intentions connected by mutual beliefs (as Lagerspetz (1995), for example, maintains) or as intentions which are already in a collective form (as Searle (1996, 2010) states, following on the work of Raimo Tuomela and Margareth Gilbert: see (Tuomela 1995; Gilbert 1989)).

Now, if constitutive rules and collective intentionality are intended as explanatory tools for the ontology of institutions, this should work also for law and legal facts—and, in fact, these authors draw from the legal domain many examples of institutional facts. Indeed, the question of how the concept of constitutive rule can be of help in explaining legal phenomena has already been treated to a certain extent, for example by contemporary scholars who have argued for an institutional conception of law (Ruiter 2001). However, this is not how we want to make use of this concept here. In this paper, we will instead inquire whether constitutive rules can be found to have a useful explanatory role with regard to some practices of legal interpretation. Can an explanation of how constitutive rule typically behave shed some light on the behavior of legal concepts in the context of a given legal system? Would such an explanation be able to explain typical forms of legal interpretation and argumentation? In the pages that follow, we will try to make some steps in this direction.

## 11.2 Ontological Versus Analytical Use of Constitutive Rules

Imagine that a person, or a group of persons, have an idea for a game. They discuss this idea at length, and in the end try to formalize it into a coherent and recognizable sets of rules. Just as in chess, or in thousands of other games, these rules define the basic elements of the game by determining how these elements can be used by players, what their effect is, and so on. Now, the group of game designers make a great deal of playtesting, and many problems arise regarding the complexity, balance, and deepness of the game as constituted by the rules so far conceived. The game designers conceive some solutions to these problems, modify the rules, make more playtesting, and proceed along this way, in a long series of trial and errors, by modifying the original set of rules. Eventually they arrive at a final set of rules on which all of them agree. Hence, they write down these rules in plain English and have the game published by an important game-publishing house: Its title is GAME. A large amount of people read the presentation of GAME in specialized journals, buy it, start reading the rules and play. After some time, an entire domain of practice and discourse has arisen. Tournaments of GAME are organized, a lot of forum discussion on the Internet is brought forward by a consistent group of fans (that we may call the "GAME community"), the meaning of the rules of GAME goes through a continuous process of interpretation and re-interpretation, errata and further extensions of GAME are published in order to further improve the original version. What is more, the entire discussion on GAME, namely, the linguistic exchange that takes place in the GAME community forum, makes consistent use of terms and concepts that no one who is not acquainted with the core rules of GAME can understand. An entire technical lexicon is developed by the rules of GAME, one which is widely used within the GAME community and whose usage makes its members resemble the initiates of an esoteric sect.

Clearly, something along the lines of the GAME example happens all the time in the games market, and with suitable modifications something very similar happens in other important domains of institutional life, such as law, for example. It is certainly true for example that, while in the legal domain norms are interpreted, thus giving the impression that no rule exists before their decisions, and while legal customs emerging from social practices play an essential part in the everyday practice of legal communities, nevertheless instances of statutes defining new roles and procedures, enacted by the legislator for specific purposes and giving place to an entirely new technical lexicon, are ubiquitous in all legal systems. And these last cases fall exactly within the scope of the GAME example. Now, we take it to be evident that, without the rules of GAME, all the activity that we have described to revolve around GAME could not have taken place. Those rules have been essential in creating a practice and an entire domain of discourse, in a way that simple regulative rules cannot be. The technical lexicon that members of the GAME community use all day has been created by the rules of GAME, and all the GAME players must know what those rules are about in order to play correctly. It is indeed difficult to explain the GAME example—and the other cases of institutions traceable to it—without recurring to the notion of constitutive rule.

Clearly, however, institutions traceable to the GAME example are instances of artifactual institutions—that is, they are created from scratch (and possibly subsequently modified) through some sort of authoritative systems. But consider another classic example of institution (one which was used both by Santi Romano and MacCormick): the institution of queue, that is, the practice by which persons who arrive later at a place in which goods are provided place themselves immediately before the last arrived, thus creating a continuous line of persons. Consider now this rule:

> In a queue, the person who stands at the end of the line is the last in accessing goods. (11.1)

Would this be a constitutive rule of queue? It depends on whether, without that rule, the activity of queue could not have taken place, just as GAME could not have existed without its rules. But it is not clear whether that of queue is an institutional practice born independently of rules—through habits, for example, and customs—or whether it has been created through a given and explicit set of rules.

Now, the point we would like to stress here is the following. If the institution of queue is an institutional practice which is born independently of rules—a customary practice, for example, internalized through habits and by imitation—then (11.1) cannot properly be constitutive but is rather as a formalization ex post of an already-existing practice. On the contrary, if the institution of queue has been created through a given set of rules, and if (11.1) has had a role in this genealogical process just as the rules of GAME, then (11.1) can properly be said to be constitutive.

This leads us to a distinction, which up to now has not received sufficient attention in the discussion on constitutive rules. Depending on the nature of the institution and its genealogy, the statement of constitutive rules can represent either rules which are genuinely constitutive of an institution or are a mere description of it, whatever structure it may have.[1] In the former case, the statement of a constitutive rule has a performative (and hence constitutive) illocutionary force; in the latter case, the statement of a constitutive rule has an assertive illocutionary force, being nothing more than an ex-post reconstruction of that practice, a reconstruction which can be true or false.

This distinction corresponds to a distinction between two possible uses of the concept of constitutive rule: an ontological and an analytical one. The ontological use is made when constitutive rules are taken to explain the very genealogy of an institution; the analytical use is made when constitutive rules are taken to describe that institution, independently of ontological questions such as whether it has been indeed created through rules or instead had an independent standing.

In this paper, when considering whether constitutive rules can shed some lights on the process through which legal interpretation and argumentation shape legal concepts, we will mainly make an analytical use of the concept of constitutive rules. Hence, we do not necessarily subscribe here to the idea that these concepts are

[1] Hence, constitutive rules in this second sense are similar to semantic rules describing institutional concepts: each of such rules does not constitute the reality of the institution—a reality that may very well depend on phenomena that are different from rules, such as imitation, empathy or behavioral responses—but defines its concepts and makes them cognitively graspable and so usable. Perhaps, this intuition can be compared to Ross (1957)'s well known account of legal intermediate concepts: see (Sartor 2006). However, a comparison with Alf Ross's work is out of the scope of this paper.

entirely and explicitly constituted through well-formalized rules. Instead, we simply use constitutive rules—with their typical features—as analytical tools to describe the dynamics of legal concepts through typical forms of legal interpretation (without taking a stance on the ontology of law, which is a separate matter).

## 11.3 How Constitutive Rules Behave: Conditions, Conceptual Holism and Defeasibility

In this section, we will briefly present some features of the process through which constitutive rules typically constitute concepts, so as to inquire in the following sections whether and to what extent these features can find an application in the domain of legal concepts. To this end, and for the sake of simplicity, we will make reference to the (quite typical) example of chess.

Let us consider the following rule, which is constitutive of the concept of "checkmate" in chess:

A checkmate is made when the king is attacked in such a way that no move will leave it unattacked. (11.2)

Clearly, this rule sets down conditions of application for the sortal term "checkmate," and hence specifies under what conditions a checkmate occurs during a match of chess. Typically, these conditions are necessary, and indeed (11.2) set down a necessary (and sufficient) condition for a checkmate to obtain. But suppose that in chess you can make a checkmate in different ways, and that separate rules (11.2.1), …,(11.2.k) determine these different ways. Now, clearly, (11.2.1), …,(11.2.k) would set down different conditions for a checkmate, each sufficient and not necessary. However, if we merged (11.2.1), …,(11.2.k) into a single rule (11.2.z), collecting all the conditions under which a checkmate can obtain in a disjunctive form, then this rule would still set down a necessary and sufficient condition in disjunctive form. Hence, in creating a concept (corresponding to a sortal institutional term), constitutive rules set down necessary or sufficient conditions, and in the end for the concept to be completely constituted necessary and sufficient conditions must be determined. This is our first premise.

However, the fact that constitutive rules jointly determine necessary and sufficient conditions for the application of a sortal term (and hence in this way create a concept) does not entail that all these conditions must correspond to conditions of subsistence of a given institutional object, state of affairs, property, relation, etc. That is, semantic conditions do not always strictly correspond to ontological conditions of subsistence.

Consider this rule of chess:

A checkmate COUNTS AS victory in chess. (11.3)

This, too, is a constitutive rule of checkmate, just as (11.2). This rule certainly sets down a necessary condition for the application of the term checkmate: you cannot call a checkmate on your adversary and concluding that he won. However, this rule sets down not a necessary condition for a checkmate to happen but rather the immediate consequence of checkmate. Hence, constitutive rules create the concepts of institutional elements by determining both their typical conditions of subsistence and their typical institutional consequences.

Our third consideration is that constitutive rules set down the application conditions of an institutional concept defeasibly, that is, depending on other contextual considerations. The new premise defeating the normal institutional consequences that are set down by constitutive rules can be a simple fact or another institutional fact whose concept is rule-constituted. Examples can be many: if, during a match of chess, no move of the king would leave it unattacked this counts as a checkmate, but only if the previous move was regular. If, during an auction, a person raises his hand this normally counts as a bid, but only if that person did not raise his hand to scratch his head.

Fourth, constitutive rules come in systems, and the way in which they constitute a concept is holistic. Consider again rule (11.2): it defines checkmate by appealing to other elements of the game of chess such as the "king," the concept of "attack," and that of "move." And these elements have their own constitutive rules; for example, the king has among its own constitutive rules:

The black king is the piece whose initial position on the chessboard is e8. (11.4)

The kings may either move to any adjoining square not taken by any of the opponent's pieces, or they may move by castling but may not do so more than once over the course of a match.

These constitutive rules of the king refer to the concept of "castling," which has its own constitutive rules. And part of the definition of an attack presupposes that the concept of "king" is already in place:

The king is under attack when an opponent's piece can capture it with its next move. (11.5)

This behavior of constitutive rules is typical of conceptual holism: you cannot say to have the complete meaning of an institutional term without knowing the whole system of constitutive rules and the web of concepts with which the meaning of that term is intertwined. Now, as said, the complete system of constitutive rules determines all the conditions for application of an institutional sortal term, each of which can be sufficient or necessary but all of which are sufficient and necessary. If you have access to this system from the start, as happens with simple institutions that are constructed artificially (chess and other games are good examples), determining the whole system of these conditions is relatively simple. Hence an ontological use of constitutive rules normally presuppose that you know the content of all those rules, because, if you can explain the role that these rules have had in the genealogy of a given institution, then you should be able to determine them with relative ease. But, in making an analytical use of constitutive rules, that is, in using constitutive rules as ex-post formalizations and representations of the semantic structure of institutional concepts, we will have to admit that the whole system of constitutive rules of an institutional concepts is very often indeterminate: You do not have the whole set of its necessary and sufficient conditions of application, but rather fallible theories and reconstructions of portions of this system, in the form of inferential chains of concepts connected by constitutive rules. This is often the case with legal concepts, whose content is often determined not simply through explicit rules but also through interpretive practices that connect those concepts among themselves and with other concepts of ordinary language.

We can summarize the just-mentioned features of constitutive rules under four points:

1. Constitutive rules create institutional concepts by determining the necessary and sufficient conditions for the application of a given institutional sortal term.
2. Constitutive rules create institutional concepts by determining typically both conditions of subsistence and institutional consequences of a given institutional element.
3. Constitutive rules are defeasible rules.
4. Constitutive rules constitute in systems: Their meaning-creation process is holistic.

With some caveats, the most important of which has just been made with regard to conceptual holism, all these four points can be useful in making both an ontological and an analytical use of constitutive rules. In the following sections, we will inquire whether these features of constitutive rules can be useful in explaining how legal concepts evolve through typical forms of legal interpretation.

## 11.4 Building Blocks

As usual, we represent legal rules with conditional structures such as $b_1, \ldots, b_n \Rightarrow l$ (if $b_1, \ldots, b_n$ hold, then $l$ follows). As is well-known, the assumption that the conditions of legal rules give a complete description of their applicability is too strong, due to the complexities and dynamics of the world (Sartor 2005). Legal rules cannot take into account all the possible conditions where they should or should not be applied, because the legislator cannot consider all the possible contexts which are exceptional, namely, he cannot foresee unexpected changes of the world and of the ontology of concepts the rules refer to.

In this paper we represent arguments supporting the extensive and restrictive interpretations of legal provisions by devising a reasoning framework consisting of the following components:

- A mechanism for reasoning about constitutive rules and legal concepts;
- A mechanism for reasoning about regulative legal rules;
- A mechanism for reasoning about the goals of regulative legal rules.

The basic intuition is that the distinction between regulative and constitutive rules suggests that the extensive and the restrictive interpretations do not amount to revising regulative legal rules. Since they require to interpret legal concepts, they amount to revising constitutive rules (Sartor 2006).

### 11.4.1 Constitutive Rules

Constitutive rules typically have the following form (Searle 1996): $r$: $a_1, \ldots, a_n \Rightarrow b$. For example, a bicycle is considered as a vehicle according to the following constitutive rule:

$$Bike \Rightarrow Vehicle.$$

In the law, constitutive rules may either specify conceptual links between "brute" facts or acts (i.e., non-institutional facts or acts whose status is independent of the existence of any constitutive rule; example: being over 18 years) and types of institutional facts or acts (e.g., being adult), or rather specify conceptual links where institutional facts or acts (e.g., a contract made by person $j$ in the name of person $k$) have the same effects of other institutional facts or acts (e.g., a contract made by $k$). This view basically implies that the consequents of constitutive rules always correspond to institutional facts or acts.

As we previously recalled, constitutive rules may provide

1. **Sufficient conditions to obtain a concept** (here, Bid):

$$Auction,\ Raise\_Hand \Rightarrow Bid$$

2. **Necessary conditions to obtain a concept** (here, King):

$$King \Rightarrow Move\_OneSquare\_InAnyDirection$$

3. **Necessary and sufficient conditions to obtain a concept**: this is possible when we take the whole theory of constitutive rules as a unique system characterizing a concept.

However, there exists another important type of constitutive rules, those which determine

4. **Possible conditions to obtain a concept** (here, Vehicle):

$$Horse \leadsto Vehicle.$$

The occurrence of a horse alone is not sufficient for supporting even the defeasible conclusion that we have a vehicle, but the rule suggests that this is possible. Note that we represent this type of rules using the *defeaters*, namely, special rules marked with the arrow $\rightsquigarrow$, which are not meant to derive conclusions, but to provide reasons against the opposite. Indeed, if *Horse* is a good reason *to prevent* the conclusion that this is *not* a vehicle, this is nothing but saying that a horse is possibly a vehicle (Governatori and Rotolo 2008a; Governatori et al. 2005).

The above comment on the role of defeaters leads us to consider ways for representing the defeasibility of constitutive rules. As we have already argued, consider again the following example:

$$Auction,\ Raise\_Hand \Rightarrow Bid$$
$$Auction,\ Raise\_Hand,\ Scratch\_Head \Rightarrow \neg Bid.$$

Of course, raising one hand in any auction counts as a bid, but this does not hold if one raises one hand and scratches her own head; when both the above rules apply, we have a conflict in which the second rule should prevail. To do so, it is possible in our framework to establish the relative strength of rules by stating that one rule *overrides* or is *stronger* than other (conflicting) rules.

## *11.4.2 Regulative Legal Rules*

For the sake of simplicity, we will assume that regulative legal rules only impose duties and prohibitions, and state permissions (Governatori and Rotolo 2008a; Governatori et al. 2009). For instance, the rule

$$Vehicle, Park \Rightarrow \mathrm{OBL}\neg Enter$$

states the defeasible prohibition for vehicles to enter parks.

Two important issues can be mentioned in regard to the regulative legal rules:

- The mentioned idea of rule holism can be enriched by considering the interplay between constitutive and regulative rules;
- Regulative legal rules work like partial plans of the legislator in order to achieve or promote goals.

As regards the first question, Fig. 11.1 illustrates the idea. Indeed, the conceptual characterization of the applicability conditions of a given regulative rule may involve other regulative rules insofar as these conditions are conceptually linked to the applicability conditions of such other regulative rules.

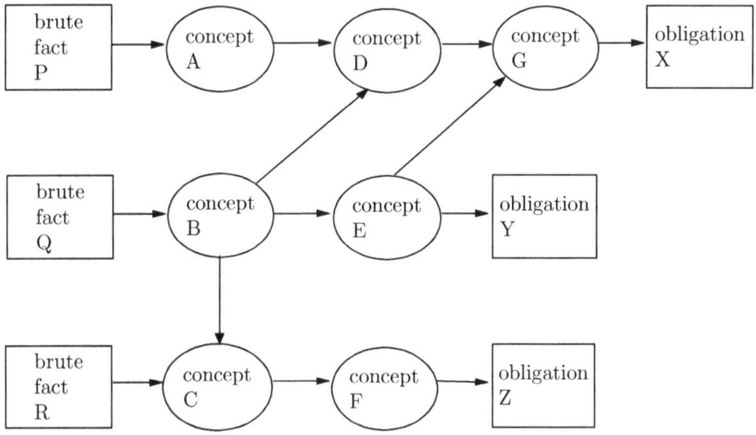


**Fig. 11.1** Interplay between constitutive and regulative rules

From a logical point of view, the following set of rules reframes the contents of Fig. 11.1:

$$\begin{array}{llll} P \Rightarrow A & A \Rightarrow D & D \Rightarrow G & G \Rightarrow \text{OBL}X \\ Q \Rightarrow B & B \Rightarrow E & & E \Rightarrow \text{OBL}Y \\ R \Rightarrow C & C \Rightarrow F & & F \Rightarrow \text{OBL}Z \\ B \Rightarrow D & E \Rightarrow G & B \Rightarrow C & \end{array}$$

If we have $Q$ and there are good reasons to attack the argument saying that $Q$ counts as $B$, then we prevent the conclusion that $Y$ is obligatory, but we may also undermine arguments supporting the conclusions that $Z$ and $X$ are obligatory.

The second point is briefly discussed in the following subsection.

### *11.4.3 Reasoning About the Goals of Regulative Legal Rules*

As it is usually acknowledged in legal theory (Peczenik 1989; Sartor 2005), we assign goals to regulative legal rules. Such a building block should enable us to check whether some situations promote goals or their negations. For our purpose it is sufficient here to introduce a suitable set of rules for goals (Governatori and Rotolo 2008b) which should be used to establish what are the effects of situations where legal rules are violated or complied with, and, in doing so, to see whether they are consistent with the goals. In other words, we have to devise a set of rules like $d_1, \ldots, d_n \Rightarrow_G e$: if applicable in a given context, this rule allows for deriving the goal $e$, meaning that $e$ is promoted by $d_1, \ldots, d_n$. Consider again the rule

$$Vehicle, Park \Rightarrow \text{OBL}\neg Enter$$

and suppose that its goal is **pedestrian_safety**.[2] Consider now that following set $R$ of rules for goals:

$$R = \{x : Bike, Park, Enter \Rightarrow_G \textbf{fast\_circulation},$$
$$y : NarrowSpace, UnprotectedChildArea,$$
$$\textbf{fast\_circulation} \Rightarrow_G \neg\textbf{pedestrian\_safety}\}$$

Rule $x$ states that entering parks with bikes promotes the fast circulation of people in those parks; rule $y$ says that, if fast circulation is promoted and parks have narrow spaces and unprotected children's play areas, then the promoted goal is the negation of pedestrians safety. If both rules are applicable, then allowing bikes to enter parks would promote a goal which is incompatible with the goal of the regulative legal rule prohibiting vehicles to enter.

### *11.4.4 Defeasible Argumentation*

In this paper we assume that reasoning with all the types of rules we have so far mentioned obeys some basic rules of defeasible inference and can be used to build arguments and counter-arguments in a dialectical setting.

In particular, in line with (Governatori and Rotolo 2008a; Governatori et al. 2009), we assume that any $q$ is a defeasible conclusion when three conditions are satisfied. First, we need to consider possible reasoning chains in support of $\neg q$, and show that $\neg q$ is not indisputable. Second, we require that there must be a defeasible rule for $q$ which can be applied. Third, we must consider the set of all rules which are not known to be inapplicable and which permit to get $\neg q$. Essentially, each such a rule $s$ attacks the conclusion $q$. For $q$ to be a conclusion, $s$ must be counterattacked by a rule $t$ for $q$ with the following properties: (1) $t$ must be applicable, and (2) $t$ must be stronger than $s$. Thus each attack on the conclusion $q$ must be counterattacked by a stronger rule. In other words, $r$ and the rules $t$ form a team (for $q$) that defeats the rules $s$.

## 11.5 Interpreting Legal Concepts Means Revising Theories: The Idea

In the context of judicial argumentation in continental legal systems, it is typically assumed that the set of legal regulative rules is kept to be prima facie fixed: any judge or court, during the interpretation process, can argue about the applicability conditions of regulative rules but cannot either add new regulative rules nor cancel them: only legislators have the power to do it.

[2]For clarity's sake, we use in this section bold type expressions to denote goals.

Applying a regulative legal rule such as $r : b_1, \ldots, b_n \Rightarrow \mathrm{OBL}\neg l$ to a case $H$ requires to establish if $H$ matches, via the constitutive rules, with the applicability conditions $b_1, \ldots, b_n$ of $r$. However, there can be some discrepancy between the literal meaning of $b_1, \ldots, b_n$ and the goal assigned to the rule $r$ by the legislator. If so, even though the facts in $H$ match with $b_1, \ldots, b_n$, the occurrence of $l$ in $H$ might not amount to a genuine a violation of $r$ because the other facts in $H$ should not match with $b_1, \ldots, b_n$. A non-literal interpretation of $b_1, \ldots, b_n$ would exclude $H$ as a circumstance falling within the scope of $r$, since the goal of the norm would be achieved anyway: *lex magis dixit quam voluit*, the law said more than what the legislator was meaning to say. Analogously, not all cases in which $H$ mismatches with $b_1, \ldots, b_n$ are not violations. We could have that *lex minus dixit quam voluit*, the law said less than what the legislator was meaning to say: here a non-literal, goal-based interpretation of $r$ would lead to broaden its applicability scope to match $H$, thus making the agent a violator (Peczenik 1989).

Let us begin to illustrate the argumentative process supporting extensive and restrictive interpretation of a legal regulative rule by considering the following simple running example.[3]

*Example 11.1 (Bike in a park).* Suppose Mary enters a park with her bike, thus apparently violating the rule below:

$$r_0 : \mathit{Vehicle}, \mathit{Park} \Rightarrow \mathrm{OBL}\neg \mathit{Enter}$$

Police stops her when she is still on her bike in the park and fines her. Suppose the concept of "park" is indisputably defined, but Mary thinks that the fine is unreasonable because she thinks that here the category "vehicle" should not cover bikes.

### 11.5.1 Restricting the Applicability of Regulative Rules

In a first case, the set $T$ of constitutive rules characterizing the concept of vehicle allows us to derive that any bike is indeed a vehicle:

$$\begin{aligned} T = \{ & r_1 : \mathit{Bike} \Rightarrow \mathit{Vehicle}, \\ & r_2 : \mathit{2\_wheels}, \mathit{Transport}, \neg \mathit{Engine} \Rightarrow \mathit{Bike}\} \end{aligned}$$

If $T$ is the case, the judge could argue that Mary should be fined, as $r_0$ clearly applies to her.

[3] The remainder of this section informally discusses the logical framework originally presented in (Boella et al. 2010a,b). A more advanced way for revising theories of defeasible rules has also been recently proposed in Rotolo (2011).

But suppose that the goal/value of $r_0$ is to reduce pollution. In court, the judge has to establish if Mary violated $r_0$ or not. The judge can show that, if Mary's case fulfills the applicability conditions of $r_0$ (Mary's bike is a vehicle) then a goal which is incompatible with the goal assigned to $r_0$ would be promoted. For example, prohibiting to circulate with bikes in parks would encourage people to get around parks by car and then walk. This would be against the goal of $r_0$ and so the judge has good reasons to exclude that bikes are vehicles when $r_0$ should be applied. Accordingly, when arguing in this way, the judge may interpret $r_0$ by reducing its applicability conditions as far as Mary's case is concerned, and so by contracting $T$ in order to obtain in $T$ that Mary's bike is not a vehicle in the context of the current case.

### 11.5.2 Expanding the Applicability of Regulative Rules

Alternatively, the characterization of the concept of vehicle could exclude that bikes are vehicles and the goal of $r_0$ could be the safety of people walking in the park:

$$T' = \{r_2 : \mathit{2\_wheels}, \mathit{Transport}, \neg \mathit{Engine} \Rightarrow \mathit{Bike},$$
$$r_3 : \mathit{Bike} \Rightarrow \neg \mathit{Vehicle},$$
$$r_4 : \mathit{Transport} \rightsquigarrow \mathit{Vehicle}\}$$

where $r_3$ overrides $r_4$

$T'$ also includes $r_4$, which states that, if we know that something has the purpose of transport, then we have reasons *against* arguing that it is *not* a vehicle (i.e., reasons to block other rules which would lead to exclude that this something is a vehicle). However, in $T'$ $r_4$ is weaker than $r_3$, and so, if we have a bike, we conclude by $r_3$ that we do not have a vehicle.

Now, suppose the judge has to settle Mary's case starting from $T'$. Again, the goal of legal rules such as $r_0$ may be decisive. The judge could argue that Mary should not be fined, as $r_0$ clearly does not apply. But suppose that, since $r_0$ is not fulfilled, this would be against the goal of $r_0$, which is now pedestrians' safety. In this case, the judge has rather good reasons to consider bikes as vehicles when $r_0$ is considered. Hence, the judge may interpret $r_0$ by broadening its applicability conditions as far as Mary's case is concerned, and so by revising $T'$ in such a way as Mary's bike is a vehicle.

### 11.5.3 Revision Procedure and Its Constraints

Sections 11.5.1 and 11.5.2 informally illustrate how to restrict or expand legal concepts and provide the reader with the basic intuitions behind restrictive and extensive legal interpretation. But such interpretive arguments are far from simple and can be formulated in a more complete and complex way. This is what we will do in this section.

Before illustrating in some more detail the procedures for revising theories, let us preliminarily introduce three notions which we will use in the remainder (argument, goal demotion and promotion).

**Definition 11.1 (Argument).** Given a set $R$ of rules and a set $H$ of facts, an argument based on $R$ and $H$ for a conclusion $\phi$ is a tree, where

- Nodes correspond to literals and arcs correspond to the rules used to obtain these literals or to the defeaters blocking the complementary literals;
- The root corresponds to $\phi$;
- The leaf nodes to the primitive premises (facts), and
- For every node corresponding to any literal $\psi$, if its children are $\psi_1, \ldots, \psi_n$, then there is a rule whose antecedents are these literals.

  An argument is *positive* iff no defeater is used in it.

  A *constitutive argument* is an argument where all the used rules are constitutive rules. A *goal argument* is an argument where all the used rules are goal rules.

*Remark 11.1.* Consider the following:

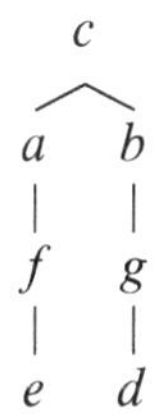


$$r : e \Rightarrow f$$
$$s : f \Rightarrow a$$
$$t : d \Rightarrow g$$
$$u : g \Rightarrow b$$
$$w : a, b \Rightarrow c$$

The tree on the left side is the argument for the literal $c$ we can build using the rules $r$, $s$, $t$, $u$, $w$ on the right side (provided that $e$ and $d$ hold, i.e., are in $H$). Note that defeaters are permitted to occur in arguments. Indeed, a defeater cannot prove anything but only block conclusions, but we want to select here also those arguments in which defeaters can be replaced, for instance, by defeasible rules in order to reinstate or introduce new conclusions.

**Definition 11.2 (Goal Demotion and Promotion).** Let $H = \{f_1, \ldots, f_m\}$ be a set of facts, $r : b_1, \ldots, b_n \Rightarrow \text{OBL}l$ be a regulative legal rule, and $g$ one of the goals of $r$.

*H demotes the goal* $g$ iff

- There is no positive goal argument for $\neg g$ whenever $H$ do not hold;
- There is at least one positive goal argument for $\neg g$ whenever $H$ hold.

*H promotes the goal* $g$ iff

- There is no positive goal argument for $g$ whenever $H$ do not hold;
- There is at least one positive goal argument for $g$ whenever $H$ hold.

The procedure for revising the theories that characterize legal concepts can be framed in general as follows.

**Definition 11.3 (Applicability Restriction).** Let $r : b_1, \ldots, b_n \Rightarrow \text{OBL}l$ be a legal regulative rule, $g$ be one of the goals of $r$, $R^c$ the set of constitutive rules characterizing $b_1, \ldots, b_n$, and $H = \{f_1, \ldots, f_m\}$ be the set of facts of a case. If

1. $H$ makes $r$ applicable;
2. Either
   (a) $H \cup \{\neg l\}$ and $H \cup \{l\}$ *demote* $g$ and there exists any $b_k$ in the applicability conditions for $r$ such that $b_k$ occurs in every positive goal argument $\mathscr{C}$ for $\neg g$ built using both the available rules and either $H \cup \{\neg l\}$ or $H \cup \{l\}$;
   (b) $H \cup \{\neg l\}$ *promotes* $g$ and $H \cup \{l\}$ *demotes* $g$, and there exists any $b_k$ in the applicability conditions for $r$ such that $b_k$ occurs in every positive goal argument $\mathscr{C}$ for $g$ built using both the available rules and $H \cup \{\neg l\}$, or in every positive goal argument $\mathscr{C}'$ for $\neg g$ built using both the available rules and $H \cup \{l\}$;
   (c) $H \cup \{\neg l\}$ and $H \cup \{l\}$ *promote* $g$ and there exists a $b_k$ in the applicability conditions for $r$ such that such that $b_k$ occurs in every positive goal argument $\mathscr{C}$ for $g$ built using both the available rules and either $H \cup \{\neg l\}$ or $H \cup \{l\}$;

then the restriction of the applicability conditions of $r$ with respect to the case $H$ amounts to revising $R^c$ as follows:

$$R'^c = R^c \cup \{r : f_1, \ldots, f_m \rightsquigarrow \neg b_k\}$$

where all $r$ override any other conflicting constitutive rule, and

3. There is no positive goal argument for any other goal $\neg g'$ built using $H$ and $R'^c$, where $g'$ is not less important than $g$ and is the goal assigned to any regulative legal rule $z$ applicable to $H$.

*Remark 11.2.* We have three situations in which the applicability conditions of a regulative legal rule should be restricted (sub-conditions (a), (b), and (c) under point 2 above).

First, we have that the goal of $r$ is demoted not only by $\neg l$ but also by complying with the regulative legal rule; moreover, there exists at least one of the antecedents of the legal rule which is used in all goal arguments, in which either $l$ or $\neg l$ occur, to prove $\neg g$ (the goal violation of the legal rule). Thus, we have reasons to block the constitutive rules supporting this antecedent.

Second, we have that the violation of $r$ ($\neg l$) unexpectedly promotes the goal $g$ of this rue, while compliance ($l$) doesn't; moreover, there exists at least one of the antecedents of the legal rule which is used in all goal arguments, in which $l$ occurs, to support $g$ (the goal promotion of the legal rule), while an antecedent is used in all goal arguments, in which $\neg l$ occurs, to support $\neg g$ (the goal demotion of the legal rule). Thus, we have reasons to block the constitutive rules supporting such antecedents.

Finally, we have that the goal of the norm is promoted independently from the fulfillment or violation of the norm.

The resulting revision is however subject to the final constraint that no other goal $g'$ of any applicable regulative rule would be demoted if $g'$ is at least important as $g$.

**Definition 11.4 (Applicability Extension).** Let $r : b_1, \ldots, b_n \Rightarrow \text{OBL}l$ be a legal regulative rule, $g$ be one of the goals of $r$, $R^c$ the set of constitutive rules characterizing $b_1, \ldots, b_n$, and $H = \{f_1, \ldots, f_m\}$ be the set of facts of a case. If

1. There exists a subset $\{b_k, \ldots, b_{k+j}\}$ of all the applicability conditions $\{b_1, \ldots, b_n\}$ of $r$ for which there is no positive constitutive argument built using $H$ and $R^c$;
2. $H \cup \{\neg l\}$ *demote* $g$;
3. $H \cup \{l\}$ *promote* $g$;
4. There exist the non-positive constitutive arguments $\mathscr{C}_k, \ldots, \mathscr{C}_{k+j}$ built using $H$ and $R^c$ for $b_k, \ldots b_{k+j}$, such that each element of $H$ occurs in each of such arguments;

then the expansion of the applicability conditions of $r$ with respect to the case $H$ amounts to revising $R^c$ as follows: for each argument $\mathscr{C}_h$ among $\mathscr{C}_k, \ldots, \mathscr{C}_{k+j}$, there is a defeater $r' : d_1, \ldots, d_n \rightsquigarrow e$ occurring in $\mathscr{C}_h$ such that

$$R'^c = R^c - \{r' : d_1, \ldots, d_n \rightsquigarrow e\} \cup \{r' : d_1, \ldots, d_n \Rightarrow e\}$$

where all $r'$ override any other conflicting constitutive rule, and

5. There is no positive goal argument for any other goal $\neg g'$ built using $H$ and $R'^c$ where $g'$ is not less important than $g$ and is the goal assigned to any regulative legal rule $z$ applicable to $H$.

*Remark 11.3.* This definition considers the situation where a regulative legal rule $r$ is only partially applicable since some of the conditions cannot be matched by the facts $H$ (1). However, in this situation, not respecting $r$ (i.e., $\neg l$) leads to demoting the goal $g$ of this rule (2). This would be avoided by complying with $r$, i.e., by achieving $l$ (3). Moreover, the constitutive rules suggest that some elements of the context could be interpreted as the missing applicability conditions of the rule $r$ (4). Thus, the theory should be expanded by transforming some defeater rules, among the constitutive rules, into standard rules. The resulting theory is however subject to the final constraint that no other more important goal $g'$ of any norm would be demoted.

To sum up (let's still bear in mind the case of Mary's bike):

1. Revisions of theories never amount to removing rules;
2. There is no other goal $g'$ such that
   - The revision of $T$ (or of $T'$) promotes $r_0$'s goal $g$ which is incompatible, in the application context of $r_0$, with respect to the goal $g'$ of any applicable rule $r$, and
   - $g$ is not more important than $g'$;
3. Our set of constitutive rules should suggest us that the concept of *Bike* can be subsumed under the concept of *Vehicle*.

Point 1 is crucial when we have to handle explicit constitutive rules that correspond to legal definitions stated by the legislator. Clearly, in this case a judge or a court have no power to remove them: such legal definitions are authoritative. However, we may add exceptions by exploiting the defeasible character of constitutive rules. Notice, however, that in many cases revising concepts is inferentially equivalent to changing regulative rules.

Point 2 above states that, if by restricting or extending the concept of *Bike*, we undermine at least one equally or more important goal, which is supposed to be promoted by any applicable rule, then such a restriction or extension is not acceptable. This limit is provided by teleological reasoning (Sartor 2005; Peczenik 1989) and excludes that we can re-balance goals against the balance originally made by the legislator.

Point 3 above is rather connected with the fact that the set of constitutive rules should inherently provide some conceptual limits for any interpretation. Indeed, suppose that Mary enters the park with a gun. We could have reasons for arguing that entering with a gun is dangerous for all people in the park, and so for pedestrians too. However, this is not enough, of course, for arguing that guns are vehicles. In other words, if we do not have any other legal rules prohibiting to enter parks with guns, this behaviour will be permitted. Hence, point 3 has to do with Hart (1994)'s theory of penumbra: we have a core of cases which can be clearly classified as belonging to the legal concept and a penumbra of hard cases, whose membership in the concept can be disputed; but hard cases should exhibit some conceptual link with the core of cases. This idea is formally captured here by confining the revision of the set of constitutive rules only to those situations where such a set, though failing to prove that a bike is a vehicle, already contains reasoning chains suggesting that this may be the case. For example, if we have

$$r_2 : \mathit{2\_wheels}, \mathit{Transport}, \neg \mathit{Engine} \Rightarrow \mathit{Bike}$$
$$r_5 : \mathit{Bike} \leadsto \mathit{Vehicle}$$

$r_5$ states that, if we know that something is a bike, this is not sufficient to prove that it is a vehicle ($r_5$ is a defeater), but $r_5$ is sufficient to block other arguments and rules which would lead to exclude that we have a vehicle. This means that, possibly, if we have a bike, then it could not be unreasonable to consider it as a vehicle. Hence, the revision would require, for example, that $r_5$ be replaced by

$$r'_5 : Bike \Rightarrow Vehicle.$$

## 11.6 Refining the Argumentation Model

The model so far described simplifies the argumentative procedure behind the extensive and restrictive interpretation of statutory law. In fact, it

1. Assumes that the goals of regulative legal rules is clearly identifiable or is given;
2. Takes for granted that a method exists for formulating theories of constitutive rules that characterize concepts;
3. Does not consider the fact that we may have a legal as well as an ordinary understanding of the same concepts and that such different understandings may conflict;
4. Does not guarantee that there is only one suitable revised theory that promotes the goal of the regulative legal rule at hand, and does not offer any criteria for choosing among different and alternative revised theories.

It goes without saying that we cannot address here all the above research issues. Some of them have been already investigated. For instance, the idea that legal rules are supposed to promote goals is quite standard in legal theory and several models for identifying such goals have been discussed in the literature (Peczenik 1989; Sartor 2005, 2006; Bench-Capon 2002).

Issue (2) is far from obvious but it will not be addressed here. Formal and argumentation techniques have been in particular proposed in order to construct theories of rules from judicial precedents (Bench-Capon and Sartor 2003): we expect that similar procedures can be applied here, too.

The following two subsections briefly discuss issues (3) and (4).

### *11.6.1 Ordinary and Legal Concepts*

The law makes use of concepts that can be legal or ordinary depending on whether the legal system provides a definition of them or it just refers to their ordinary understanding in a certain community or context. Accordingly, we may identify the following cases:

1. Ordinary concepts used in the law are characterised by the semantic rules of ordinary language;
2. Legal concepts are specifically defined by the legal system (explicit legal definitions, case law, etc.); in this second case, we may have that

(a) Legal concepts do not have any ordinary understanding: e.g., *adverse possession*;
(b) Legal concepts have both a legal and an ordinary understanding: e.g., *property*;
(c) Legal concepts may recall their ordinary understanding: e.g., *furniture*.

Let us suppose that $A$ is a concept. If $LC$ and $OC$ denote, respectively, the legal and ordinary understandings of $A$, then we may have many possible interactions between $LC$ and $OC$: since we argued that concepts can be characterized as theories consisting of constitutive rules, such an interaction amounts to evaluating the relationship between different theories for the concept $A$. Some (but not all) of the most significant relationships are illustrated in Fig. 11.2a–f.

Consider Fig. 11.2a. This case is clearly unproblematic, as it does not raise any conflict between $LC$ and $OC$: the legal and ordinary understandings of $A$ coincide and correspond to a single constitutive rule stating that any instance of $A$ counts as an instance of another concept $B$ (such a rule thus provides a necessary condition for things to be $A$s). Consider now Fig. 11.2b. Here things do not look harder but can be more complex. In fact, the legal understanding of $A$ still amounts to a theory consisting of $A \Rightarrow B$, but the ordinary understanding of $A$ includes, too, a rule which clarifies the concept $B$ to which $A$ is linked. (This illustrates the idea behind the holistic reading of concepts.) Figure 11.2c, d deal with a case where no theory includes the other but there is still some overlapping. The first case (Fig. 11.2c) corresponds to the case in which the two understandings suggest that $X$ is a defeasible sufficient reason for things to be $A$s, even though $LC$ links $A$ with $B$ while $OC$ states that $X$ is also a defeasible sufficient reason for things to be $B$s; the second case is indeed problematic, since $LC$ and $OC$ agree on the same rule ($X \Rightarrow A$) but disagree on how $A$ and $B$ are related. (Suppose that $A =$ "bicycle" and $B =$ "vehicle": the legal system states that bicycles are vehicles but the ordinary understanding of a vehicle does not include bikes.) Finally, Fig. 11.2e, f consider when $LC$ and $OC$ are disjoint. While the first case is trivial (there is no ordinary understanding of $A$), the second is problematic since the two theories disagree on how $A$ and $B$ are related.

In all cases where $LC$ and $OC$ are different or, worse, incompatible, we have to address the problem of what understanding is more satisfactory. A rather simple answer to this question would be in line with the authoritative nature of the law and of the legislator: the more preferred option is of course the one that is suggested by the legal system. However, this solution is far from obvious, especially when the interpreter has good arguments to resort to any restrictive or extensive interpretation of $A$, namely, has good arguments to reject the actual version of $LC$ as a good theory for $A$ in the current case.

A more cautious approach that still gives priority to $LC$ over $OC$ consists not in choosing between them, but rather in aggregating them into a new single theory.

Indeed,

- $OC$ can be crucial for characterizing undefined concepts in $LC$ by using suitable rules of $OC$;

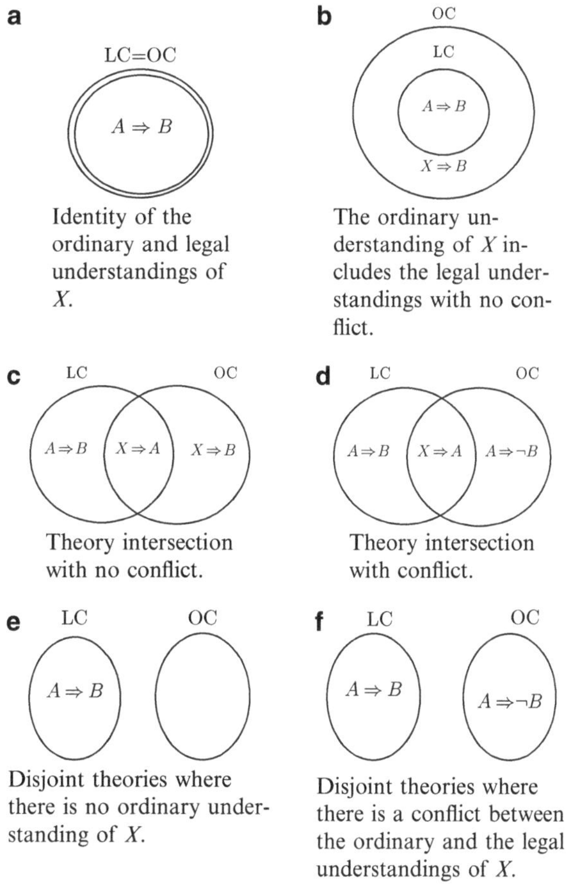


**Fig. 11.2** Some relations between theories. (**a**) Identity of the ordinary and legal understandings of $X$. (**b**) The ordinary understanding of $X$ includes the legal understandings with no conflict. (**c**) Theory intersection with no conflict. (**d**) Theory intersection with conflict. (**e**) Disjoint theories where there is no ordinary understanding of $X$. (**f**) Disjoint theories where there is a conflict between the ordinary and the legal understandings of $X$

- $OC$ rules can be decisive to root legal concepts in our ordinary experience, in the domain of empirical concepts, and link them with paradigmatic examples (legal concepts usually are inferentially connected with ordinary concepts).

The above two arguments are at the core of any holistic theory of institutional concepts, as they imply that all legal concepts are meaningful insofar as they are related to other (not necessarily legal) concepts and refer directly or indirectly to non-legal (brute or empirical) concepts.

Theory aggregation can be in general a complex, and sometimes unsolvable problem, but when tractable it can be handled by roughly adopting the following guidelines.

**Definition 11.5 (Theory aggregation).** Let $A$ be a legal concept and $LC$ and $OC$ be its legal and ordinary understandings. The aggregation of $LC$ with $OC$ is defined by the following procedure:

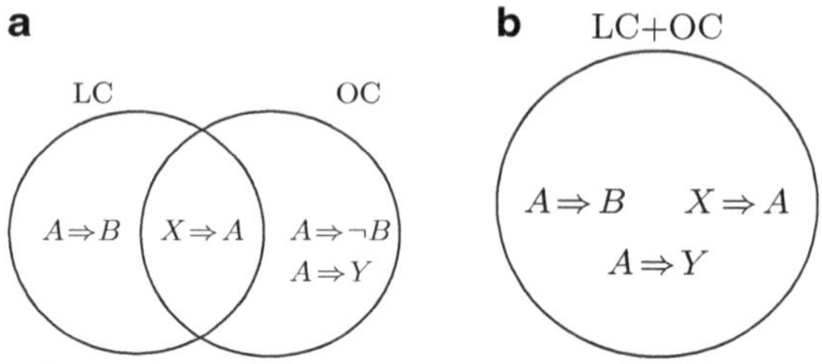


*LC* and *OC* agree on rule $X \Rightarrow A$ and disagree on the link between $A$ and $B$.

The aggregation preserves all rules in *LC* and consistently adds *OC* rules as much as possible.

**Fig. 11.3** Aggregation of $LC$ with $OC$. (**a**) $LC$ and $OC$ agree on rule $X \Rightarrow A$ and disagree on the link between $A$ and $B$. (**b**) The aggregation preserves all rules in $LC$ and consistently adds $OC$ rules as much as possible

- Take the $LC$ and $OC$ rules and state that $LC$ rules should prevail over $OC$ rules in case of conflict;
- When no clear priority can be given between $LC$ and $OC$ rules, aggregate $LC$ with $OC$ by maximizing the set of $OC$ rules into a new consistent theory.

An example of theory aggregation which meets the above guidelines is given in Fig. 11.3a, b.

## *11.6.2 Arguments to the Best Theory*

A simple inspection of Definitions 11.3, 11.4, and 11.5 shows that there exist cases where more resulting theories are available for

- Aggregating the legal and ordinary understandings of concepts;
- Revising the given theories of constitutive rules in order to align concepts with the goals of regulative legal rules.

The combination of the above two reasons raises the crucial question of how to choose among many possible theory revisions. Clearly, this problem can take the form of a dialectical process where the players exchange arguments and counter-arguments to establish which is the best theory supporting or excluding the extensive or restrictive interpretation of a legal rule (Prakken and Sartor 2004, Sect. 4).

Even though in a different context of judicial reasoning, some suggested to adapt criteria classically proposed for evaluating scientific theories (Bench-Capon and Sartor 2003), such as:

Explanatory power: This criterion was adopted in legal case-based reasoning to determine a measure of the number of cases explained. Here, such a criterion may correspond to the idea of theory inclusiveness, which can be measured, for example, by the number of concepts that occur in the theory or by the number of regulative legal rules whose applicability conditions are conceptually characterized by the theory at hand.

Consistency and teleological coherence: This criterion has been already implemented, as it requires that theories of constitutive rules are internally consistent and support coherent solutions with respect to the goals of the regulative legal rules.

Simplicity: This criterion could be measured in terms of the number of rules occurring in a theory; in some cases, such a criterion may work in the opposite direction of the explanatory power, since simplicity can lead to decreasing the number of concepts occurring in a theory. In such cases, we will need ways to solve the conflict between these two criteria. For example, we could give priority to explanatory power but by imposing to minimize the number of rules in case more options are available.

However, at least two other criteria should be considered:

Minimal change: This criterion comes from standard revision theory, which assumes that, to adjust theories, we should change them as little as possible. In rule-based theories, two basic strategies can be the following ones: (a) keep the set of rules as close as possible to the original one, (b) minimize the changes of the set of conclusions obtained from the theory. Notice that the first option is independent of the facts of the case, whereas the other is context-dependent, since different facts may fire different rules. These two options do not always lead to the same results: suppose $H$ includes $a$ and consider

$$\begin{aligned} R^c = \{r &: a \Rightarrow b \\ s &: b \Rightarrow e \\ t &: b \Rightarrow d \\ z &: b \Rightarrow e\} \end{aligned}$$

If we want to block $e$ (we want to restrict the interpretation of a concept), we have two options: add either two defeaters to override respectively $s$ and $z$, or only one defeater that overrides $r$. The first option is better in terms of minimizing the change of conclusions (we only drop $e$), while the second one is better, as only one defeater is added (but two conclusions are dropped: $b$ and $e$). Perhaps, in the present context, the first alternative should be preferred, since we are dealing with judicial reasoning, which is context-dependent.

Theory connectedness: This can be roughly measured by the number of links (rules) that connect each concept with the others. Intuitively, this is a desirable property, since it reflects the systematic character of legal systems. However, this criterion can be in conflict with the one that aims at minimizing changes.

Consider the following example:

$$r_0 : \mathit{Vehicle}, \mathit{Park} \Rightarrow \mathrm{OBL}\neg \mathit{Enter}$$

but suppose that $r_0$ if applied to *Bike* is against the goal $\neg$*pollution*

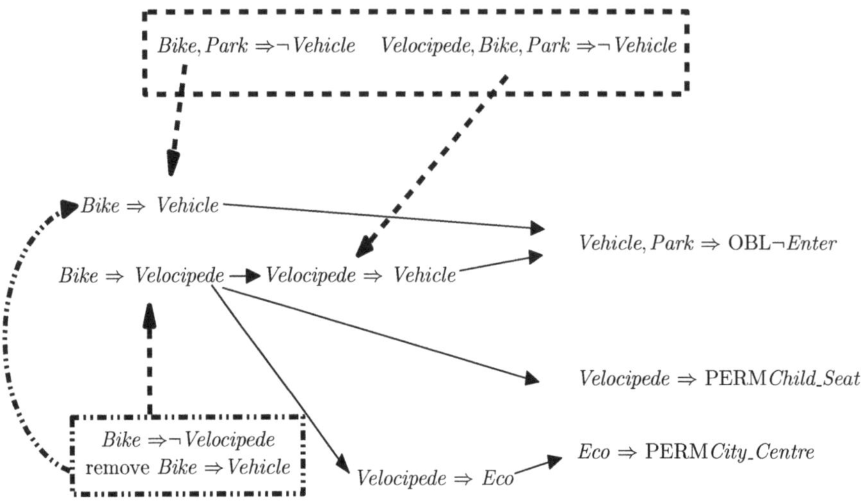


**Fig. 11.4** Multiple theories

Figure 11.4 illustrates two alternatives that restrict the concept of vehicle, thus excluding that a bike is a vehicle.

- Assume that the goals of the permissions are less important than $\neg$*pollution*; then
- The best option is the one in the dashed box on to of the figure, because the resulting theory better satisfies the following requirements
  - Minimal change,
  - Inclusiveness,
  - Connectedness.

## 11.7 Related Work and Conclusions

In this paper we proposed a framework for reconstructing the arguments supporting the extensive and restrictive interpretations of legal provisions. The contribution is based on the idea that the interpretation of legal concepts may require to change the constitutive rules defining them. Indeed, if our ontology does not classify a bike as a vehicle, but we have reasons that this is the case, then this implicitly leads to conclude that the ontology must be revised and that a bike, at least in the contexts under consideration, is a vehicle. The revision procedure presented in this paper are driven and constrained by considering the goal of the regulative legal rules in which these concepts occur.

The possibility to model legal and normative ontologies via constitutive rules has a solid philosophical background (see Searle 1996; Sartor 2006). In the field of logic and argumentation theory, the only work which addressed the problem of the penumbra of legal concepts within a complete theory of constitutive rules is Grossi (2007). Grossi (2007) provides a very complex modal account of counts-as rules in which the problem of the penumbra is analysed in terms of the notion of context. A "penumbral meaning" is then nothing else but the set of individuals on which the contextual interpretation of the concept varies. However, Grossi (2007) does not explain how the different extensions of a concept are related to the contexts depending on the regulative norm whose violation is discussed. In addition, what is lacking in that work is that it does not address the problem of the dynamics of constitutive rules and does not consider the role of normative goals in determining the applicability conditions of legal rules.

Several works in the literature of AI and Law have considered the role of teleological reasoning in the legal interpretation. Indeed, this idea is standard in legal theory and the goals of legal rules are recognized by jurists as decisive in clarifying the scope of the legal concepts that qualify the applicability conditions for those rules (Bench-Capon 2002; Prakken 2002; Skalak and Rissland 1992; Hage 1997). Bench-Capon (2002) and Prakken (2002) use goals and values in frameworks of case based reasoning for modelling precedents mainly in a common law context. Skalak and Rissland (1992) analyses a number of legal arguments even in statutory law, which include cases close to the ones discussed here. The proposal which is closer to our contribution is Hage (1997). In (Hage 1997) Jaap Hage addresses, among others, the problem of reconstructing extensive and restrictive interpretation. This is done in Reason-Based Logic, a logical formalism that can deal with rules and reasons: the idea is that the satisfaction of rules' applicability conditions is usually a reason for application of these rules, but there can also be other (and possibly competing) reasons, among which we have the goals that led the legislator to make the rules.

All these approaches highlight the importance of rule goals, and (Hage 1997), in particular, follows this idea to formalise extensive and restrictive interpretation. However, it seems that no work so far has attempted to couple this view with a framework for reasoning with counts-as rules and their dynamics.

## References

Bench-Capon, T. 2002. The missing link revisited: The role of teleology in representing legal argument. *Artificial Intelligence and Law* 10(1–3):79–94.

Bench-Capon, T., and G. Sartor. 2003. A model of legal reasoning with cases incorporating theories and values. *Artificial Intelligence* 150:97–143.

Boella, G., Governatori, G., Rotolo, A., and L. van der Torre. 2010a. Lex minus dixit quam voluit, lex magis dixit quam voluit: A formal study on legal compliance and interpretation. In *AI approaches to the complexity of legal systems*, Complex systems, the semantic web, ontologies, argumentation, and dialogue, vol. 6237, 162–183. Berlin: Springer.

Boella, G., Governatori, G., Rotolo, A., and L. van der Torre. 2010b. A logical understanding of legal interpretation. In *Principles of knowledge representation and reasoning: Proceedings of the twelfth international conference, KR 2010*. Menlo Park: AAAI Press.

Gilbert, M. 1989. *On social facts*. Princeton: Princeton University Press.
Governatori, G., and A. Rotolo. 2008a. BIO logical agents: Norms, beliefs, intentions in defeasible logic. *Autonomous Agents and Multi-Agent Systems* 17(1): 36–69.
Governatori, G., and A. Rotolo. 2008b. A computational framework for institutional agency. *Artificial Intelligence and Law* 16(1): 25–52.
Governatori, G., Rotolo, A., and G. Sartor. 2005. Temporalised normative positions in defeasible logic. In *Proceedings of the ICAIL 2005*, 25–34. New York: ACM Press.
Governatori, G., Padmanabhan, V., Rotolo, A., and A. Sattar. 2009. A defeasible logic for modelling policy-based intentions and motivational attitudes. *Logic Journal of the IGPL* 17(3):227–265.
Grossi, D. 2007. Desigining invisible hancuffs. Formal investigations in institutions and organizations for multi-agent systems. Ph. D. thesis, Utrecht University.
Hage, J. 1997. *Reasoning with rules: An essay on legal reasoning and its underlying logic*. Dordrecht: Kluwer.
Hart, H. L. A. 1994. *The concept of law*. Oxford: Clarendon.
Lagerspetz, E. 1995. *The opposite mirrors*. Dordrecht: Kluwer.
MacCormick, N. 2005. *Rhetoric and the rule of law: A theory of legal reasoning*. Oxford: Oxford University Press.
Peczenik, A. 1989. *On law and reason*. Dordrecht: Kluwer.
Prakken, H. 2002. An exercise in formalising teleological case-based reasoning. *Artificial Intelligence and Law* 10:113–133.
Prakken, H., and G. Sartor. 2004. The three faces of defeasibility in the law. *Ratio Juris* 17: 118–139.
Ross, A. 1957. Tû-tû. *Harvard Law Review* 70:812–825.
Rotolo, A. 2011. Norm compliance of rule-based cognitive agents. In *Proceedings of the twenty-second international joint conference on artificial intelligence*. Menlo Park: AAAI Press.
Ruiter, D. W. P. 2001. *Legal institutions*. Dordrecht: Kluwer.
Sartor, G. 2005. *Legal reasoning: A cognitive approach to the law*. Dordrecht: Springer.
Sartor, G. 2006. Fundamental legal concepts: A formal and teleological characterisation. *Artificial Intelligence and Law* 14(1–2):101–142.
Searle, J. R. 1964. How to derive "ought" from "is". *Philosophical Review* 73(1):43–58.
Searle, J. R. 1996. *The construction of social reality*. New York: The Free Press.
Searle, J. R. 2010. *Making the social world: The structure of human civilization*. Oxford: Oxford University Press.
Skalak, D. B., and E. L. Rissland. 1992. Arguments and cases: An inevitable intertwining. *Artificial Intelligence and Law* 1:3–44.
Tuomela, R. 1995. *The importance of us: A philosophical study of basic social notions*, Stanford series in philosophy. Stanford: Stanford University Press.

# Chapter 12
# Is Balancing a Method of Rational Justification *sui generis*?

## On the Structure of Justification by Balancing

**Jan Sieckmann**

## 12.1 Introduction

Reasoning with conflicting normative requirements presents a central problem of practical and, in particular, legal argumentation.[1] It takes the form of balancing.[2] However, the method of balancing is a matter of dispute. It is criticized as irrational and arbitrary[3] – a critique, however, that is not warranted.[4] No doubt the method of balancing ensures a certain degree of rationality of normative judgment, although it cannot in each case guarantee a single right answer. It is not as clear, however, whether balancing constitutes a form of reasoning *sui generis*, aside from that of subsumption and deduction. Is balancing a type of rational justification on its own, as distinct from the method of subsumption? Or can it be reduced to some form of inferential reasoning, thus presenting a complex form of subsumption?

Subsumption and deduction have usually been regarded as the basic logical form of legal argumentation. Since Ronald Dworkin's critique of the "model of rules",[5] however, support has increased for the thesis that balancing constitutes another basic

[1]See, for example, Dworkin (1986), Besson (2005).

[2]On balancing in particular Alexy (2002, 2003a, 2009), Sieckmann (1995, 2004, 2007, 2010b), Clérico (2001), Bernal Pulido (2004, 2006a, b).

[3]See the critiques, for example, of Jestaedt (2007), Schlink (2001), Habermas (1996), Guibourg (2010).

[4]For a defence of the rationality of balancing see, for example, Alexy (2009), Bernal Pulido (2006b), Sieckmann (1995, 2007, 2010b). See also in this volume the contribution of Bruce Anderson.

[5]The discussion on balancing was instigated by Ronald Dworkin (1978, 22pp.). However, Dworkin contributed little to the further analysis of balancing and offers a model of interpretation that does not make a clear distinction between subsumption and balancing, see Dworkin (1986).

J. Sieckmann (✉)
Faculty of Business, Economics and Law, University of Erlangen, Erlangen, Germany
e-mail: jansieckmann@yahoo.de

C. Dahlman and E. Feteris (eds.), *Legal Argumentation Theory: Cross-Disciplinary Perspectives*, Law and Philosophy Library 102, DOI 10.1007/978-94-007-4670-1_12,

form of legal argumentation, apart from that of subsumption.[6] In particular, Robert Alexy (2003b) has emphasized the difference between subsumption and balancing as modes of legal reasoning. In later writings, however, Alexy has taken the view that rational balancing is possible only if it follows an inferential scheme that connects the factors of balancing with its result, and has offered the "weight formula" as an analogue to the scheme of deduction.[7] This casts into doubt the thesis that balancing is a peculiar form of reasoning, a reasoning that is distinct from subsumption and deduction. The "weight formula" presents an arithmetical function, and the factors of balancing are represented accordingly by numbers. In addition, Alexy (2009, 17) sustains that the numbers represent judgments or propositions regarding the factors of the balancing. Since the representation of an arithmetic function by means of judgments or propositions can hardly be anything else but a deductive argument, the difference between balancing and subsumption seems to fade.[8]

By contrast, this paper will argue that the balancing of normative arguments indeed constitutes a specific form of reasoning, which may be called "autonomous reasoning" and cannot be reduced to a type of argument where the result is inferred from premises or criteria established without a balancing.[9] Subsequently, this paper will analyse the structure of justification presented by autonomous balancing, and will argue the following theses:

(1) The basic structure of the justification of norms resulting from autonomous balancing consists in the support of this norm by a normative argument, that is, an argument requiring that one ought to accept the norm in question as definitively valid.
(2) Normative arguments consist of sets of reiterated requirements for the validity of norms.
(3) The structure of reiterated requirements for the validity of norms constitutes a form of procedural validity, that is, if a normative argument of this structure is presented it cannot be rejected outright, but can only be attacked by counter-arguments.
(4) The substantive justification of normative arguments follows from interest-based claims of autonomous agents.
(5) The justification of a normative judgment based on the balancing of normative arguments consists of the requirement of validity included in the prevailing normative argument.

---

[6]Sieckmann (1990, 18), Stück (1998).

[7]Alexy (2009, 16). The "weight formula" has been criticized in various respects. See, for example, Bolaños (2010), Moreso (2007), Riehm (2006), Sieckmann (2010b). The point made here does not depend, however, on these critiques, but concerns the more general issue of whether, and to which extent, a deductive or inferential reconstruction of balancing is possible.

[8]This also corresponds to the thesis of Klatt and Schmidt that uncertainty does not exist with regard to balancing, because balancing according to the "weight formula" consists in a mere mathematical calculation. See Klatt and Schmidt (2010, 45f.).

[9]See also Sieckmann (2004, 2009).

## 12.2 The Structure of Balancing

The general idea of balancing is that of determining the priority among competing demands or requirements according to their importance in the concrete case.

For example, if someone says about someone else that he or she is lying, the right to personal honour, demanding protection against insults, conflicts with the right to free speech, demanding that everyone ought to be allowed to say what he or she thinks. Both rights cannot co-exist unrestrictedly. Hence we have a conflict of rights. Both rights apply to the case but cannot dictate the solution. They can hold only in principle, requiring a certain solution, but both are in need of being weighed and balanced against each other.

The basic principle of balancing states that, whenever two requirements are in conflict, the one deserving priority in the case in question is that whose fulfilment is more important in the circumstances of this case, or, as one might also say, the one that is stronger or has the greater weight in the concrete case.[10] One might regard this as a rule and infer the result by applying it,[11] subsuming the facts that determine the weight in the concrete case under this rule. However, the crucial problem of balancing is not one of subsumption, but how to determine the weight or importance given to the conflicting requirements in a concrete case. Is it possible to determine these weights without a balancing, or does it again depend on balancing? Two fundamentally different accounts of balancing compete in this respect, which may be called "rule-based balancing" and "autonomous balancing".

### *12.2.1 Rule-Based Balancing*

Rule-based balancing assumes that one can infer the correct result of the balancing from the combination of factors of balancing. It determines the importance of the competing requirements in the concrete case according to certain criteria, which determine the "factors of balancing". The result follows from the application of these criteria. The argument has inferential structure. In its fully developed form, balancing follows an inferential scheme that defines the correct solution for any combination of the factors of balancing.[12]

However, the rule-based approach to balancing has two drawbacks. Firstly, it is doubtful whether the relevant factors can be determined independently from

---

[10]See Sieckmann (2010b). One may also speak of the "value of fulfilment" that is assigned to a particular solution of the balancing problem, see Sieckmann (1995).

[11]Any argument can be presented in deductive or inferential form. The crucial point is that this presentation remains incomplete in so far as the argument includes non-inferential elements. In particular, it refers to the determination of relative weight, strength or importance that the agent doing the balancing makes.

[12]See, in particular, Alexy (2009), who describes his "weight formula" as an inferential scheme.

balancing, without regard to the correctness of the result of the balancing.[13] Secondly, if the rule-based approach is feasible, the consequence would be that balancing is not a method of justification on its own, but merely a special case of subsumption and deduction. Accordingly, the only way to understand balancing as a method *sui generis* is the notion of autonomous balancing.

### *12.2.2 Autonomous Balancing*

By contrast to rule-based balancing, autonomous balancing does not presuppose premises that substantively determine the balancing of normative arguments, but consists in establishing a priority among the conflicting arguments that does not follow from given criteria. The determination of the importance of the conflicting requirements is thus itself a matter of balancing. The structure of autonomous balancing includes three elements: first, the arguments to be balanced against each other; second, the procedure of balancing aimed at establishing a priority among the conflicting arguments; and, third, the definitive norm that results from the balancing and the priority established.[14]

In order to determine a definitive solution, a priority must be established among the competing requirements, regarding their relative weights and the facts of the case.[15]

For example, one might assume that if the offensive assertion was false then the right to personal honour deserves priority. Even if the assertion was sincere but nevertheless wrong and there are no special circumstances that legitimize the offensive speech, the right to personal honour will be given priority over that of free speech.

---

[13]An argument on this point refers to the abstract weights of the conflicting requirements, which are factors relevant to the balancing that can only be determined by means of balancing. They are not properties of arguments, norms, or principles that are independent from any conflict. See also Barry (1990). Rather, they are abstractions from the determination of relative weights of conflicting norms in previous or hypothetical cases. However, the abstract weights established on the basis of previous decisions or hypothetical cases cannot command the weighting in the actual balancing. Treating them as strictly binding would contradict the idea of autonomy. Individual autonomy implies the right to form a normative judgment on one's own, see Sieckmann (2007). It would be to deny this right if we were to assume that the individual judgment was strictly bound by previous determinations. It is thus the idea of autonomy that excludes to reduce balancing to some form of inferential reasoning, such as subsumption and deduction.

[14]In more detail see Sieckmann (2004, 2009).

[15]Thus, the balancing requires not only the conflicting arguments but also supplementary arguments concerning the relative weight and the degree of fulfilment or non-fulfilment of the requirements included in the conflicting arguments.

In legal context,[16] the competing normative arguments are usually called "principles", in the sense that they express norms that are valid only in principle and need to be balanced against competing arguments.[17] In the example above, these are:

$P_1$: Everyone has the right to free speech.
$P_2$: Everyone has the right to personal honour.

The principle $P_1$ implies a requirement of a particular normative consequent, namely that the speech be permitted (R). The principle $P_2$ implies a requirement of the opposing consequent ($\neg$R). The normative situation comprises of a number of facts of the case $F_1, \ldots,$ Fn. A subset of these facts forms the condition (C) under which one principle receives priority over the other with respect to the normative issue of whether a particular speech is permitted or forbidden.

The priority relation can be defined in various ways, as a priority among principles[18] or between possible results. The latter conforms better to the idea of normative arguments as reasons for particular results of the balancing. Accordingly, the priority is stated with regard to the legal consequences of the conflicting principles, that is, with regard to the possible solutions of the balancing. Such a priority depends on certain conditions C and on the conflicting principles or normative arguments. Thus, the notation will be

$$\text{PRIOR}\,(R/\neg R)\,C, P_1, P_2.$$

In the example: On the balancing of the principles of free speech and personal honour in the case of a speech that is not false, the permission of speech receives priority over its prohibition.

The priority among the competing arguments determines which rule takes priority in the case in question. This rule may support the consequence R under a certain condition C:

$$R/C,$$

or it may support the opposite consequence Non-R under some condition C:

$$\neg R/C,$$

[16] By contrast, in moral discourse the term "principle" is often used to denote norms of strict validity. One can explain the difference by the fact that principles are often regarded as important norms of general character, and that in law, in order to count as legally valid, a normative argument must be sufficiently strong to establish an obligation of law-applying organs to take this argument into account in their legal reasoning. Important arguments usually have a wide range of application, so that they may well be called "principles". By contrast, in moral reasoning any legitimate interest-based claim of an autonomous agent counts, but not all such claims qualify as principles. See Sieckmann (2010a).

[17] On the notion of principles see Sieckmann (2011).

[18] See the "law of competing principles" *(Kollisionsgesetz)* in Alexy (2002).

The important point is that the validity of this rule is established only as the result of the procedure of balancing and is not derived from pre-determined criteria. Since it is based on the reasoning of an autonomous agent (A), the type of validity of the result of the balancing is, for example, should R be chosen:

$$\mathrm{VAL}_{\mathrm{DEF,A}}\,(\mathrm{R}/\mathrm{C})\,.$$

Hence, the result of the balancing is a normative judgment of the agent doing the balancing. Since it is in first place merely an individual, subjective judgment, but nevertheless claims to state a norm valid also for other agents, the question arises whether, and in which sense, such a judgment can be claimed to be rationally justified.

## 12.3 Justification of Autonomous Judgments

The thesis that balancing constitutes a form of argument on its own depends on the fact that it not only has a logical structure distinct from that of subsumption and deduction, but also presents a form of rational justification. Autonomous balancing has been defined by a distinctive logical structure. The remaining issue is, accordingly, whether one can understand it as a form of rational justification. Addressing this question requires some clarification as to what we might understand by the notion of justification.

### *12.3.1 The Notion of Justification*

In general, "justification" consists in an argument for something that is a possible object of choice, such as acts, beliefs, or some states of affair.[19] Regarding normative judgments, that is, judgments that one ought or ought not to do something, the justification consists in an argument that aims to show that one ought to accept as correct such a judgment. This includes several aspects. First, one must distinguish the structure or form of justification and its validity. The structure of justification provides the criterion for identifying justifications and distinguishing them from other phenomena. The issue of validity is whether some justification (in the structural sense) has the justificatory effect it purports to have. As to the issue of validity, a justification may be valid subjectively or objectively. In a subjective

[19]The philosophical discussion of the notion of justification seems to be concerned primarily with the justification of beliefs. See Alston (1989), Audi (1993). By contrast, focussing exclusively on reasons for action, Raz (1999, 15). In any case, the issue of justification only occurs if one asks whether one should or may hold some belief. The choice of beliefs may be seen as a special case of action. With regard to states of affairs, it makes no sense to ask for a justification if they cannot be brought about or changed by some sort of action. Therefore, the justification of actions seems to be elementary.

sense, a justification consists in any argument that someone advances in order to show that an act is correct. The justification is valid according to the perspective of the respective agent. By contrast, a justification is objectively valid if every reasonable agent must accept it as correct in the sense of being at least defensible. With regard to normative judgments, one must further distinguish between objective validity in the weak sense – that everyone must accept the judgment in question as defensible, and objective validity in the strong sense – that every reasonable agent must accept the purported norm as being valid. If a justification is objectively valid in the strong sense, it would be mistaken to deny the validity of the alleged norm. If it is objectively valid only in the weak sense, one cannot show the corresponding judgment to be mistaken, but different views may equally count as correct.

A rational justification of a normative judgment must be valid at least in the weak objective sense. Although the mere presentation of arguments displays some form of rationality, a normative judgment can count as rationally justified only if it is at least defensible. This must include the justification of the normative claim made on others by means of this judgment.

With regard to balancing, a crucial issue is whether one can reasonably claim correctness of such a judgment and, correspondingly, validity for the norm it proposes. Or will such a claim always be mistaken and hence irrational?

In order to address this issue, one must distinguish between, on the one hand, the rational critique of balancing judgments and, on the other, positive judgments claiming the correctness of a certain result (Sieckmann 1995). There is no doubt that there are formal criteria of correct balancing with which judgments based on balancing must comply. They include, in particular, criteria of Pareto-optimality, coherence, and universalizability, but also procedural criteria of intersubjective reflection. These criteria allow one to control and criticize judgments as mistaken or incorrect and, accordingly, to deny the validity of the stated norm.[20] The crucial point, however, is whether balancing judgments can be positively justified as being correct and, accordingly, the validity of substantive norms can be directly established by means of balancing. Addressing this issue requires clarification of how justification is possible.

## 12.3.2 Types of Justification: Inferences, Facts, Arguments

One can distinguish three elementary forms of justification: justification by means of inference, facts, and arguments, or, as one might also say, logic, truth, and arguments.[21]

[20]In some cases, the critique of balancing judgments might even imply positive normative statements as to which norm is valid. For example, if public agencies need a justification for interfering with individual rights, balancing them with competing arguments, but the balancing is faulty and therefore does not yield the justification required, then it follows that the interference is prohibited.

[21]The expansion of the realm of rational argumentation beyond logic and empirical facts one finds also in the "New Rhetoric" of Perelman, who draws upon the Aristotelian dialectic against the

Justification by inference means to explicate what has already been accepted. The paradigm case is that of deductive inference. Deductive inference allows one to infer a conclusion from a set of premises in accordance with the rules of deductive logic.[22] Such an inference does not introduce new content, but is possible only because the conclusion is already included in the set of premises. Its formal structure may be represented as:

$$\Gamma \Rightarrow C,$$

where "Γ" presents a set of sentences and "C" a consequence of this set.

Justification by reference to facts consists in showing that a certain sentence corresponds to what may be called "the world". That is, there is something (a state of affairs "x") that satisfies the sentence in question, thus making it true. The structure of the justification of an assertion of a sentence "S" is:

$$\exists x \text{ SATISF}(S, x).$$ [23]

Justification by argument means that one can correctly claim that everyone should accept a certain conclusion as the result of the argument. Thus, arguments set out what ought to be accepted as the result of discourse. The structure of such a justification is:

$$A \text{ because } OA,$$

where "A" represents an action required by a norm that A ought to be done (OA).

One should also note that justification by means of inference or facts constitute arguments. This, however, is due to the fact that one ought to accept these inferences or facts as correct. Thus, it seems that the basic form of normative justification is that of arguments in the sense pointed out above – in short, that of normative arguments.

### *12.3.3 The Form of Normative Arguments*

What is the characteristic of normative arguments as a third or – as suggested above – the most elementary form of justification? The thesis that I will advance here is:

---

Cartesian limitation of rationality to analytical and empirical arguments. See Perelman y Olbrechts-Tyteca (1971). However, the following analysis is not concerned with the ideas of Perelman or Aristotle, but only with the analysis of arguments that figure as reasons for judgments based on balancing.

[22]There are alternatives to deductive logic, but the idea of logical inference based on certain premises and inference rules remains the same. See, for example, Prakken (1997); Hage (1997), on non-monotonic reasoning.

[23]One might simply write ∃x Sx, using S as a predicate about state of affairs as object. This would not conform, however, with the usual distinction between sentences and predicates.

(TR) Arguments have the structure of reiterated requirements of accepting a certain result as valid.

The idea of this "reiteration thesis" (TR) is as follows[24]: Any argument involves what one ought to accept as the result of the argument. Thus, arguments are normative. The result is presented in the form of some proposition (p). The issue is, accordingly, which proposition one ought to (O) accept (ACC) as true or, with regard to norms, which norm (N) one ought to accept as valid (VAL).

Arguments will accordingly include a structure that can be represented as:

One ought to accept p.
O ACC p.

With regard to norms, this structure is:

One ought to accept the validity of N.
O ACC (VAL N).

Since in autonomous reasoning the validity of norms depends on the acceptance of autonomous agents, the basic structure of arguments regarding the validity of norms may be represented simply as:

N ought to be valid.
O VAL N.

Such arguments include requirements as to which norm one ought to accept as definitively valid, in short, requirements for validity.[25] Accordingly, normative argumentation in its most elementary form is a procedure where individuals make normative claims requiring that a particular norm be definitively valid.[26]

For example, in the case of offensive speech, the principle of free speech demands that the speech be permitted, and the principle of the protection of personal honour demands that offensive speech be forbidden. Both include a requirement for the validity of a particular norm, which is the prohibition or the permission of a certain speech, respectively. The normative arguments claim that these norms ought to be accepted as valid.

A crucial point is that normative arguments are not statements as to the definitive validity of norms. Statements of the definitive validity of a particular norm exclude the definitive validity of incompatible norms.

If, for example, in a normative system offensive speech is definitively forbidden, it cannot at the same time be definitively permitted.

Accordingly, normative statements of definitively valid norms must be consistent if they are to be used as arguments. However, incompatible norms, that is, norms that

---

[24]See also Sieckmann (2005, 2009, 2011).

[25]Accordingly, "requirement for validity" should in general, if not otherwise indicated, be read as "requirement for definitive validity".

[26]Validity is understood here in a normative sense, that is, as the implication that a valid norm ought to be applied and followed.

imply requirements Op and O¬p, cannot have definitive validity at the same time, for the norm contents p and ¬p cannot be fulfilled at the same time. Therefore, the definitive validity of one excludes the definitive validity of the other:

$$VAL_{DEF}(Op) \rightarrow \neg VAL_{DEF}(\neg Op),$$

and statements as to their definitive validity would be inconsistent. Consequently, incompatible norms cannot at the same time be stated as definitively valid. Since normative arguments are used in a situation of conflict, they cannot have the structure of statements of definitive validity of the norm in question.[27]

The negative characterization of normative arguments, which contrasts them with normative statements, calls on the other hand for a positive characterization of the structure and type of validity of normative arguments. They cannot include statements of definitive validity regarding the norm resulting from the balancing, but must have some form of validity and cannot be mere norms in a semantic sense without any assignment of validity.[28] In this situation, the most plausible alternative is that their claim to validity rests on higher order requirements for validity.[29] With regard to each requirement for validity of a certain order there must be a requirement of higher order that demands its definitive validity. Thus, an infinite set of requirements for validity is necessary to constitute a valid normative argument.

For example, in the case of an offensive speech, the principle of free speech demands that the speech be permitted. Such a normative claim must have some form of validity, but cannot be definitively valid. Its character of validity is that the normative claim included in it must again be supported by a requirement for validity of higher order, stating that one ought to accept the normative claim in question as valid, and so on. By repeating this structure an infinite chain of reiterated requirements for validity results, each of them backed by a requirement for validity of higher order.

Accordingly, the validity of a normative argument presupposes the reiteration of requirements of validity regarding a particular norm. With regard to each requirement for validity of a certain order there must be a requirement of higher order that demands its definitive validity.

This conception of normative arguments is distinct from that of arguments as a set of premises from which a conclusion follows logically. The connection between

---

[27] Although one finds attempts to analyse normative conflicts by means of normative statements or propositions, for example, by means of optimising requirements, prima facie- or pro tanto-norms, or defeasible norms, these conceptions weaken the content or the character of validity of the respective norms in a way that makes them incapable of figuring as arguments in the situation of conflict. See Sieckmann (2011).

[28] As to this notion see Sieckmann (1990).

[29] This holds if normative arguments are constructed as a compound of deontic operator (O), norm content (p), and ascription of validity (VAL). A more complex analytical framework might offer further alternatives, as Alexy (2000) suggests. However, it is not clear what this framework might be and, anyway, it is not plausible to use a more complex framework if a more elementary framework is available.

normative arguments and the result of the balancing is not a logical conclusion, but a procedural act of accepting what ought to be accepted. The procedural character of normative justification is an essential feature of autonomous reasoning, for autonomous agents must be in a position to form their own normative judgments, and the validity of a norm must therefore, in some way, depend on their judgments.[30] Since logical inferences do not reflect the structure of such procedures, the relation between arguments and results must be defined in a different way. What is required is a procedural inference, which consists in accepting what one ought to accept.

Summing up, normative arguments have the structure of reiterated requirements for validity. A normative argument consists of a set of norms including

(1) a norm N that is argued for,
(2) a second-order norm requiring the definitive validity of the norm N as the result of the balancing,
(3) a third-order norm requiring the validity of the second-order norm,
(4) a fourth-order norm requiring the validity of the third-order norm,

and so on.

The possibility of saturating this structure is the specific criterion for the validity of normative arguments. That is, a normative argument is valid if the claim contained in it can be supported by an unlimited chain of requirements for validity of higher order. Hence the claim of a normative argument is that the normative demand in question can be supported by requirements for validity of ever higher order. This is expressed by the structure ... O $VAL_{DEF}$ N.

## *12.3.4 The Impact of Normative Arguments*

The reiteration of requirements of validity of norms constitutes the form of normative arguments, the possibility of saturating this structure the type of its validity. What is the impact or effect of such an argument – that is, supposing it to be valid, how does it change the argumentative situation?

The reiteration of requirements of validity constitutes procedural validity of an argument in the sense that the requirement in question cannot be ignored or rejected outright, but must be attacked by counter-arguments if one is not prepared to accept its conclusion. Whether the argument is in fact valid depends, of course, on its justification in substance, just like deductive arguments or empirical arguments depend on the truth of the premises they include. Even disregarding the issue of substantive validity, however, the use of an argument with the structure of reiterated requirements of validity makes a difference regarding the structure of the argumentation.

[30]Thus, rational discourse or other forms of participatory procedures are not merely an instrument to get a correct or, at least, a better result, but they are constitutive elements of normative justification.

The idea behind this thesis is that the structure of reiterated requirements for validity provides a basis to counter the sceptical strategy of attacking any argument by asking why one should accept that argument. If someone suggests that given condition C one has the right to free speech a sceptic will ask why. If the proponent gives an argument the sceptic will again react with a "why"-question, and so on. This leads to the well-known trilemma of justification, which consists in the problem that any argument will end in a circle, an infinite regress, or a break-off of argument (Albert 1980, 13). The account of normative arguments as reiterated requirements for validity may serve as a device against the sceptical strategy of asking "why"-questions, since it is based on the possibility of adducing an unlimited number of arguments.[31] Hence, one can answer any "why"-question with a new argument. The proponent will never be forced to concede that he can give no further argument.

One might object that the reiteration of requirements for validity only leads to an infinite regress, which is one horn of the trilemma of justification. This seems indeed to be correct. But the question is whose problem is this regress. The role of normative arguments in a justificatory procedure is distinct from that of normative statements. The aim of making a normative argument is not to end the argumentation but to commence or continue with it. For this purpose it is necessary to show that the argument in question must be considered and cannot be rejected right from the start by questioning its validity. The necessity of taking an argument into account follows if,

- taken on its own, the argument is sufficient to decide the issue, that is, if it determines the result if no counter-argument is advanced, and
- the argument can be supported by arguments of ever higher order, that is, if one is able to reiterate the requirement for validity O $VAL_{DEF}N$ at any higher level of argumentation.

If the reiteration is possible, then any question as to why one should consider the argument can be answered, and as soon as this becomes clear the sceptical strategy of asking "why"-questions looses sense. In addition, if the time comes to make a decision, the only relevant argument is that advanced by the proponent. The sceptic has not offered a counter-argument, and since the argument of the proponent is apt to decide the issue, this argument prevails. Accordingly, the only way to refute an argument of reiterated structure is to present counter-arguments, and hence to enter into an argumentation.[32]

---

[31]There are various suggestions how to cope with this problem. See, for example, Buchwald (1990, 232ff.). However, the question of whether the trilemma of justification can be resolved within deductive reasoning is beyond the scope of the present analysis. The point here is that autonomous reasoning presents a complete model of normative justification, in which the trilemma of justification does not occur.

[32]By contrast, normative statements claim to state what is definitively valid. They claim to state the result of an argumentation and, thus, to finish it, and not to open or continue it. This difference is important because the sceptical strategy of "why"-questions has different effects for normative statements than for normative arguments. If someone makes a normative statement, thus

To conclude, the reiteration of requirements for validity results in an infinite structure, where each requirement for validity is backed by another one of higher order. However, this does not undermine the position of the proponent but that of the sceptical opponent. Thus, the structure of normative arguments as reiterated requirements for validity provides the key for a complete model of the justification of norms, starting with interest-based normative arguments and resulting in statements of definitively valid norms.

### 12.3.5 The Justification of Normative Arguments

The procedural validity of a normative argument does not yet constitute its substantive validity, that is, the need to balance it with competing arguments. Procedural validity may be attacked on the basis of the foundation of the argument. It could be said that, although it displays the form of an argument and therefore cannot be excluded from consideration in a rational discourse, it is based on mistaken assumptions or has no importance at all. Arguments to be balanced against each other must have not only procedural validity, but also a substantive justification, which supports their importance and their force against competing arguments.

The substantive justification of normative arguments follows from the interest-based claims of autonomous agents. Normative arguments based on interests display the structure of reiterated requirements of validity. If one accepts that interests imply a demand that they ought to be respected, one will also have to assume that there is an interest in the validity of the norm which demands respect for those interests, and an interest in the validity of the higher-order-norm, and so on. The possibility of reiterating interest-based demands results from two premises:

(1) An interest of an autonomous agent justifies a demand that this interest be realised and, consequently, a corresponding normative argument for the definitive validity of the norm in question.
(2) Together with a first-order interest, there is an interest of higher-order in the definitive validity of the requirement for validity of a norm protecting the first-order interest.

The first premise, that autonomous agents may advance interest-based claims and that these claims ought to be recognized as arguments, can be justified by means of

claiming to end an argumentation, he must be able to support this claim in a finite number of steps; otherwise, he looses the argument. If, by contrast, someone opens an argumentation with a normative argument, the sceptical strategy will never bring him into the difficulty of presenting a new argument. A first order requirement for validity of N is different from a second order requirement, and so on. Each of them is supported by the possibility of reiteration. Hence the proponent can always present a new argument. This does not make much sense. But this is not the problem of the proponent. It is the sceptic who blocks further argumentation by provoking a senseless reiteration. This, however, is irrational. Therefore, one cannot rationally ask "why"-questions demanding further arguments if the proponent can show that he is able to present a normative argument supported by reiterated requirements for validity.

the conception of autonomous reasoning. Since the validity of a norm depends in some way on the consent of autonomous agents and these agents, if reasonable, will not consent to an argument that treats their interests as irrelevant, the validity of a norm can only be established if it is recognized that the interests advanced by autonomous agents ought to be realised. Accordingly, autonomous agents have the normative power or competence[33] to introduce interest-based claims as normative arguments, thus bringing other agents under the obligation to consider these claims as arguments.

The second premise, which connects a first-order interest with a higher-order interest in the validity of a norm protecting the first-order interest, follows as a requirement of rationality. The norm protecting the first-order interest serves to promote the realisation of this interest. This holds in the case of a conflict of interests and if the normative protection serves to promote the realisation of the interest in question. This positive effect is proven by the fact that argument about norms actually takes place. If norms were irrelevant for realising interests, such disputes would not make sense. Therefore, at least in general,[34] the second premise holds. Based on these premises, one can develop the reiterative structure of normative arguments. In order to do this, some determinations are in order.

| | |
|---|---|
| INT(Z): | There is an interest of an autonomous agent in a state of affairs Z. |
| $VAL_{ARG}OZ$: | The requirement of Z is valid as a normative argument. |
| $INT(VAL_{ARG}OZ)$: | There is an interest in the definitive validity of the requirement of Z. |

The normative position of a rational agent who defends his interests in a normative argumentation then will develop as follows:

| | |
|---|---|
| (1) INT(Z) | |
| (2) $INT(Z) \rightarrow VAL_{ARG}OZ$ | |
| (3) $INT(Z) \rightarrow INT(VAL_{DEF}OZ)$ | |
| (4) $VAL_{ARG}OZ$ | Inference from (1), (2) |
| (5) $INT(VAL_{DEF}OZ)$ | Inference from (1), (3) |
| (6) $INT(VAL_{DEF}OZ) \rightarrow VAL_{ARG}OVAL_{DEF}OZ$ | Inference from (2), replacing Z by $VAL_{DEF}OZ$ |
| (7) $VAL_{ARG}OVAL_{DEF}OZ$ | Inference from (5), (6) |

In general, a requirement for validity of level $i+1$ can be generated by inserting $VAL_{DEF}OZ$ for Z in a requirement for validity of level i.[35]

[33]Normative power in the sense of Hohfeld as the capability to change the normative situation. See Hohfeld (1923).

[34]There may be exceptional cases in which interests are not furthered by the existence of norms demanding respect for them.

[35]This structure holds for teleological arguments in general. If the validity of a norm serves to guide action, and the fulfilment of the required action serves a particular goal, the validity of the norm is demanded as a means to fulfil this goal. However, interests are special because in an autonomy-

### 12.3.6 The Justification of Normative Judgments

How can one justify a normative judgment based on the balancing of normative arguments if there are no pre-determined criteria from which it could be derived, that is, how is the justification of autonomous judgments possible?

Part of the claim to correctness of an autonomous judgment is that, although free and not pre-determined by established norms, it is required by the stronger of the competing normative arguments and, hence, ought to be accepted. This claim includes, in accordance with the requirements of normative justification, formal and normative elements. An agent making a normative judgment must, firstly, claim that the judgment complies with the formal requirements of a correct balancing and, secondly, that it is required by the normative arguments that the agent regards as stronger in the concrete case and therefore is the judgment that one ought to make or accept.[36]

Normative judgments include a claim that the result of the balancing be accepted as definitively valid. One must distinguish this claim from that included in a normative statement.

For example, the result of a balancing might be expressed as:

(1) In situation C, which includes the fact that an offensive speech is not negligently based on false assumptions, the principle of liberty of expression deserves priority with respect to the question of whether offensive speech is allowed.

This can be expressed in the form of a normative requirement:

(1′) In situation C, the offensive expression ought to be permitted.

---

based theory they must necessarily be accepted as a basis of valid arguments. Interests are whatever autonomous agents demand to be realised and respected in procedures of normative justification. One must acknowledge these claims at least in principle if there should be any chance of finding a result that must be accepted by the autonomous agents involved.

Autonomous interests are the primary and, presumably, the only source of normative arguments. By contrast, arguments directly referring to religious or traditional authority, which are not supported by autonomous interests, do not have the structure of reiterated requirements for validity. Such arguments refer to an authoritative act that claims to be a final justification and are not meant to contribute to an argumentation. Thus, an interesting result of the conception of normative arguments as reiterated requirements for validity is that precisely those normative claims are disqualified as normative arguments that have been the main target of the reason-based tradition of enlightenment.

[36]More elegantly, one might say that the result is required by the stronger of the competing normative arguments. This, however, would suggest that the strength of the argument is an objective criterion, which could be applied by the agent involved. By contrast, it is important to emphasize that the strength of the argument is to be determined by the agent himself in his balancing. For this reason, the argument cannot be presented as an inference. An argument "I regard argument A to be stronger than the competing arguments. Therefore, everyone ought to accept the result supported by A." would not be justified as a logical inference. Still, it is justified as a claim made by an autonomous agent.

On the other hand, one might make a normative statement:

(2) In situation C, the offensive expression is permitted.

Within the structure of the balancing of normative arguments, the normative statement, that is, (2), of what is actually permitted, prohibited, or required, is not included in the normative judgment, that is, (1) or (1′), but complies with the normative requirement expressed by that judgment. The step from normative judgment to a normative statement requires a procedural act of determining which norm is definitively valid. The claim to (substantive) correctness of normative judgments thus can be stated as follows:

(CCNJ) Someone making a normative judgment based on the balancing of normative arguments must claim its normative correctness in the sense that the stated norm ought to be accepted as definitively valid.

The necessity of such a claim follows from the structure of normative arguments as reiterated requirements for validity. If a normative argument is preferred to a conflicting one because of its greater relative weight in a given situation C, the resulting priority relation and the corresponding norm R/C are required by the prevailing argument. This argument demands that the stated norm ought to be valid. Thus, a normative judgment includes a requirement that the proposed priority ought to be accepted. Since this is the implication of the prevailing normative argument, it has the status of a normative argument. Its structure is

$$\ldots \text{O VAL}\,(\text{R}/\text{C})\,\text{P1}, \text{P2}.$$

In fact, the prevailing argument requires an even wider-ranging norm that covers the complete norm-content of the normative argument, that is, . . . O VAL(R). However, the norm established by the balancing is limited to the range of application in which the argument receives priority, represented by the condition C. Since it is included in the wider-ranging norm, it is also required by the prevailing argument.

Summing up, a normative judgment based on the balancing of normative arguments raises a claim not only to formal correctness in the sense of compliance with the standards of rational decision-making, but also a claim to normative correctness in the sense that it is required by the prevailing normative arguments. Autonomous agents cannot avoid making such claims in their normative judgments.

## 12.4 Conclusion

The central thesis advanced here is that balancing constitutes a method of rational justification on its own, not to be reduced to some form of inferential reasoning, but consisting in the justification of a certain result by means of normative arguments and judgments. This is based on several elements:

- the distinction between rule-based balancing and autonomous balancing;
- the rejection of rule-based balancing as a form of inferential reasoning;
- the distinction of logical inference, facts, and arguments as elementary forms of justification;
- the notion of normative arguments as reiterated requirements for validity;
- the resolution of the trilemma of justification based on the reiterative structure of normative arguments;
- the substantive validity of normative arguments based on interest-based claims of autonomous agents;
- the claim to correctness of normative judgments resulting from the balancing of normative arguments.

With these elements one can construct a form of justification by balancing that does not presuppose criteria from which the result can be derived by means of logical inference. Hence autonomous balancing presents a method of justification on its own, which is not reducible to inferential reasoning.

**Acknowledgments** I would like to thank the editors of this volume for their substantive comments that helped to improve on this paper, and Justin Newton for advice on matters of English style.

## References

Albert, H. 1980. *Traktat über kritische Vernunft*, 4th ed. Tübingen: Mohr.
Alexy, R. 2000. On the structure of legal principles. *Ratio Juris* 13: 294–304.
Alexy, R. 2002. *Theory of fundamental rights*. Oxford: Oxford University Press (orig. Theorie der Grundrechte, 1985).
Alexy, R. 2003a. Die Gewichtsformel. In *Gedächtnisschrift für Jürgen Sonnenschein*, ed. J. Jickeli, P. Kreutz, and D. Reuter, 771–792. Berlin: De Gruyter.
Alexy, R. 2003b. On balancing and subsumption. *A Structural Comparison. Ratio Juris* 16: 433–449.
Alexy, R. 2009. Die Konstruktion von Grundrechten. In *Grundrechte, Prinzipien und Argumentation. Studien zur Rechtstheorie Robert Alexys*, ed. L. Clérico and J. Sieckmann, 9–19. Baden-Baden: Nomos.
Alston, W. 1989. *Justification. Essays in the theory of knowledge*. Ithaca: Cornell University Press.
Audi, R. 1993. *The structure of justification*. Cambridge: Cambridge University Press.
Barry, B. 1990. *Political argument*, 2nd ed. New York et al: Harvester/Wheatsheaf.
Bernal Pulido, C. 2004. The structure and the limits of balancing. *ARSP-Beih.* 97: 79–84.
Bernal Pulido, C. 2006a. On Alexy's weight formula. In *Arguing fundamental rights*, ed. A.J. Menendez and E.O. Eriksen, 101–110. Dordrecht: Springer.
Bernal Pulido, C. 2006b. The rationality of balancing. *ARSP* 92: 195–208.
Besson, S. 2005. *The morality of conflict. Reasonable disagreement and the law*. Oxford/Portland (Oregon): Hart Publishing.
Bolaños, B. 2010. Balancing and legal decision theory. In *Legal reasoning: The methods of balancing,* ed. J. Sieckmann, *ARSP-Beih.* 124: 63–72. Stuttgart: Steiner.
Buchwald, D. 1990. *Der Begriff der rationalen juristischen Begründung*. Baden-Baden: Nomos.
Clérico, L. 2001. *Die Struktur der Verhältnismäßigkeit*. Baden-Baden: Nomos.
Dworkin, R. *Taking rights seriously*. 2nd ed. Cambridge (Mass.): Harvard University Press.
Dworkin, R. *Law's empire*. London: Fontana Press.

Guibourg, R. 2010. On Alexy's weighing formula. In *Legal reasoning: The methods of balancing*, ed. J. Sieckmann, *ARSP-Beih.* 124: 145–159. Stuttgart: Steiner.

Habermas, J. 1996. *Between facts and norms*. Cambridge: MIT Press (orig. *Faktizität und Geltung*. 4ed., 1994).

Hage, J. 1997. *Reasoning with rules*. Dordrecht: Kluwer.

Hohfeld, W. N. 1923. *Fundamental legal conceptions as applied in legal reasoning and other legal essays*. New Haven: Yale University Press.

Jestaedt, M. 2007. Die Abwägungslehre – ihre Stärken und ihre Schwächen. In *Staat im Wort. Festschrift Isensee*, ed. O. Depenheuer et al., 253–275. Heidelberg: Müller.

Klatt, M., and J. Schmidt. 2010. *Spielräume im Öffentlichen Recht*. Tübingen: Mohr.

Moreso, J.J. 2007. Alexy y la aritmética dc la ponderación. In *Derechos sociales y ponderación*, ed. Robert Alexy et al., 223–248. Madrid: Fundación Coloquio Jurídico Europeo.

Perelman, C., and L. Olbrechts-Tyteca. 1971. *The new rhetoric. A treatise on argumentation*. Notre Dame/London: University of Notre Dame Press.

Prakken, H. 1997. *Logical tools for modelling legal argument. A study of defeasible reasoning in law*. Dordrecht/Boston/London: Kluwer.

Raz, J. 1999. *Practical reasons and norms*, 3rd ed. Oxford: Oxford University Press.

Riehm, T. 2006. *Abwägungsentscheidungen in der praktischen Rechtsanwendung. Argumentation – Beweis – Wertung*. München: Beck.

Schlink, B. 2001. Der Grundsatz der Verhältnismäßigkeit. In *Festschrift 50 Jahre Bundesverfassungsgericht*, vol. 2, ed. P. Badura and H. Dreier, 445–465. Tübingen: Mohr.

Sieckmann, J.-R. 1990. *Regelmodelle und Prinzipienmodelle des Rechtssystems*. Baden-Baden: Nomos.

Sieckmann, J.-R. 1995. Zur Struktur und Begründung von Abwägungsurteilen. *Rechtstheorie* 26: 45–69.

Sieckmann, J.-R. 2004. Autonome Abwägung. In *ARSP* 90: 66–85.

Sieckmann, J-R. 2005. Principles as normative arguments. In *Values, rights and duties in legal and philosophical discourse*, ed. C. Dahlman and W. Krawietz. Rechtstheorie Beih. 21: 197–210. Berlin: Duncker & Humblot.

Sieckmann, J.-R. 2007. The concept of autonomy. In *Law and legal cultures in the 21st century: Diversity and unity*, ed. T. Gizbert-Studnicki and J. Stelmach, 149–170. Warszawa: Oficina/Kluwers.

Sieckmann, J.-R. 2009. *Recht als normatives system*. Baden-Baden: Nomos.

Sieckmann, J.-R. 2010a. The theory of principles – A framework for autonomous reasoning. In *On the nature of principles*, ed. M. Borowski, *ARSP-Beih.* 119: 49–61. Stuttgart: Steiner.

Sieckmann, J-R. 2010b. Balancing, optimisation, and Alexy's "Weight Formula". In *Legal reasoning: The methods of balancing*, ed. J. Sieckmann, *ARSP-Beih.* 124: 103–119. Stuttgart: Steiner.

Sieckmann, J.-R. 2011. Prinzipien, ideales Sollen und normative Argumente. *ARSP* 97: 178–197.

Stück, H. 1998. Subsumtion und Abwägung. *ARSP* 84: 405–419.

# Chapter 13
# Arguing on Facts: Truth, Trials and Adversary Procedures

**Giovanni Tuzet**

*We resist the pipes of Pan, because we care about Truth.*
(Simon Blackburn)

## 13.1 Introduction

What is the point of arguing about facts in a trial? According to traditional wisdom a trial aims to find out the truth about the disputed facts; therefore, factual argumentation in a trial context is supposed to provide a true representation of the relevant facts. The facts have to be reconstructed on the basis of the evidence at disposal; one should give an accurate description of their features and a true explanation why they are so, providing arguments that support these claims. So, if the traditional account is correct, legal argumentation on facts is truth-oriented. Factual claims made on trial are committed to truth, even if, of course, they may fail in giving a true representation of what is at stake.

But today many scholars claim that finding the truth is not among the aims or the functions of a trial. What should be done by judges, they say, is to assess the evidence presented and make a decision on what is at stake. This critical line of thought emphasizes the differences between inquiry and advocacy, truth and justice, scientific dialogue and legal conflict. One of the reasons presented in favor of this view is the nature of the adversary system in legal proceedings: parties are conceived as "fighters", and judges as "referees" who do not participate in the collection of the evidence and must avoid any "inquisitorial" procedure in deciding cases. Because of this, it is said, trials do not and cannot aim at truth. Nor is it a function of adversary procedures.

G. Tuzet (✉)
Philosophy of Law, Department of Legal Studies, Bocconi University, Milan, Italy
e-mail: giovanni.tuzet@unibocconi.it

C. Dahlman and E. Feteris (eds.), *Legal Argumentation Theory: Cross-Disciplinary Perspectives*, Law and Philosophy Library 102, DOI 10.1007/978-94-007-4670-1_13,

In the same spirit, as a consequence, legal argumentation is conceived as a "fight" device that parties use to win the case, not as a dialogical effort for a true representation of what is at stake.

But according to the traditional view adversary procedures such as cross-examination are the best means we have to find out the truth. I will try to defend this traditional view claiming that: (1) truth is a necessary condition of substantive justice, (2) legal argumentation on facts is truth-oriented, and (3) fallibilism requires adversary procedures. Before going into this, let me clarify some issues about law and truth.

## 13.2 Law and Truth

What is the relation between law and truth? One can conceive of it in several ways.[1] For instance, one can ask whether law is founded on some truth (you could call it "Truth in law") and whether there are any truths about law ("Truth of law"). Or, starting from the institutional features of legal systems, one could ask about the relation between, in turn, truth and jurisdiction, truth and legislation, and truth and constitution.[2] All these issues require some concept of both law and truth, of course. Among them I would like to point out the following:

(1) whether legal norms are truth-apt, that is, capable of being true or false;
(2) whether, and to what extent, law could be based or founded on some truth;
(3) whether there is truth in legal interpretation and argumentation;
(4) whether truth is an aim of a legal trial.

As to (1), non-cognitivist philosophers in legal and moral matters claim that norms are neither true nor false. The classical positivist way to put this is to say that legal norms are commands and, as such, are not truth-apt.[3] A command like "Open the door!" is neither true nor false. To put it in the contemporary philosophical jargon, it has a world-to-word direction of fit. An assertion like "The door is open" can be true or false, but norms and commands in general cannot.[4]

---

[1]Cf. e.g. Patterson (1996), Pintore (1996), Haack (2003a).

[2]It is clear that different legal theories have different views on these matters. A legal theory based on moral realism will say, for instance, that there are truths about constitutional values, while non-cognitivist views will reject this claim.

[3]However there are reasons not to reduce norms to imperatives or commands: (i) norms do not necessarily depend on a subject stating them, while genuine imperatives do; (ii) norms can be premises or conclusions in logical inferences, but imperatives *qua* imperatives cannot; (iii) norms can be iterated, while imperatives cannot (it does make sense to say "It should be that *p* should be", while it does not to say "I order that I order that *p*").

[4]A positivist can perfectly admit, however, that a norm-proposition (a proposition to the effect that a certain norm exists) is true or false. See in particular von Wright (1991) and Jørgensen (1938).

On the contrary, non-positivist and cognitivist philosophers in these matters often claim that norms are truth-apt.[5] However, if these views imply some correspondence theory of truth, it is clear what the truth-bearers would be (the norms themselves) but it is quite mysterious, in my opinion, what the truth-makers would be (normative facts? objective values?): one should not conflate a *norm* with the *fact* that a norm has been enacted, for the enactment makes true a statement about it but not the norm itself.

Concerning (2), instead, I would say that even if law is not truth-apt one could reasonably ask whether a law could be based or founded on some truth. Think about law and economics analysis, for instance: one could claim that legal norms and institutions are founded on economic facts and their corresponding truths. Even admitting that norms are neither true nor false, one could say they are legal means to social ends given certain economic facts. If the facts were different, such norms would or should be different in order to achieve those ends. Here the analysis takes often a normative turn: the point is not to give an explanation of given norms and institutions but, rather, a normative picture of how the law should be to achieve those ends given certain economic truths. In any case, what would be admitted is that, to some extent, laws or legal norms could be based on truth.

As to (3), I will be very brief here and point out that cognitivist views of interpretation respond in the affirmative while non-cognitivist ones strongly deny that there could be any truth in legal interpretation. According to people like the Legal Realists and their skeptical progeny interpretive statements are rather judgments of value or political acts, while Dworkinians claim that our interpretive efforts aim at truth and our best interpretive statements, providing the best explanation and justification of our legal materials and practices, are certainly true.[6] Similar views can be held about legal argumentation, to which I will come back below.

Now it is (4) the main issue I want to discuss in the present paper. It is not on legal norms and their relation to truth. It is about facts; to be sure, about legally relevant facts in a trial context. A fact is legally relevant when, according to the logical structure of a conditional, a norm prescribes that a certain legal consequence follow from the type of fact considered in the antecedent of the conditional. Then in a trial a judge should see whether (it is proven that) the fact in hand is a token of that type. If this account is correct, one is committed to say that truth is an aim of a trial. For the judge should see whether it is true or false that the fact in hand instantiates the type of fact from which a certain legal consequence should follow according to the law. But in our times the claim that truth is an aim of a trial has been put into question and rejected by several legal scholars. I will deal with this in the following.

---

[5]See e.g. Kalinowski (1967).

[6]See e.g. Llewellyn (1950) and Guastini (2005) on the one hand, and Dworkin (1986, 1996) on the other. Cf. also Endicott (2005).

## 13.3 Inquiry or Advocacy?

In some recent papers, focusing on the U.S. legal culture, Susan Haack has claimed that science is concerned with inquiry and an open-ended search for truth, whereas law is concerned with advocacy and a need of finality in settling disputes.[7] "Inquiry starts with a question and seeks out evidence, aiming to arrive at an answer; advocacy, aiming to persuade, starts with a proposition to be defended and marshals the best evidence it can in its favor" (Haack 2009, 13). Inquiry and advocacy are very different attitudcs and activities.

One of the reasons she presents in favor of this view is the nature of the adversary system in the U.S. legal trials, or, as she calls it, "the adversarialism of the U.S. legal culture" (Haack 2004a, 17).[8] In the adversary system parties are not interested in the search and discovery of truth, but rather in the outcome of the case. Some authors (not Haack herself) qualify parties as "fighters": what these want is to win their case, not to find or point out what really happened.[9] To this end they have to provide good evidence and good arguments, so as to persuade judges or juries. Accordingly, some authors think of judges as "referees" who do not participate in the collection of the evidence and must avoid any "inquisitorial" procedure in deciding cases. A trial for Haack (2008, 563) isn't exactly a "search for truth": rather, it is better described "as a late stage of a whole process of determining a defendant's guilt or liability". Why "a late stage"? Because the process starts with the search and collection of the favorable evidence by the parties, who then try to persuade the finder of fact.

So, for Haack inquiry is the core business of science and advocacy is the one of law (or of attorneys at least). Science is truth-oriented, while law is outcome-oriented or, at best, justice-oriented.

Haack (2007, 14) recognizes with Bentham that "factual truth is an essential element of substantive justice; it really matters that the person who is punished be the person who actually committed the crime or caused the injury". She acknowledges that substantive justice requires truth, for an application of law is correct when, *inter alia*, the relevant factual reconstruction is true.[10] If you want, to put it in abstract philosophical terms, factual truth is a necessary (even not sufficient) condition of justice. But Haack also claims that adversary procedures like cross-examination (as they are actually run in the U.S.) are not a good means to that end. Therefore, if I understand correctly, there is a tension within law itself: justice requires truth, but trials hardly deliver it.

---

[7] Cf. Haack (2003b, 2004a, 2004b, 2007, 2008, 2009).

[8] She says that "there are deep tensions between the goals and values of the scientific enterprise and the culture of the law, especially the culture of the U.S. legal system" (Haack 2009, 2).

[9] See e.g. Frank (1949).

[10] "Justice requires just laws, of course, and just administration of those laws; but it also requires factual truth" (Haack 2004a, 15).

These claims recall the critique of the adversary system made several decades ago by Jerome Frank in particular.[11] As is well-known, Frank was a Legal Realist who was skeptical not only about rules but also about facts. Rule-skeptics contested that legal rules univocally determine the outcome of a case. Fact-skeptics like Frank contested that actual legal procedures permit us to find out the truth on trial and to predict future decisions. This is due, in his opinion, to a variety of factors: in part to the epistemic problems involved in such activities as reconstructing the past, relying on testimony, etc. (what he called "the elusiveness of the facts on which decisions turn"); in part to judicial discretion; and in part to the legal features of the adversary system where parties are fighters and the winner is not the one who has a right to that but the one who is most persuasive and rich enough to get the best advocates and the best evidence in his favor.[12]

In the same spirit, legal argumentation could be conceived as a "fight" device that parties use to win the case, not as a dialogical effort for a true representation of what is at stake.

How to avoid the drawbacks of adversarialism? Frank's way out was to make appeal to the judge's discretion and sense of justice. Haack's proposal is to slightly move the U.S. legal system in the direction of a more "continental" approach, giving the judges some "inquisitorial" powers or encouraging them to use such powers when needed (for instance to appoint independent experts in matters of scientific evidence assessment).[13] I do not want to discuss these proposals however. I would rather like to discuss some of their assumptions and the skeptical claims about truth on trial.

## 13.4 Truth on Trial?

Because of the features outlined above it is held that trials do not and cannot aim at truth, at least in the systems where trials are shaped along the lines of the adversary model. I have some objections against this view. On the one hand I lack the competence to go into a technical discussion of the U.S. legal procedure or of the procedure of other positive systems; on the other hand I have some methodological and conceptual worries about the view in question.

First of all, a *methodological* point. As I understand them, such claims as those made by Haack seem to contrast the pathology of the adversary system with the physiology of science. Science is taken in its ideal dynamics, made of disinterested inquirers who search for truth and critically assess their own or others' empirical hypotheses without any sort of prejudice. This is of course ideal science, not

---

[11]See Frank (1930, 1949).

[12]Frank (1949). Note that there is a tension in claiming at the same time that uncertainty comes from judicial discretion and judicial "laissez-faire".

[13]See in particular Haack (2004a, 24–25).

necessarily real science. (But Haack is well aware that science, like every human enterprise, is susceptible to corruption). Law instead is taken in its real dynamics, made of interested litigators who pursue their own success and do not care about justice in its own sake. Now, is this a fair comparison and assessment? Would things be different if we were to consider the physiology of the adversary system and the pathology of science? The same problem appears if we compare the adversary and the inquisitorial system. Haack's proposal makes appeal to unbiased and scrupulous judges who reasonably use their inquisitorial powers. This is the physiology of the inquisitorial system. What about biased or even malicious judges who abuse their powers to favor the outcome they like? History provides a lot of examples of such a pathological drift. A fair comparison would require taking either the physiology of both or their pathology.

In the second place, I think that the skeptical accounts are partial if they do not take into account the role of judges: litigators pursue their own interests, it is clear, but judges should pursue justice. I would call this the *partiality* objection. The skeptical accounts stress the role of the parties in a trial and underestimate, in my opinion, the judicial point of view. From the point of view of the judge, very simply, justice should be made and this requires that the factual reconstruction be true. This means, to be sure, that the accused in a criminal case can be legally convicted only if (it has been proven that) he did what he is accused of; otherwise, given the principles of our legal systems, he should be acquitted (think of a killing case). And it means that the plaintiff in a civil case is entitled to win only if (it has been proven that) what he claims is true (think of an injury case). Notwithstanding the different standards of proof in criminal and civil cases, it is impossible to think of a correct application of the law on the basis of false premises, because there is a conceptual relation between justice and truth, according to which the latter is a necessary condition of the former. So, according to my argument, even if truth is not *the* goal of a trial, it is *one of its* goals. The first of these is making justice, but if a true representation of the case or a true reconstruction of what happened are necessary conditions of a just decision, then determining such truths is one of the goals of a trial.[14] This is the point of view judges should have.

This brings us to a further critical claim. From a *conceptual* point of view the skeptical accounts neglect the relation between truth and proof. It is undisputable that in our (adversary) systems both plaintiffs and public prosecutors have to prove what they claim. They have the so-called burden of proof.[15] What is disputed (somehow inexplicably in my view) are the consequences of this: some scholars

[14]To be just, a normative conclusion needs to follow not only from an acceptable normative premise, but also from a true factual premise. Were the minor premise false, the norm would be applied to the wrong situation. In the Italian literature, see Taruffo (1992) defending this thesis for the civil cases and Ferrajoli (1989) for the criminal ones. Furthermore Ferrajoli claims that truth is required both on legal and factual claims (which is different from saying that legal norms themselves could be true); for a critique of Ferrajoli on this issue see Villa (1999, 152–8, 181–191).

[15]I make abstraction from some technicalities like the distinction between burden of proof and burden of production. They do not touch on the present conceptual point. Cf. Prakken and Sartor (2006).

claim that given the burden of proof one is committed to recognize that trials do not aim at truth but, rather, at dispute resolution according to some positive rules. These include not only the burden of proof rules, but also those on the admissibility of evidence, the assessment of evidence and the standards of proof. So it would be right to say that a legal decision in favor of the plaintiff or prosecutor is legally correct when the burden of proof has been satisfied by the plaintiff or prosecutor, regardless of truth; or, to put it differently, when the claim has been proven according to the relevant standard, regardless of truth. Now, it is certainly true that our legal systems include such rules but I cannot see why truth would become immaterial given those rules. My argument focuses on the conceptual relation between truth and proof. Is it possible to prove that *p* and, at the same time, claim that it is false that *p*? Such a conjunctive claim would sound rather paradoxical, or even contradictory. Why? Because of the conceptual relation of truth and proof: to prove that *p*, is to prove that it is true that *p*.

However some prominent scholars contend that the conceptual relation between truth and proof does not hold in legal matters. In particular Jordi Ferrer (2004, 38–41) has claimed that the sentence "It is proven that *p*" is not synonymous with "It is true that *p*", but synonymous with "There is sufficient evidence in favor of *p*".[16] If this is right, it can perfectly happen that it is proven that *p* while it is false that *p*; this happens when the standards of proof are met but in fact it is false that *p*. One could reply that the relevant difference in such cases is between being proven and being *considered as* proven; in such cases, when the standard is met but in fact it is false that *p*, it is not proven that *p* but it is erroneously considered as proven (unless there is a justified divergence of substantive truth and judicial findings, as I will say in the next section). Moreover, suppose you are a party in a trial: the act of presenting some evidence and the speech act of describing such evidence as relevant[17] to the factual issue in hand commits you to say that what you claim about such evidence is true. Otherwise it would be fine to say things like "I have the proof that *p* but it is false that *p*". According to our conceptual framework, if I am right, it is legitimate to draw an inference not only from "I claim that *p*" to "I claim that it is true that *p*", but also from "I have the proof that *p*" to "I have the proof that it is true that *p*".[18] This is not to equate truth with proof, but to recognize that an evidentiary claim implies the concept of truth and a truth-claim. To show this, it is useful to reformulate the so-called Moore's paradox. Such a paradox is known from a passage of Wittgenstein's *Philosophical Investigations* (second part, X). It concerns the relation between reality and belief, the paradox being, in my reading, that a conceptual difference such as the difference between reality and belief implies nevertheless a certain connection between the two, so as to make some statements paradoxical as the following:

(A) It rains but I believe it does not.

[16] See also Ferrer (2006) and Pardo (2010).

[17] Because it directly proves what is at stake or permits to draw an inference about it.

[18] This could be easily put in inferentialist terms. Cf. Canale and Tuzet (2007).

We can reformulate Moore's paradox considering the relation between truth and proof:

(B) I have the proof that *p* but it is not true that *p*.

Such a statement as (B) is paradoxical by virtue of the conceptual relation between truth and proof. *If I claim I have the proof that* p *I am conceptually committed to claim that it is true that* p *and I am not entitled to claim that it is false*. This goes beyond the criminal-civil divide and the different standards of proof. No one, both in civil and criminal cases, would ever claim something like (B), or to have a false proof of the fact he is trying to prove.[19]

This could be rephrased in terms of argumentation. Imagine someone who claims, first, that he has the proof that *p* and, second, that one can infer from it that it is false that *p*. It would be not only strange but also self-defeating. The idea of providing an argument for *p* and for not-*p* at the same time is a very bad one. One has to give arguments for (the truth of) *p* and avoid arguments that lead to the opposite conclusion.

In sum, I would say that truth is (*i*) a conceptual presupposition of assertive discourse in general and of factual claims in particular (in a trial context as well), and (*ii*) a goal of our epistemic practices in general and of evidentiary ones in particular (in a trial context as well, with the specification that truth on trial is not pursued for itself but for the sake of justice).[20]

## 13.5 Substantive Truth vs. Formal Truth

Now the reader may ask what concept of truth is at stake here. In the preceding pages I almost implicitly used a *correspondence theory of truth*. A statement or a belief is true when it corresponds to the fact it is about. The correspondence idea has some problems from a philosophical point of view but we don't need to address them here.[21] It suffices to say, in my opinion, that a correspondentist concept of truth

[19]As a counter-argument, Christian Dahlman suggested me to consider the following: That there is legal proof that *p* means that there is a legal obligation to act as if it were true that *p*; but, given that it is logically possible to have an obligation to lie, this does not show that there is a necessary conceptual connection between truth and legal proof. To my impression, in the possible world of a lie-obligation the concept of proof would be different indeed; I deal with the concept of proof that is used in our epistemic and legal practices, where to claim that it is proven that *p* is to claim that it is true that *p* and there is sufficient evidence for it.

[20]"The truth needs to be found not for its own sake but for the application of rules and principles" (Pastore 2003, 333–4). But Pastore supports an epistemic concept of truth. "Truth is an ideal that consists in the warranted assertibility of statements" (Pastore 2003, 335).

[21]Cf. Horwich (1998), Engel (2002), Künne (2003). Notice that a minimalist or disquotationalist conception of truth rules out the difference between cognitivism and non-cognitivism in normative matters. "Expressivism in ethics says that ordinary moral judgements such as 'torture is wrong' are *not* truth-apt: they are neither true nor false, but are expressions of feeling or emotions. But, on

is the one we use in our ordinary discursive and inferential practices. Does the same hold for truth-claims in a legal trial?

Well, things are more complicated on trial. Correspondingly, legal argumentation on truth is more complicated than everyday argumentation on truth. There is a well-known distinction between *formal* and *substantive* truth. The former consists in judicial findings; the latter in correspondence with facts. Some scholars take the distinction to mean that a trial is only concerned with formal truth.[22] I subscribe to the view of those who contend that both are legally important. Robert Summers (1999, 497), in particular, has claimed that a primary function of trial court procedures and of rules of evidence in cases before courts in which facts are in dispute "is to find the truth" in a substantive sense. This is the case not only for reasons of justice (just application of the law) but also for reasons of utility.[23]

Therefore, in a well designed system "judicial findings of formal legal truth generally coincide with substantive truth in particular cases" (Summers 1999, 498).[24] But formal legal truth may, in a particular case, fail to coincide with substantive truth. This may happen for "pathological" motives (e.g. lack of competence of the triers of fact) but also for good reasons (e.g. protection of fundamental rights). Summers (1999, 501ff.) calls the latter situation "rational divergence". Some rules of exclusion in common law countries determine a right-oriented divergence (think of evidence being excluded because illegally collected). But some of the divergences are also truth-oriented. Such is the case of hearsay evidence exclusion.

> It is, of course, true that to exclude hearsay evidence in some particular case may be to defeat the truth. Yet one rationale for the general exclusion of hearsay evidence is simply that the fact-finder is likely to accord such evidence too much weight, given that the party who would merely be quoted in court is not actually present before the court and so is not available for cross examination. And another rationale, also truth serving in nature is that exclusion of hearsay may induce the hearsay's proponent to introduce instead the live testimony of the witness who would then be subject to cross examination (Summers 1999, 502–503).

So, some divergences are rational because they are designed to protect some fundamental rights and some are rational for epistemic reasons: according to Summers it is rational to exclude a kind of evidence which is not reliable in general (like hearsay evidence) even if in a particular case it might be the only way to find the truth. So *coincidence of substantive and formal truth is the rule and divergence is the exception*. Such divergences are the price we pay for the fact that the law has many purposes that sometimes conflict with one another and substantive truth is one

---

the minimalist picture, if truth-aptness amounts just to 'syntactic discipline', the expressivist view is automatically ruled out. This can be seen easily if truth-aptness is just a matter of satisfaction of the disquotational schema" (Engel 2002, 82).

[22]See e.g. Carnelutti (1915, 31–36) and Kelsen (1945, 135–136).

[23]"If a rule of law is judicially applied to the true facts it envisions, the rule can also be tested for the adequacy of its formulation and for the soundness of any means-goal hypothesis it embodies" (Summers 1999, 498).

[24]But one may suspect this is unrealistic.

among them.[25] This has important consequences for legal argumentation on facts: arguing on facts may consist in arguing either on substantive or on formal truth, depending on the case; in particular, in the latter situation, one has to argue that there are good reasons to exclude some evidence and to stick to formal truth.

In the light of this our previous claim should be made weaker. Substantive truth is a necessary condition of justice except in those cases in which the discovery of substantive truth would undermine a fundamental value protected by the law and deemed as more important than discovering the truth in a particular case.

A similar point could be made in philosophy about truth and justification.[26] Richard Rorty has claimed among others that there is no practical difference between truth and justification: even if it is possible in principle to distinguish truth from justification, what we aim at in our discursive practice are justified beliefs and assertions.[27] But imagine that "*p*" stands for "*A* killed *B*". If "*p*" is true, it is correct to convict *A*. If "*p*" is false, it is not correct. Now imagine that it is justified to believe that *p*, but "*p*" is false. It might be justified to believe that *p* since there might be some (in fact deceptive) evidence to that conclusion. Would it be correct to convict *A* in such a case? Our intuitions may differ, but even those who claim that it would be legally correct should give a specific argument for that, for instance the distinction between formal and substantive truth and the possibility of some justified exceptions to their coincidence. This supports the claim that truth and justification are not the same and their difference *makes* indeed a practical difference. The same holds for substantive and formal truth, and it is false that only the latter is relevant to law.

Eugenio Bulygin has made the point very clearly.[28] He says that the fact that a proposition has been proven in court does not entail its truth (one could say, better: the fact that it has been considered as proven does not entail its truth), where truth is intended in the correspondentist sense via the semantic rules that link our words and sentences to reality.[29] He gives the example of Dmitri Karamazov, who was accused and convicted for a crime he did not commit.

---

[25]"If the system is well designed, and if, in a particular case of divergence, relevant rationales for such divergence are in play, the divergence is merely the price we pay for having a complex multi-purpose system in which actual truth, and what legally follows from it, comprise but one value among a variety of important values competing for legal realization" (Summers 1999, 511).

[26]On the conceptual distinction between truth and justification, cf. Engel's remarks in Engel and Rorty (2005, 38–40). Cf. Wright (1992).

[27]See his remarks in Engel and Rorty (2005, 72–73). *Contra*, see Haack (2004b, 43).

[28]Bulygin (1985, 162): "it may be true that *A* ought to pay his tax and that he did not pay it and yet the judge ought not to sentence him (if e.g. it has not been proved in court), and vice versa, it may be true that the judge ought to sentence *A* for not having paid his tax, though it is not true that he did not pay it."

[29]"The semantic rules determine to what individuals the names 'Tom' and 'Peter' refer and what relation is designated by the predicate 'killed'. The sentence 'Tom killed Peter' is true if and only if the individual referred to by 'Tom' stands in the relation designated by the predicate 'killed' to the individual referred to by 'Peter'. What a judge says about Tom's killing Peter is absolutely irrelevant for the truth of this sentence. So in order to find out whether the sentence

> He did not kill his father and so, according to the penal law, he ought not to be punished. But there was a certain amount of evidence against him and the jury decided that he had killed his father. Once this decision had been taken, the judge was under an obligation to sentence him to prison. So he did and his decision was perfectly lawful, i.e. it was justified by the law of procedure, though not by the penal law (Bulygin 1985, 162).[30]

This is an interesting way to put the matter: the decision was justified by procedural law, not by criminal law. There was a divergence in that case between substantive and formal truth, to put it in Summers' terms. Does it follow from this and similar cases that substantive truth is immaterial in court? Not at all. Two considerations are in order for Bulygin: first, what has to be proven in criminal cases is determined by criminal and not by procedural law; secondly, the fact that the jury decision, though lawful, was not justified by criminal law "enables us to say that it was wrong, that a judicial mistake had been made in the case of Dmitri Karamazov" (Bulygin 1985, 163).[31] I completely agree with this and would repeat Summers' diagnosis: this is a price we pay for the fact that law is a multi-purpose system, where the purposes of criminal law sometimes conflict with those of procedural law, where the purpose of final decisions conflicts with the purpose of correctness, etc.

Something similar has been pointed out by Mirjan Damaška: given that it is possible to discover the truth (notwithstanding the difficulties stressed by Frank and other fact-skeptics), he wonders (1998, 301ff.) if it is really important to do that. He thinks it is (for reasons of justice and utility, as I understand him) with some exceptions however:

1. the litigation with a heavy law-making component, in which the reconstruction of what happened is rather unimportant – in the U.S. 1965 case *Griswold* vs. *Connecticut*, for example, whether an individual instructed a couple to use contraceptives "is not nearly as important as the chance to determine the constitutionality of a criminal statute banning this activity" (Damaška 1998, 303);
2. the civil lawsuits in which conflict-resolution is more important than truth-discovery – given also that in such cases "litigants are sovereign in determining what is in issue between them through admissions, stipulations and settlements" (Damaška 1998, 304);
3. the criminal cases where an individual has to be protected from the abuse of power by public officials – given that "the criminal process also serves a variety of needs and values that are independent from and potentially in conflict with the drive toward fact-finding accuracy" (Damaška 1998, 305).

'Tom killed Peter' is true the judge must know the semantic rules of the language (must understand the language) and he must discover certain facts" (Bulygin 1995, 20).

[30]Cf. Bulygin (1995, 20–24).

[31]Such a decision produces its legal effects (what was stressed by Kelsen) but this does not mean it is correct.

One can easily see that the multi-purpose diagnosis applies also here, and my weaker claim should take these exceptions into account as well: factual truth is a necessary condition of justice except in those cases in which it is less important than other legal purposes that are in conflict with it. In such cases arguments on facts would be different than elsewhere because they would focus on the normative features of the facts, so to say, rather than on the facts themselves trying to provide a true explanation of them.

But notice that some truth-claims are also made in such cases: to protect an individual from the abuse of power by public officials, one has to claim that (it is true that) such an individual is in need of protection and is entitled to this by the law; to give conflict-resolution more importance than truth-discovery in certain civil lawsuits, one has to claim that (it is true that) the case in hand is of the relevant sort, the parties want to determine a certain settlement and the law gives them the power to do it; and even in deciding a constitutional case one has to claim that (it is true that) some principles apply to the case, should be balanced in a certain way, etc. Of course the truth-makers of such normative claims, when these are true, are different from, and somehow more problematic than, the ones of factual claims on what happened. However what strikes me as conceptually wrong is to say that those claims are not truth-apt and legal decisions in such cases dispense with truth altogether.

## 13.6 Legal Argumentation and Fallibilism

I have given some arguments in favor of the view that truth is a necessary condition of justice. Now I would like to show that legal argumentation is truth-oriented and that fallibilism requires adversary procedures.

If the above account is correct, indeed, *legal fact-finding aims at truth and so does legal argumentation concerning the relevant facts* (unless it has been shown there are good reasons to dispense with substantive truth and stick instead to formal truth). Factual argumentation in law starts from the evidence at disposal and tries to provide the best explanation of it.[32] What happened? Who killed Dmitri Karamazov's father? What was the drug that caused the injury? And so on. Empirical hypotheses are made and should be assessed on trial. The fighting parties usually provide conflicting hypotheses that judges or jurors consider and assess. As I contended elsewhere,[33] the first inferential step of the fact-finding process is abductive: abductions are drawn from the evidence to a hypothesis capable of explaining it. Now abduction is an uncertain inference, a non-deductive device whose tentative conclusions should be carefully checked by further inferential steps

---

[32]See Pardo and Allen (2008). Cf. Bex et al. (2010).

[33]See Tuzet (2005). On evidentiary reasoning as abductive cf. Pastore (2003, 340).

and empirical tests.[34] Judges and jurors undertake a *reductio ad unum* process in which the (epistemically and legally) best explanation of the evidence is to be selected.

What are the argumentative features of such an inferential process? Given that abductions aim at true explanatory hypotheses, an easy answer to this question would be that abductive in particular and factual argumentation in general is truth-oriented as well. (Or at least one could say that argumentative claims are truth-claims even if insincerely made: if I argue that *p* I argue that it is true that *p*, no matter what I really think about it). But this answer does not take into account the specific features of a trial and, more in detail, the features of a trial according to the adversary model.

A trial context is a conflict context. In this sense it is true that it does not consist of a dialogical or collaborative effort for a true representation of what is at stake. Parties are "fighters" (who have to follow some rules anyway) and trial argumentation has dialectical and rhetorical aspects that are absent from scientific argumentation. Nor is trial argumentation the *ex post* elaboration of an individual mind, as it goes for judicial argumentation justifying the decision that was made;[35] it is constitutively dialectical and conflicting. This is remarkably true of the adversary trial, if judges are mere "referees" who do not participate in the fight. Now recall the first objection I made to Haack's account: it contrasts the pathology of the adversary system with the physiology of science and with the physiology of the inquisitorial system. To this objection one could reply that what we are discussing is in fact adversarial physiology, not pathology! It is perfectly normal that parties fight for their case. The system is designed for this, not for the collaborative discovery of truth. Legal argumentation on trial is not supposed to be a disinterested effort for truth and justice. It is supposed to be an effort for success. It is advocacy, not inquiry. Or so the reply goes.

But somewhere Haack is less critical against the adversary system, when she claims (2004b, 61) for instance that the way of adversarialism and exclusionary rules "is not an inherently bad way to determine the truth in legal disputes; but as it presently works it isn't nearly as good a way as we would ideally like it to be". One of the reasons for this is that neither system is perfect, of course; what matters, focusing in particular on the system of exclusionary rules, is what parties do in fact: considering Bentham's strategy for which no species of evidence whatsoever ought to be excluded, "just as the inclusive strategy that Bentham urges would work poorly unless the advocates for the parties do a decent job of seeking out relevant evidence and of revealing the flaws in the dubious stuff admitted along with everything else, so too the exclusionary strategy built into our rules of evidence will also work poorly unless the parties do a decent job of challenging dubious stuff to get it excluded" (Haack 2004b, 61). No rule produces a decent result without people who do a decent job. This is fine, but there is something more.

---

[34]"*No* standard of proof can fully eliminate the uncertainty or render the kind of abductive inferences used in legal reasoning truth-preserving" (Laudan 2005, 356).

[35]Cf. Feteris (1999) in particular.

When Haack criticizes the epistemological confusions in some U.S. Supreme Court's decisions as *Daubert* and the bad methodologies supported by them, she seems to agree on the fundamental thesis that legal proceedings *should aim at truth*.[36] But she seems to deny that the adversary procedure is a good means to the end of truth. Now this view goes against the traditional opinion on the epistemic virtues of the adversary system and of its components like cross-examination, according to which they are the best means we have to discover the truth.[37] So, in the traditional view, the rationale for the adversary system is not only legal and moral (to give everyone the opportunity to discuss his case before an impartial judge or jury) but also epistemic, since cross-examination and adversary procedures permit us to find out the truth much better than inquisitorial or other procedures do. Wigmore's dictum that "Cross-examination is the greatest legal engine ever invented for the discovery of truth" is often quoted to this effect. Now, apart from the technicalities of cross-examination and other legal devices, I would like to indicate an argument which is in my opinion crucial for supporting adversary procedures. The argument is *fallibilism* and is very simple: given that humans are fallible, adversary procedures are epistemically more reliable than inquisitorial ones.

"Fallibilism" as a slogan was introduced in contemporary philosophy by Charles Peirce. His pragmatist philosophy emphasized the epistemic limitations of human cognition and, at the same time, resisted a skeptical position on knowledge. Haack is well aware of it and of the distinction between fallibilism as a theoretical claim about human cognition (human liability to hold false beliefs) and as a methodological caveat (we cannot ever be sure of what we believe, since we are fallible, so we should be open to belief revision in the light of new evidence).[38] But she seems to forget about it when she deals with adversary and inquisitorial models. True, she does not support inquisitorial models as such but rather suggests to introduce inquisitorial correctives in adversary systems, or, as she calls them, "adaptations of adversarialism" (in particular, court-appointed experts in matters of scientific evidence).[39] Moreover another pragmatist philosopher, William James, stressed the human need of making decisions in due time and, in particular, the legal need to settle questions one way or another:

> in human affairs in general the need of acting is seldom so urgent that a false belief to act on is better than no belief at all. Law courts, indeed, have to decide on the best evidence attainable for the moment, because a judge's duty is to make law as well as to ascertain it, and (as a learned judge once said to me) few cases are worth spending much time over: the great thing is to have them decided on *any* acceptable principle, and got out of the way.[40]

---

[36]See in particular Haack (2004b, 2009). In the Italian literature cf. Taruffo (2009).

[37]"Adversarial procedure is the best aid to truth-finding" (Pastore 2003, 341). Cf. e.g. Twining (2006, 85–86).

[38]See e.g. Haack (2009, 2). On Peirce's fallibilism see also Tiercelin (2005).

[39]See again Haack (2004a). Cf. Haack (2003b).

[40]This is a passage from § VIII of *The Will to Believe* (1897), now in James (1968, 728).

This recalls Haack's contrast between the open-ended fallibilism of science and the law's concern for finality: Peirce's fallibilist pragmatism fits science and our epistemic life; James' humanist pragmatism fits our practical life. Therefore Peirce's fallibilism seems to support Haack's position and the idea that trial procedures (or at least adversary procedures) are not a good means to the end of truth. But I think we should remind of fallibilism when we compare adversarial with inquisitorial procedures. It is in practice impossible to measure their error rates, but I believe it is a fair guess to say that the former is a better guarantee than the latter against fact-finder's errors.[41]

To resume. When I argue for "*p*" I argue for the truth of "*p*" and, since I am fallible as any other human, the best way to decide about "*p*" is to confront the different opinions about it. The adversary system is designed for this.

So, if the traditional view is correct, legal argumentation on factual claims is truth-oriented and fallibilism requires adversary procedures. Then judicial reasoning and argumentation can be conceived as *ex post* efforts to give an adequate justification to the decision made, both in hard and easy cases, on the basis of what the parties discussed on trial.[42]

**Acknowledgments** Previous drafts of this paper were presented in the following conferences: "25th IVR World Congress of Philosophy of Law and Social Philosophy" (Frankfurt am Main, Goethe University, August 2011), "Romanistik im Dialog. XXXII. Romanistentag" (Berlin, Humboldt University, September 2011), "International Conference on Legal Theory and Legal Argumentation" (Nova Gorica, European Faculty of Law, November 2011); I wish to thank the organizers and the participants in these conferences for their helpful comments. I also owe a special thank to Federico Arena and Susan Haack, for having read and commented a first draft of this work.

[41]Cf. Laudan (2006). But once Peirce defined "atrocious" the adversary legal procedure according to which bias and counter-bias would be favorable to the extraction of truth (see Haack 2004b, 49). In correspondence Haack has remarked that given the limitations of time and resources an adversarial process can be, not a perfect way of arriving at the truth but, a good-enough way; but this in her view depends on some assumptions which are rarely true in practice, e.g. that both sides have roughly equal resources.

[42]See Moreso (1996, 93): "in neither hard nor easy cases can logic alone tell us which are the applicable normative premises, nor whether the statements describing the facts of the case are true (the scope of external justification); but in both cases logic serves to test whether steps taken from the premises to the conclusion are correct (the role of internal justification)."

## References


Bex, F., et al. 2010. A hybrid formal theory of arguments, stories and criminal evidence. *Artificial Intelligence and Law* 23: 123–152.
Bulygin, E. 1985. Norms and logic: Kelsen and Weinberger on the ontology of norms. *Law and Philosophy* 4: 145–163.
Bulygin, E. 1995. Cognition and interpretation of law. In *Cognition and interpretation of law*, ed. L. Gianformaggio and S.L. Paulson, 11–35. Turin: Giappichelli.
Canale, D., and G. Tuzet. 2007. On legal inferentialism. Toward a pragmatics of semantic content in legal interpretation? *Ratio Juris* 20: 32–44.
Carnelutti, F. 1915. *La prova civile*. Rome: Athenaeum.
Damaška, M. 1998. Truth in adjudication. *Hastings Law Journal* 49: 289–308.
Dworkin, R. 1986. *Law's empire*. Cambridge/London: Harvard University Press.
Dworkin, R. 1996. Objectivity and truth: You'd better believe it. *Philosophy and Public Affairs* 25: 87–139.
Endicott, T. 2005. The one true interpretation. In *Analisi e diritto 2005*, ed. P. Comanducci and R. Guastini, 127–137. Turin: Giappichelli.
Engel, P. 2002. *Truth*. Bucks: Acumen.
Engel, P., and R. Rorty. 2005. *À quoi bon la vérité*. Paris: Grasset.
Ferrajoli, L. 1989. *Diritto e ragione. Teoria del garantismo penale*. Rome-Bari: Laterza.
Ferrer, J. 2004. It is proven that p. The notion of proven fact in the law. *Associations* 8: 29–54.
Ferrer, J. 2006. Legal proof and fact finders' beliefs. *Legal Theory* 12: 293–314.
Feteris, E.T. 1999. *Fundamentals of legal argumentation*. Dordrecht: Kluwer Academic Press.
Frank, J. 1930. *Law and the modern mind*. New York: Brentano's.
Frank, J. 1949. *Courts on trial. Myth and reality in American justice*. Princeton: Princeton University Press.
Guastini, R. 2005. A sceptical view of legal interpretation. In *Analisi e diritto 2005*, ed. P. Comanducci and R. Guastini, 139–144. Turin: Giappichelli.
Haack, S. 2003a. Truth, truths, "truth", and "truths" in the Law. *Harvard Journal of Law and Public Policy* 26: 17–22.
Haack, S. 2003b. Inquiry and advocacy, fallibilism and finality: Culture and inference in science and the law. *Law, Probability and Risk* 2: 205–214.
Haack, S. 2004a. Truth and justice, inquiry and advocacy, science and law. *Ratio Juris* 17: 15–26.
Haack, S. 2004b. Epistemology legalized: Or, truth, justice, and the American way. *The American Journal of Jurisprudence* 49: 43–61.
Haack, S. 2007. On logic in the law: "Something, but not all". *Ratio Juris* 20: 1–31.
Haack, S. 2008. Of truth, in science and in law. *Brooklyn Law Review* 73: 563–586.
Haack, S. 2009. Irreconcilable differences? The troubled marriage of science and law. *Law and Contemporary Problems* 72: 1–23.
Horwich, P. 1998. *Truth*, 2nd ed. Oxford: Oxford University Press.
James, W. 1968. *Writings*, ed. J. McDermott. New York: The Modern Library.
Jørgensen, J. 1938. Imperatives and logic. *Erkenntnis* 7: 288–296.
Kalinowski, G. 1967. *Le problème de la vérité en morale et en droit*. Lyon: Emmanuel Vitte.
Kelsen, H. 1945. *General theory of law and state*. Cambridge: Harvard University Press.
Künne, W. 2003. *Conceptions of truth*. Oxford: Clarendon.
Laudan, L. 2005. The presumption of innocence: Material or probatory? *Legal Theory* 11: 333–361.
Laudan, L. 2006. *Truth, error, and criminal law. An essay in legal epistemology*. Cambridge: Cambridge University Press.
Llewellyn, K.N. 1950. Remarks on the theory of appellate decision and the rules and canons about how statutes are to be construed. *Vanderbilt Law Review* 3: 395–406.
Moreso, J.J. 1996. On relevance and justification of legal decisions. *Erkenntnis* 44: 73–100.
Pardo, M. 2010. The Gettier problem and legal proof. *Legal Theory* 16: 37–57.

Pardo, M., and R. Allen. 2008. Juridical proof and the best explanation. *Law and Philosophy* 27: 223–268.
Pastore, B. 2003. Truth in adjudication. In *The legitimacy of truth*, ed. R. Dottori, 333–344. Münster: Lit.
Patterson, D. 1996. *Law and truth*. Oxford: Oxford University Press.
Pintore, A. 1996. *Il diritto senza verità*. Turin: Giappichelli.
Prakken, H., and G. Sartor. 2006. Presumptions and burdens of proof. In *Proceedings of the 19th annual conference on legal knowledge and information systems (Jurix)*, ed. T. Van Engers, 21–30. Amsterdam: Ios Press.
Summers, R.S. 1999. Formal legal truth and substantive truth in judicial fact-finding – their justified divergence in some particular cases. *Law and Philosophy* 18: 497–511.
Taruffo, M. 1992. *La prova dei fatti giuridici*. Milan: Giuffrè.
Taruffo, M. 2009. *La semplice verità. Il giudice e la costruzione dei fatti*. Rome-Bari: Laterza.
Tiercelin, C. 2005. *Le doute en question*. Paris-Tel-Aviv: Éditions de l'éclat.
Tuzet, G. 2005. Abduction and deduction: Epistemic justice *vs*. political justice? *Rechtstheorie* 21: 211–221.
Twining, W. 2006. *Rethinking evidence*, 2nd ed. Cambridge: Cambridge University Press.
Villa, V. 1999. *Costruttivismo e teorie del diritto*. Turin: Giappichelli.
von Wright, G.H. 1991. Is there a logic of norms? *Ratio Juris* 4: 1–15.
Wright, C. 1992. *Truth and objectivity*. Cambridge/London: Harvard University Press.

# About the Authors

**Bruce Anderson**'s published work has focused on the discovery process in legal reasoning. Recently he has been investigating connections between visual art and law. He is a Professor of Business Law at Saint Mary's University, Halifax, Nova Scotia, Canada.

**FlaviaCarbonell Bellolio** is professor of Legal Theory and Legal Philosophy at the Faculty of Law, University Alberto Hurtado, Chile. She is Director of the Law Department. She is a member of the board of the Chilean Association of Legal and Social Philosophy. She holds a LLM from the Centre for Political and Constitutional Studies, Spain, and a Master in Public Law from the Universidad Carlos III, Madrid, as well as a specialization in Legal Argumentation from the Universidad de Alicante, Spain. Among Carbonell's publications are "Coherence and post-sovereign legal argumentation", In. Menéndez, A. & Fossum, J. (eds.), *Law and Democracy in Neil D. MacCormick's Legal and Political Theory*, Springer, 2011, pp. 159–182; F. Carbonell, R. Letelier, "Principios jurídicos e interpretación democrática del derecho" ("Legal Principles and Democratic Interpretation of Law"), In. F. Carbonell, R. Coloma, R. Letelier (eds.), *Principios Jurídicos. Análisis y Crítica* (Legal Principles. Analysis and Criticism), Santiago, Abeledo Perrot, Thomson Reuters, 2011, pp. 155–184.

**Carlos Bernal** is a senior lecturer at Macquarie Law School (Sydney, Australia). He has research interests in the fields of jurisprudence, torts, theory of action and constitutional theory. He has published widely in all these fields in seven different languages. His qualifications include a LL.B. from the University Externado of Colombia (Bogota) (1996), a S.J.D. from the University of Salamanca (Spain) (2001) and a M.A. (2008) and a Ph.D. in Philosophy (2011) from the University of Florida (U.S.A).

**Thomas Bustamante** is a Tenured Adjunct Professor of Legal Theory at the Federal University of Minas Gerais, Brazil, and a member of the research programme on Legal Theory and Legal Philosophy at the Law School of the same university. From 2008 to 2010, he has been a Lecturer at the University of Aberdeen,

C. Dahlman and E. Feteris (eds.), *Legal Argumentation Theory: Cross-Disciplinary Perspectives*, Law and Philosophy Library 102, DOI 10.1007/978-94-007-4670-1,

UK, where he still holds an honorary position. Amongst Prof. Bustamante's key publications are his books *Argumentação Contra Legem: A Teoria do Discurso e a Justificação Jurídica nos Casos mais Difíceis* [Contra Legem Legal Arguments: Discourse Theory and Legal Justification in the Hardest Cases], *Teoria do Direito e Decisão Racional: Temas de Teoria da Argumentação Jurídica* [Legal Theory and Rational Decision-Making: Essays on Legal Argumentation], and *Teoria do Precedente: O peso da Jurisprudência na Argumentação Jurídica* [A Theory of Precedent: The Weight of the Case Law in Legal Argumentation].

**Christian Dahlman** (professor in jurisprudence), **David Reidhav** (assistant professor in jurisprudence) and **Lena Wahlberg** (assistant professor in jurisprudence and medical law) teach legal argumentation at the faculty of law at Lund University (Sweden). They are currently conducting a research project on ad hominem arguments, funded by the Swedish Research Council (Vetenskapsrådet).

**Eveline T. Feteris** received her Ph.D. in Humanities at the University of Amsterdam. She is an Associate Professor at the Department of Speech Communication, Argumentation Theory and Rhetoric and a member of the research programme Argumentation and Discourse and the research school of the International Learned Institute of Argumentation Studies (ILIAS). She is director of the research masters's programme Text and Communication. She is a member of the editorial board of the journal Argumentation, the journal Argumentation in Context and the journal Language, Law and Interdisciplinary Practice. She is a member of the editorial board of the series Argumentation in Context of John Benjamins. Among Feteris key publications are *Fundamentals of Legal Argumentation: A Survey of Theories of Justification of Judicial Decisions*, Dordrecht: Springer Netherlands 1999; E.T. Feteris, H. Kloosterhuis, H.J. Plug, *Argumentation and the application of legal rules*, Amsterdam: Sic Sat, 2009. Address: Department of Speech Communication, Argumentation Theory and Rethoric, Spuistraat 134, 1012 VB Amsterdam, Netherlands. Email: e.t.feteris@uva.nl.

**Jaap Hage** Department Foundations and Methods of Law, University of Maastricht, Maastricht, Netherlands.

**Harm Kloosterhuis** studied Argumentation Theory (MA and PhD) and Law (LLM). He is lecturer and researcher at the Erasmus School of Law Rotterdam and lecturer at the University of Aruba. His main areas of research are legal argumentation theory, legal theory and speech act theory. His publications include *Reconstructing Interpretative Argumentation in Legal Decisions* (2006) and *Argumentation and the Application of Legal Rules* (2009, co-edited with E.T. Feteris and H.J. Plug). His articles on legal theory and argumentation theory have been published in *Argumentation*, *Ratio Juris* and *Artificial Intelligence and Law*.

**Marko Novak** is an associate professor of legal theory and constitutional law at the Faculty of Law in Nova Gorica, where he is director of the Legal Theory Department and Vice-Dean for Student Affairs. His major publications in the area of legal argumentation include: The Promising Gifts of Precedents. In *Changes in Culture and Techniques of Judicial Decision-Making*. 2003. Priban, J, Roberts, P.,

Young J. (Eds.). Ashgate, Dartmouth Publishing; Limiting Courts: Toward Greater Consistency of Adjudcation in the Civil Law System. In *Logic, Argumentation and Interpretation.* 2005. Joseph Aguilo-Regla (Ed.). Nomos, Franz Steiner Verlag; Three Models of Balancing (in Constitutional Review). 2010. *Ratio Juris.* Vol. 23, No. 1; *Pravna argumentacija v praksi [Legal Argumentation in Practice].* 2010. Ljubljana: Planet GV.

**Antonino Rotolo** CIRSFID, University of Bologna, Bologna, Italy.

**Corrado Roversi** CIRSFID, University of Bologna, Bologna, Italy.

**Frederick Schauer** IS David and Mary Harrison Distinguished Professor of Law at the University of Virginia. He is also Frank Stanton Professor of the First Amendment, Emeritus, at the Kennedy School of Government, Harvard University, where he taught from 1990 to 2008, served as Academic Dean and Acting Dean, and also taught at the Harvard Law School. Previously he was Professor of Law at the University of Michigan, and has also been Fischel-Neil Distinguished Visiting Professor of Law at the University of Chicago, Morton Distinguished Visiting Professor of the Humanities at Dartmouth College, Distinguished Visiting Professor at the University of Toronto, Distinguished Visitor at New York University, and Eastman Professor and Fellow of Balliol College at Oxford University. A Fellow of the American Academy of Arts and Sciences and former holder of a Guggenheim Fellowship, Schauer is the author of The Law of Obscenity (1976), Free Speech: A Philosophical Enquiry (1982), Playing By the Rules: A Philosophical Examination of Rule-Based Decision-Making in Law and in Life (1991), Profiles, Probabilities, and Stereotypes (2003), and Thinking Like a Lawyer: A New Introduction to Legal Reasoning (2009). He was founding co-editor of the journal Legal Theory, has served as chair of the Section on Constitutional Law of the Association of American Law Schools and of the Committee on Philosophy and Law of the American Philosophical Association. In 2006 Schauer was author of the Foreword to the Harvard Law Review's Supreme Court issue, and has written numerous articles on freedom of speech and press, constitutional law and theory, evidence, legal reasoning, and the philosophy of law. His books have been translated into Italian, Spanish, Portuguese, and Turkish, and his scholarship was the subject of a book (Rules and Reasoning: Essays in Honour of Fred Schauer, Linda Meyer, ed., Hart Publishing, 1999) and special issues of the Notre Dame, Connecticut, and Quinnipiac Law Reviews, Politeia, and the Harvard Journal of Law and Public Policy.

**Jan Sieckmann** is Professor for Public Law at the University of Erlangen and Visiting Professor for Constitutional Law and Legal Philosophy at the Faculty of Law of the University of Buenos Aires. Among Sieckmann's key publications are *Regelmodelle und Prinzipienmodelle des Rechtssystems, Baden-Baden, Nomos, 1990; Modelle des Eigentumsschutzes, Baden-Baden, Nomos, 1998; El modelo de los principios del derecho, Bogotá, Univ. Externado de Colombia, 2006; Recht als normatives System, Baden-Baden, Nomos, 2009. Also he edited various books on the theory of principles and of balancing, in particular J. Sieckmann (ed.),*

*Die Prinzipientheorie der Grundrechte. Studien zur Grundrechtstheorie Robert Alexys, Baden-Baden, Nomos, 2007; L. Clérico/J. Sieckmann (Hg.), Grundrechte, Prinzipien und Argumentation. Studien zur Rechtstheorie Robert Alexys, Baden-Baden, Nomos, 2009; J. Sieckmann (ed.), Legal Reasoning: The Methods of Balancing, ARSP-Beiheft 124, Stuttgart, Steiner Verlag, 2010.*

**Giovanni Tuzet** is Assistant Professor in Philosophy of Law at Bocconi University. He studied law and philosophy in Turin and Paris and wrote his Ph.D. thesis on Peirce's theory of inference. Formerly post-doc researcher at the universities of Lausanne, Switzerland, and Ferrara, Italy, he teaches at Bocconi Philosophy of Law, Legal Hermeneutics and Legal Argumentation.

He is a member of the editorial board of the series "Argumentation in Context" (John Benjamins). His publications include the book *The Rules of Inference. Inferentialism in Law and Philosophy* (edited with D. Canale, Milan: Egea 2009) and several papers on legal reasoning and legal argumentation in journals like *Ratio Juris*, *Informal Logic*, *Argumentation* and *Analisi e diritto*.

# Name Index




C. Dahlman and E. Feteris (eds.), *Legal Argumentation Theory: Cross-Disciplinary Perspectives*, Law and Philosophy Library 102, DOI 10.1007/978-94-007-4670-1,

# Subject Index




C. Dahlman and E. Feteris (eds.), *Legal Argumentation Theory: Cross-Disciplinary Perspectives*, Law and Philosophy Library 102, DOI 10.1007/978-94-007-4670-1,

MIX
Papier aus verantwortungsvollen Quellen
Paper from responsible sources
FSC® C105338

If you have any concerns about our products,
you can contact us on
**ProductSafety@springernature.com**

In case Publisher is established outside the EU,
the EU authorized representative is:
**Springer Nature Customer Service Center GmbH**
**Europaplatz 3, 69115 Heidelberg, Germany**

Printed by Libri Plureos GmbH
in Hamburg, Germany